C000269184

Close Corporations:
A Comprehensive Guide

Second Edition

To my good friend Harry Rajak.
Kindest regards
John Henning
93-10-15
—#—

Close Corporations:
A Comprehensive Guide

Second Edition

HS Cilliers
BA LLB (Cape Town) LLD (Unisa) CA (SA)
Formerly Professor of Accounting University of South Africa

ML Benade
BA (Stell) LLB (UOVS) LLD (Unisa)
Attorney and Partner, Dyason, Pretoria
Formerly Professor of Mercantile Law University of South Africa

JJ Henning
Blur LLB LLD (UOVS)
Professor of Mercantile Law and Director of the Centre for Business Law
of the University of the Orange Free State
Attorney of the Supreme Court

JJ du Plessis
BProc LLB LLM LLD (UOVS)
Professor of Mercantile Law Rand Afrikaans University
Advocate of the Supreme Court

Butterworths
Durban
1993

Butterworth Publishers (Pty) Ltd
Reg No 91/05175/07

© 1993

ISBN 0 409 01990 9 (soft cover)

Durban
8 Walter Place, Waterval Park
Mayville 4091

Johannesburg
108 Elizabeth Avenue
Parkmore 2196

Pretoria
Suite 301, 270 Main Street
Waterkloof 0181

Cape Town
3 Gardens Business Village, Hope Street
Cape Town 8001

Typeset by Digma Publications
Printed and bound by Interpak Natal Pietermaritzburg

Preface

This second edition of *Close Corporations: A Comprehensive Guide* is a continuation of the development process in filling the market needs over a wide spectrum for an authoratative exposition on close corporations.

The first edition of the *Comprehensive Guide* was exceptionally well received. Due to the demand of specialist practitioners the work was expanded and restructured in a bilingual loose leaf format with the title *Close Corporations Service* comprising:

Part 1 Close corporations law and practice

Part 2 Specimen documents

Part 3 Close Corporations Act No. 69 of 1984

Part 4 Regulations and forms

Part 5 Amendments

Table of Statutes

Table of Cases

Bibliography

Index

A strong demand on the part of University and Technicon students, entrepreneurs using the close corporation as business form, and practitioners with a general interest in this field, for a meaningful high level overview of the close corporation available in either English or Afrikaans, became strongly evident.

It was thus logical and appropriate at this stage to publish this second edition of the *Complete Guide* in a soft cover format. This work now comprises the text of the loose leaf *Close Corporations Service* and omits the more specialised appendices which are not necessary for every day use. The text of the *Close Corporations Service* used here has been especially acclaimed for its combination of depth and full coverage of close corporation law as well as for its clarity and logical exposition.

This soft cover second edition of *Close Corporations: A Comprehensive Guide* accordingly contains the more sophisticated and integrated exposition of close corporations law, its theory and practice, the Close Corporations Act and an example of the Association Agreement.

References have been brought up to date, up to 30 September 1992.

HS CILLIERS
ML BENADE
JJ HENNING
JJ DU PLESSIS

General Contents

PART

1

Close corporations law and practice

Contents

4 Internal relations between members and the close corporation

Page

8 Accounting records and annual financial statements

9 Taxation

The concept close corporation

Objectives of the close corporation

1.01 The Close Corporations Act[1] has, with effect from 1 January 1985, introduced the close corporation as an alternative corporate form for a business venture. The stated intention of the legislature was to provide a simple, less expensive and more flexible legal form for the small enterprise consisting of a single or a small number of participants to afford them the advantages of separate legal personality. In order to promote the formation of close corporations provision was made for the conversion of existing companies into close corporations and to make it even more attractive certain tax benefits were granted where such existing companies were converted into close corporations.

The acceptance of this concept is borne out by the large number of close corporations which have been formed during the six years since the inception of the Act.[2]

1 Act 69 of 1984 (hereinafter referred to as the Act).

2 155 187 new registrations and 30 293 conversions.

1.02 The following are among the more important reasons advanced for a new legal form providing corporate personality for *small*[1] businesses:

(a) Company law has become increasingly complex in view of the circumstance that the Companies Act has developed to an ever-increasing extent to deal with problems posed or experienced by large public companies. This legislation applies to all registered companies and accordingly even the small private company is subject to these complex provisions. This is due partly to the fear of possible misuse of the private company within the context of the group system of holding companies and subsidiaries.

(b) The alternative possibility of building further exemptions for small companies into the Companies Act was considered unacceptable. It would only increase the overall complexity of the Companies Act and would aggravate the problem. The Companies Act had in effect become inappropriate for the needs of the *bona fide* small undertaking. The legal formalities have become too onerous, for example the incorporation formalities and the provisions relating to the maintenance of capital.

(c) These small undertakings are in need of a legal form which would provide the advantages of incorporation without subjecting them to the present company law "which is largely uncodified, and which is intimidating insofar as it is codified in the Companies Act".[2] This does not mean that the Close Corporations Act is a codification and therefore simplifies matters or that codification necessarily has an intimidatory effect. Although the legislature intends to simplify certain areas by means of a quasi-codification (for example the fiduciary duties and duties of care and skill owed to the corporation), large areas remain uncodified. Notably the fiduciary relationship between members and the duties and accountability of the accounting officer. It is especially with reference to the position of the accounting officer where simplicity may lead to uncertainty and confusion.[3]

(d) The aim of the Close Corporations Act 1984 is accordingly to provide "a simpler and less expensive legal form for the single entrepreneur or few participants, designed with a view to his or their needs and without burdening him or them with legal requirements that are not meaningful in his or their circumstances."[4] In this way *bona fide* small businesses may be promoted which is highly desirable in a country with growing numbers of unemployed. The close corporation is a very suitable vehicle for this purpose as it can cater alike for the unsophisticated and highly sophisticated businessman.[5]

(e) The close corporation does not affect the existence or the availability of the private company or any other existing legal form but merely creates an additional form.

1 In order to qualify for a *small* business a close corporation may have a maximum of 10 members. The number of members is the only limiting factor: the size and scope of the operations of the corporation is not at issue – a factor which detracts considerably from the admirably phrased objects for close corporations.
2 Urquhart 1984 *South African Company Law Journal* 43.
3 See 1.08 *infra*.
4 Naudé 1984 *Journal for Juridical Science (JJS)* 118.

See also Naudé 1982 *MB* 5; 1984 (2) *JJS* and 3 *Transactions of the Luyt Centre for Business Law* (1986) where the close corporation and problems connected with it are extensively discussed.
5 This is due to its flexibility. The sophisticated businessman can effect the most sophisticated internal arrangements by entering into an association agreement. Secondly, the only limit on the size of the close corporation is its number of members.

Distinctive characteristics of a close corporation

1.03 The close corporation provides a simpler and less expensive corporate form for the single entrepreneur or a few participants (who, apart from a few exceptional cases, must be natural persons). In accord with the new awareness of the socio-economic and political importance of small businesses, the legal requirements under which the close corporation operates are basic and far simpler than under the Companies Act; the Close Corporations Act comprises a mere 83 sections compared with the more than 450 sections of the Companies Act.

1.04 The following are some of the distinctive features of the close corporation:[1]

☐ As the name implies, the close corporation is a juristic person distinct from its members which consequently enjoy perpetual succession[2] and its members have limited liability in respect of the corporation's debts.[3]

☐ It is granted the capacity and powers of a natural person insofar as these are appropriate to a legal person.[4]

☐ The formation, administration and operation of a close corporation are subject to the minimum formalities, administrative requirements and duties for the participants.

☐ A single person can form a close corporation and it need not be an undertaking for gain.

☐ No shares are issued and there is no share capital.

☐ Instead of the strict rules relating to the maintenance of capital in company law, the close corporation is allowed to utilise its capital as it pleases provided it maintains the necessary solvency and liquidity. Therefore the corporation may provide financial assistance and may even itself buy a member's interest.[5]

☐ Members are allowed the greatest possible flexibility in arranging their internal relationship and the management of the close corporation.

☐ All the members have in principle an equal say in the management of the business and no provision is made for the appointment of directors. Therefore no distinction exists between the providers of capital and management.

☐ The Act is to a large extent decriminalized and members run the risk of personal liability should it appear that they have contravened the provisions of the Act or have put the close corporation or its creditors in jeopardy.[6]

☐ The common law principles relating to the fiduciary duties and duties of care and skill in managing the affairs of the corporation are to a large extent codified in the Act with the result that even the unsophisticated member knows exactly what is expected of him and his fellow members.[7]

☐ The accounting and disclosure provisions are less extensive[8] and the corporation may enjoy certain tax benefits.[9]

1 See in general *Philip Business Services CC v De Villiers* 1991 3 SA 552 (W); *Van der Merwe v DSSM Boerdery BK* 1991 2 SA 320 (T); Bleimschein & Henning 1989 *THRHR* 251, 1990 *THRHR* 567; Lessing 1990 *SA Merc LJ* 57-58; Trichard Organ & Cilliers 10 *TranCBL* (1989).
2 In other words its continuance is not affected by changes in membership.
3 Such limited liability is restricted because it may in the protection of creditors' interest be lost

should solvency not be maintained. See 6.02 *infra*.
4 S 2(4).
5 Ss 39 and 40.
6 For instance where they have abused the legal personality of the corporation or have ignored the liquidity and solvency provisions.
7 Ss 42 and 43.
8 See 8.01 *et seq*.
9 See 9.01 *et seq*.

Comparison with other business forms

Comparison with partnerships

1.05 Partnerships must consist of at least two with a maximum of 20 members and must have as an object the pursuit of gain. Companies and other corporate bodies may become partners. As a partnership does not exist as a separate legal persona the partners are personally liable for its debts and own the partnership estate. Any change in membership results in the dissolution of the partnership and each partner is in law the agent of his co-partners.[1] A close personal and fiduciary relationship exists among partners. Although members of a close corporation owe their fiduciary duties to the corporation itself the relationship as between the members *inter se* resembles that as between partners. Consequently partnership principles to a large extent govern the relationship as between members.[2] Although a partnership must submit a joint tax return the partners are taxed individually. Frequently this is to the advantage of the business and the participants. The close corporation is taxed as a separate entity on the scale applicable to companies.

1 See in general Bamford *The Law of Partnerships and Voluntary Associations in South Africa* (1982) 25 *et seq.*

2 See Ribbens *The Personal Fiduciary Character of Members' inter se Relations in the Incorporated* *Partnership* (1988). He argues that the *inter se* fiduciary relationship between members of a close corporation should receive statutory recognition.

Comparison with business trusts

1.06 As a result of the unsuitability of the company form for the needs of smaller undertakings business trusts have gained in popularity. But even with the advent of the close corporation business trusts have not disappeared since they still enjoy certain advantages which make them rather attractive propositions as compared with close corporations. Firstly, they are subject to even fewer formalities and administrative restraints than corporations. Secondly, although it is not endowed with separate legal personality it enjoys most of the advantages thereof by making use of the trustee and by limiting liability to trust property. Thirdly, the number of beneficiaries is not limited to ten or to natural persons.[1] Fourthly, the business trust may enjoy certain tax advantages which could make it an even better proposition than a close corporation.

1 There is uncertainty whether s 30(1) of the Companies Act 61 of 1973, which restricts the number of persons involved in a company, association, syndicate or partnership for gain to 20 unless registered in terms of the Companies Act or formed in pursuance of some other law, applies to trusts. See Olivier *Aspekte van die Reg insake Trust en Trustee met besondere Verwysing na die Amerikaanse Reg* (1982) 478 en Henning 3 *Transactions of the Luyt Centre for Business Law* (1986) 25 and 41 *et seq*; Theron 1990 *SALJ* 673, 1991 *TSAR* 268, 1991 *SALJ* 277.

Relative advantages and disadvantages of close corporations as compared with companies

1.07 The main relative advantages of a close corporation are as follows:

☐ Simplicity of management: there is no separate board of directors and management is the responsibility of members.

☐ Simplicity of decision-making structure: there is no prescribed annual general meeting, and although provision is made for members' meetings, most decisions can be taken informally on the basis of consultation between members (especially where there are only two or three members); fundamental matters can be reduced to a written resolution signed by all members and entered into the minute book without the need of a preceding meeting.

☐ A close corporation may under certain conditions acquire the interest of a member and may also give financial assistance to a member to acquire an interest in the corporation.

☐ Transfer and acquisitions of members' interests are not liable to stamp duty.

☐ On the conversion of a company into a corporation no transfer or stamp duties are payable in respect of the transfer of property (for example land or shares) registered in the name of the company.

☐ Distributions of income are exempt from normal income tax in the hands of members. However s 10(1)(j) of the Income Tax Amendment Act No. 101 of 1990 now provides that with effect from 1 March 1990 dividends distributed by a company are also exempt from income tax in the hands of recipient individuals and close corporations.

☐ There are no returns which need to be submitted to the Registrar of Close Corporations on a regular basis.

☐ As in the case of a company, a close corporation can hold shares in "other" limited companies, even to the extent of becoming a holding company. By virtue of the definition of members a company (with certain limited technical exceptions) cannot hold an interest in a close corporation.[1]

1 See 3.05 and 5.04.

1.08 The main relative disadvantages are as follows:

☐ The provisions governing accounting and disclosure are very sketchy; in particular the concept "in accordance with generally accepted accounting practice" is far from clear in the application as regards the annual financial statements.[1]

☐ The duties of the accounting officer, especially in relation to the annual financial statements, are not clear; there is no provision for an audit, yet the accounting officer must determine whether the annual financial statements are in accord with the accounting records, and determine whether the accounting policies applied in their preparation were those of the "generally accepted accounting practice"; it is almost impossible to envisage a report by the accounting officer which does not contain an important disclaimer.

☐ Every member is an agent of the corporation, can act on its behalf, can participate in its management and bind its credit, ultimately creating a risk for other members as insolvency of the corporation can give rise to personal liability of members.

☐ The very simplicity and informality of the corporate structure facilitates fraud and unauthorised or improper actions within the close corporation. This is exacerbated by the circumstance that in the creation of the applicable legal framework only basic and simple rules were formulated to provide corporate personality for *small* businesses, whilst the only criterion to establish the attribute "small" is a maximum membership of ten natural persons. The financial means and the scope of operations of the corporation are not at issue.

1 See 8.01 *et seq.*

2

Formation of a close corporation

Enabling Act and regulations

2.01 A close corporation acquires legal personality and corporate status by its incorporation in terms of the Close Corporations Act 1984. On being formed in accordance with the provisions of the Act and registration in terms of its provisions, a juristic person comes into existence which continues to exist as such notwithstanding changes in its membership until it is deregistered or dissolved.[1]

The Act was amended by the Close Corporations Amendment Acts (Acts 38 of 1986, 64 of 1988, 17 of 1990 and 81 of 1992) which amendments are incorporated in the discussion which follows.

Regulations further governing close corporations have been published[2] which in outline provide for the following:

(a) the requirements in respect of documents to be lodged with the registrar;

(b) the office hours of the registration office;

(c) forms to be used and fees;

(d) manner and proof of payment of prescribed fees;

(e) inspection and obtaining copies of documents kept by the registrar;

(f) preservation of records;

(g) reservation of name for a close corporation;

(h) administrative procedures to be followed in registering and amending the founding statement of the close corporation, the conversion of companies into corporations and the restoration of a corporation on the register after having been deregistered, its voluntary winding up, and the duties of an accounting officer.

1 S 2.
2 Government Notice R2487, 16 November 1984 and amended by GN R1447, 3 July 1987, GN R2098, 21 October 1988, GN R417, 10 March 1989, GN R602, 31 March 1989, GN 1392, 30 June 1989 and GN R1664, 19 June 1992.

Administration of the Act

2.02 Close corporations are registered at the close corporations registration office in Pretoria where a register of names and registration numbers and prescribed documentation concerning close corporations are kept. This office is administered by the registrar of close corporations with power of delegation.[1]

On payment of the prescribed fee any person may inspect the documents kept by the registrar, obtain a certificate from the registrar as to the contents of such a document or obtain a copy of such document.[2]

1 S 4.
2 S 5.

Formation of a close corporation

2.03 A close corporation is formed when the prescribed document (form CK1), known as the founding statement, duly completed is lodged with the registrar (in triplicate) together with the prescribed fee (presently R100,00), the form CK7 on which its name has been reserved and the written consent of the accounting officer to his appointment, whereupon it is registered in his registers.[1]

Upon registration of the founding statement the registrar must assign a registration number to the corporation and certify on its certificate of incorporation the fact of the incorporation. Such a certificate of incorporation shall upon its production be conclusive evidence that all the requirements in respect of registration have been complied with and that the corporation is duly incorporated.[2]

The original founding statement is retained by the registrar, one is returned to the corporation and the third is transmitted to the Receiver of Revenue for his purposes.

Lodging of the founding statement may be effected in person, through the post or by any one of the incorporators or by anyone on their behalf. Otherwise than in the case of the Companies Act no restrictions are imposed in this regard.

1 Ss 2, 12, 13 and reg 15.
2 S 14.

The founding statement

Form of founding statement

2.04 The founding statement in the prescribed form (CK1) serves as the charter of the close corporation and sets out its corporate structure. It must be in one of the official languages of the Republic and be signed by or on behalf of every person who is to be a member of the corporation upon its registration.[1] If it is signed on behalf of any of its members a power of attorney authorising such signature will have to be lodged at the time of the lodging of the founding statement.

1 S 12.

Contents of founding statement

2.05 The founding statement must contain the following particulars:

☐ the full name of the corporation and, if required, a literal translation of that name in the other official language and a shortened form of that name or its translation;

☐ the principal business to be carried on by the corporation;

☐ the date of the end of its financial year;

☐ the postal address and the address to which all communications and notices to the corporation may be addressed (also known as the registered office);

☐ the name and postal address of the person or firm which has consented in writing (which consent must accompany the founding statement on being lodged) to appointment as accounting officer and the name of the profession to which the accounting officer belongs which qualifies him as such;

☐ the full names, identity number (or failing such number the date of birth) and the residential and postal address of each member;

☐ the size, expressed as a percentage, of each member's interest in the corporation;

☐ particulars of the contribution of each member to the corporation, usually an amount of money or property (whether corporeal or incorporeal) or services to be rendered together with a description of such property or services and a statement of its fair value.[1]

1 S 12 and the notes to form CK1.

Keeping of copy of founding statement

2.06 The close corporation must keep a copy of its founding statement and proof of its registration at its registered office. This must be available for inspection by any person. In the case of a person who is not a member, payment of an amount determined by the corporation being not more than R1,00 may be charged. Failing to provide such access to the founding statement renders a member or officer of the corporation refusing access guilty of an offence.[1]

1 S 16.

The constitutive documents of a close corporation

2.07 The founding statement serves the same purpose as the memorandum of association and the recording of information contained in some of the registers of a company. Any change or additions to any of the matters set out in the founding statement is to be recorded with the registrar by means of the lodging of an amended founding statement (dealt with below in 2.11).

The members of a close corporation with two or more members may in addition enter into a written *association agreement* regulating internal matters of the corporation not inconsistent with the provisions of the Act. Such an agreement fulfils the role which the articles of association and a shareholders agreement would play in a company. The association agreement must be signed by or on behalf of each member and must be kept at the registered office where members may inspect it, make extracts from or copy it. Whether or not an association agreement was entered into, all the members may validly enter into any other agreement, express or implied, not inconsistent with the association agreement on any matter that may have been regulated by an association agreement.[1]

The association agreement may only be inspected as of right by members. A person dealing with the corporation shall not in law be deemed to have notice of its contents.[2]

1 S 44. See 4.01 – 4.08 below.
2 S 45.

Name of a close corporation

Name

2.08 The starting point in registering a close corporation is to reserve for it a name which is not, in the words of section 19, "in the opinion of the registrar undesirable."[1] In practice this mainly implies that it may not so closely resemble the name of another close corporation or company or offend against one of the many guidelines formulated by the registrars of companies and close corporations concerning the acceptability of names.[2] Before lodging a founding statement the approval and reservation of the name to be used must be obtained from the registrar by lodging form CK7 with him on payment of the prescribed fee, currently R50,00. The reservation is valid for two months. The duplicate of form CK7 must accompany the founding statement on being lodged for registration. If translated or shortened forms of name are to be registered forms CK7 must also be lodged in respect of each such name.

1 S 19.

2 In a document called "Directive on Names of

Companies" *Government Gazette* 4055, 19 Oct 1973. See also J C Smit 1986 *De Rebus* 489-492.

Change of name

2.09 If within one year after incorporation it appears to the registrar that a name as included in the founding statement is undesirable, he must order the corporation to change the name. An interested person may within a period of one year after the registration of a founding statement of payment of the prescribed fee apply in writing to the registrar for an order directing the corporation to change its name on the ground of undesirability or because such name is calculated to cause damage to the applicant. An interested person may also within a period of two years after registration on the same grounds apply to a court for such an order, and the court may on such application make such order as it deems fit. A person feeling aggrieved by such decision or order may within one month thereafter apply to the supreme court for relief, and the court may after the consideration of the merits make an order it deems fit.

No fee shall be payable in respect of the registration of an amended founding statement by virtue of an order of the registrar for the change of name.

The right so to apply for an order to change a name in no way detracts from the common law right to bring an action against a corporation for passing off a business, goods or services as that of another.[1]

A corporation may change its name by an appropriate amendment of its founding statement which is dealt with in 2.11.

A change of name has no effect on the rights and duties of or continuance of legal proceedings by or against a corporation. On production of a certified copy of a founding statement reflecting a change of name any registrar or officer maintaining a register must effect the necessary alterations.[2]

1 S 20.

2 S 21.

Additional requirements as to name

2.10 The following additional requirements apply to the use and publication of the name of a close corporation:

(a) the abbreviations CC and BK, in capital letters, must be subjoined to the English and Afrikaans names, respectively, of the corporation;[1]

(b) the full registered name of the corporation (or a registered literal translation) ,*and* its registration number in legible characters shall be –

☐ displayed on the outside of its registered office and every office or other place in which its business is carried on; and

☐ mentioned in all notices and other official publications, including advertisements, of the corporation and in all bills of exchange, promissory notes, endorsements, cheques and orders for money, goods or services purporting to be signed by or on behalf of the corporation, and all letters, delivery notes, invoices, receipts and letters of credit of the corporation.[2]

(c) the issue of such a notice or official publication or the signing of such a bill of exchange, promissory note, endorsement, cheque or order for money on behalf of the corporation or the issue of such a letter, delivery note, invoice, receipt or letter of credit without stating the name and registration number shall render the member or other person so acting on behalf of the corporation –

☐ guilty of an offence, and

☐ liable to the holder of the bill of exchange, promissory note, cheque or order for money, goods or services for the amount thereof, unless the amount is paid by the corporation.[3]

1 S 22; Any person carrying on business under a name or title to which such abbreviation is subjoined, or of which the words "close corporation" or "beslote korporasie" form part, shall, unless duly incorporated as a close corporation in terms of this Act, be guilty of an offence – s 22A.

2 S 23(1).

3 S 23(2). In the case of a company the failure to state the registration number does not lead to such personal liability (s 50(3)(b) of the Companies Act; *Bouwer v Andrews* 1988 4 SA 337 (E)).

Amendment of founding statement

Lodging amendment

2.11 Section 15 of the Act provides that if any change has taken place in respect of any of the particulars stated in the founding statement, an amended founding statement must be lodged with the registrar for registration in triplicate on the prescribed form (CK2).

If the change relates to a change in the principal business to be carried on, the membership of the corporation, the size of each member's interest in the corporation or the particulars of the contribution of each member the amended founding statement must be lodged within 28 days of such change and be signed by or on behalf of every member of the corporation and by or on behalf of any person who will become a member on such registration. If the change relates to the name, postal address, registered address or name and postal address of the accounting officer or the end of the financial year of the corporation the amended founding statement must first be lodged before such a change can take effect, either on date of registration or upon a later date mentioned in the statement. In the case of changes in respect of the postal or registered address of the corporation the accounting officer may sign such statement on behalf of the members if the corporation has approved of the said change and the accounting officer so certifies in writing. The accounting officer may also sign statements in respect of changes in the name or address of the accounting officer on behalf of the members, which change shall take effect upon the date mentioned in the statement.

If the change relates to the name, description of principal business or end of the financial year the prescribed fee, currently R30,00, is payable on lodging the statement; in respect of any other changes no fee is payable.

Failure to lodge amendment

2.12 If a corporation fails to lodge an amended founding statement, the registrar may on his own initiative or on application by any member or creditor of the corporation call upon the corporation to make good the default within 28 days. Failing response the registrar may direct the members to make good the default within 21 days. Failing reaction on such direction the registrar may by further written notice served on the members by registered post impose on them a penalty not exceeding R5,00 per day from the date upon which the original reminder was sent. The written notice directing the members to make good the default may be sent by the registrar to the Clerk of the Magistrate's Court in whose area of jurisdiction the registered office of the corporation is situated who shall record it and thereupon the notice shall have the effect of civil judgment of that magistrate's court against every member for the amount of the penalty in question.[1]

1 S 15(3).

Jurisdiction

2.13 The court having jurisdiction in any matter generally is the magistrate's court or supreme court within whose area of jurisdiction the registered office or main place of business of the corporation is situate.[1] If the jurisdiction of the magistrate's court is excluded because the matter in issue is something falling outside the scope of jurisdiction as limited in the Magistrates' Courts Act,[2] jurisdiction lies only with the supreme court.[3]

1 S 7, as amended by s 1, Close Corporations Amendment Act 64 of 1988.
2 Act 32 of 1944. See especially ss 29 and 46.
3 Although s 7 specifically states that the magistrate's court has jurisdiction in the *winding up* of a corporation, it has been decided in the Natal Provincial Division of the Supreme Court (*Walker v J & B Electrical and Refrigeration CC* 1988 1 SA 471 (N)) before the amendment of s 7 that the provisions of the Magistrates' Courts Act does not confer jurisdiction upon a magistrate's court to wind up a corporation, and accordingly only the supreme court would have such jurisdiction. This view of the legal position has not been stated in any of the other provinces and the decision has been criticised (*Sams Voedsel (Edms) Bpk v Bethlehem Koelkamers BK* 1989 2 SA 595 (O) 597; *Greaves v Opta Medical Co* 1989 1 SA 993 (T)). See also *J Gerber Finance (Pty) Ltd v M and M Timbers* 1987 3 SA 135 (W); *Ex parte Universal Enterprises* 1988 3 SA 969 (W); *Robinson v BRE Engineering CC* 1987 3 SA 140 (C); *Reid v Ropat Investment CC* 1988 4 SA 26 (W); Otto 1987 *De Rebus* 555; Beck 1987 *MB* 47; Henning 1987 *JJS* 107; Savvas 1987 *De Rebus* 616; Beaton 1988 *De Rebus* 215; Cilliers 1988 *De Rebus* 515; Van Loggerenberg & Van den Berg 1990 *SALJ* 97.

3

Membership and member's interest

Member's interest contrasted with a share in a limited company

3.01 Close corporations do not issue shares and therefore do not have shareholders but only members. The capital of a close corporation consists of the contributions made by its members. Instead of shares a member becomes entitled to a member's interest as a consideration for his contribution. In the case of companies with a share capital it is necessary to distinguish between shareholding and membership. In close corporations the distinction is between a member's interest and membership.

Number of members

3.02 A close corporation may be formed with one or more members but at no time may there be more than ten members.[1] Members are not even entitled to be joint holders of the same member's interest in the corporation.[2] If the maximum number is exceeded for a period of six months or more every member becomes personally liable for every debt of the corporation incurred whilst the number exceeded ten.[3]

This somewhat strict adherence to a maximum of ten members emphasises the legislature's intention that the close corporation should serve the smaller business venture in which the relationship of members *inter se* resembles that of partners. Unfortunately membership alone does not determine the size of an undertaking[4] and it is not clear why the maximum number was set at ten while partnerships are allowed a maximum of 20 (sometimes even more) members.[5]

1 S 28.
2 S 30(2).
3 S 63(c).

4 See 1.02 fn 3.
5 See further De Koker and Henning 1990 *THRHR* 547.

Requirements for membership

3.03 Subject to certain exceptions, only natural persons may be members of a corporation.[1] No juristic person or trustee of an *inter vivos* trust may directly or indirectly hold a member's interest in a close corporation.[2] Consequently a company or a close corporation may not become a member of a close corporation; if they do, they risk personal liability for corporation debts.[3] However, a close corporation may be a shareholder in a company and may thus even become a holding company and may even enter into partnerships with other companies or close corporations.

1 S 29(1). See further 3.04 – 3.05.
2 *Ibid*. The holding of a member's interest on behalf of a juristic person by means of nominees is expressly forbidden. A person holding membership for the benefit of a trust *inter vivos* as from before 13 April 1987 may continue to do so subject to certain limitations in terms of s 29(1A)

(introduced by the Close Corporations Amendment Act 17 of 1990). As to the problems experienced prior to the amendment, see Wunsh 1987 *De Rebus* 457; Henning 1987 *De Rebus* 485; Viljoen 1987 *De Rebus* 409.
3 S 63(d).

3.04 Under the following circumstances a natural person will qualify for membership:

☐ if he is entitled to a member's interest;[1]

☐ *nomine officii* as a trustee of a testamentary trust provided that no juristic person is a beneficiary of such trust;[2]

☐ *nomine officii* as a trustee, administrator, executor or curator, of an insolvent, deceased or mentally disordered member's estate or his duly appointed legal representative.[3] If the member's interest is not transferred within 28 days of his assuming office he must request the existing members to lodge an amended founding statement with the registrar designating him *nomine officii* as representative of the member in question.[4] However, even in the absence of an amended founding statement such a representative will have the power to represent the member until his member's interest has been transferred to a qualified person.[5]

As no other qualification is set for membership of a close corporation it appears that even a minor, an insolvent and other persons under legal disability may become members of a close corporation if they are qualified to hold a member's interest.[6] In contracting to become a member they would have to be represented or assisted by their legal guardians or trustees. However, subject to a few qualifications, such persons are disqualified from taking part in the management of the close corporation[7] and must be represented in the corporation by their guardians or legal representatives.[8] Notwithstanding this limitation their names must be stated in the founding statement as members. The situation envisaged in section 29(2)(c) in terms of which their members' interests must be registered in the name of a representative *nomine officii* probably only applies when a member becomes disabled or dies while a member.[9]

1 S 29(2)(a).
2 S 29(2)(b).
3 S 29(2)(c).
4 S 29(3)(c).
5 S 29(3)(e).
6 This is borne out by the provisions of s 47(1)(b)(i).

7 S 47. See 4.09 *infra*.
8 S 32.
9 See in general Oosthuizen *Beslote Korporasies* (1986) 20 (hereafter Oosthuizen). As to the possibility and consequences of "puppet" membership, see Lessing 1989 *SA Merc LJ* 242.

3.05 Juristic persons only qualify for membership under the following restricted circumstances:

☐ *nomine officii* as trustee of a testamentary trust provided that such juristic person is not directly or indirectly controlled by a beneficiary of the trust and that no juristic person is a beneficiary of such trust;[1]

☐ *nomine officii* as trustee, administrator, executor or curator of the estate of an insolvent, deceased, or mentally disordered person or of a person otherwise incapable of managing his own affairs.[2]

It must be stressed that subject to the exceptions above, a juristic person is not entitled to hold a member's interest directly or indirectly or through a nominee.[3]

1 S 29(2)(b).
2 S 29(2)(c). In terms of s 55(h) of the Insolvency Act 24 of 1936 a corporate body may not be

appointed trustee of an insolvent estate.
3 S 29(1).

Commencement of membership

3.06 Membership commences on the date of the registration of the founding statement reflecting particulars of the membership.[1] The full names and identity number, the size of the member's interest and particulars of the contribution must be recorded.[2] On the admission of a new member, or the need arising to register someone *nomine officii* as representative an amended founding statement must be registered within 28 days. It is the duty of the existing members to ensure that the amended founding statement is registered[3] and it must be signed by or on behalf of each member and by or on behalf of any person who will become a member of the corporation *on registration of the amended founding statement.*[4]

In terms of section 29(3)(a) membership commences on registration of the founding statement. The provisions of section 15(1) read with section 15(2) tends to imply that on the admission of a new member, membership may well commence on an earlier date – possibly the date that the amended founding statement was signed or the date indicated in the agreement. This follows as section 15(2) does not refer to section 12(d). However, section 15(1) does also refer to *any person who will become a member on such registration.* In light of the fact that section 29(3) deals specifically with the commencement of membership it is submitted that a new member's membership *de jure* commences at the earliest on the date of registration of the amended founding statement.[5]

1 S 29(3)(a).
2 S 12.
3 S 29(3) read with s 15(1).
4 S 15(1). As amended by s 2 of the Close Corpor-

ations Amendment Act 81 of 1992.
5 See Geach & Schoeman *Guide to the Close Corporations Act and Regulations* (1984) 520.

Certificate of member's interest

3.07 Each member must be issued with a certificate, signed by or on behalf of every member, stating the current percentage of such member's interest in the corporation.[1]

1 S 31; see also *Specimen certificate of member's interest* Part 2 p 33.

Register of members

3.08 No formal register of members need be kept but as the founding statement, which contains the names of members, must be kept up to date, the names of the present members can be easily ascertained as a copy of the founding statement must be kept open for inspection at the registered office of the corporation.[1] The most recent founding statement can be taken as the equivalent of the members' register.

The names of members must be stated in every business letter bearing the registered name of the corporation.[2]

1 See s 16. It must, however, be kept in mind that irrespective of the fact that these documents are available for inspection at the registered office of the corporation and at the office of the registrar of close corporations nobody shall be deemed to have knowledge of any paticulars thereof merely because such particulars are stated in the

documents. (The doctrine of constructive notice and its attendant complexities are thus circumvented.)
2 S 41. Contravention constitutes an offence by the corporation (s 41(2)) but it does not lead to the personal liability of members.

Member's interest

3.09 In consideration for his contribution each member acquires a member's interest in the corporation. Such an interest must be a single interest expressed as a percentage of the total and two or more persons may not be joint holders of the same member's interest.[1] The quantum of the interest is set out in the founding statement and in the certificate of member's interest.[2] A member's interest, although it must be expressed as a percentage, does not necessarily have to correspond with the percentage which his contribution bears to the total contributions of all members. The fact that it is stated that the member's interest must be a single interest implies that a person cannot acquire more than one member's interest in a single corporation.

1 S 30.
2 S 12(e) read with s 31.

Aggregate of member's interest

3.10 The aggregate of all members' interests in a corporation expressed as a percentage must at all times be 100%.[1] Therefore on the admission of a new member or the retirement of an existing member the percentage of the respective members' interests must be adjusted to attain an aggregate of 100%.[2] If the corporation acquires a member's interest from one of the existing members this must be added proportionally to the members' interests of the remaining members.[3]

1 S 38.
2 S 38.

3 S 38(c). The close corporation cannot acquire membership in itself.

Nature of member's interest

3.11 As a close corporation is a juristic person its assets are held by it and the members are not co-owners thereof. Referring to this aspect in relation to company law, the appellate division held that although a member does not have a proprietary interest in the business or assets of the company it nevertheless has a proprietary or financial interest in the company.[1] Shares in a company can be described as a share in the share capital of the company,[2] comprising a complex of rights and duties.[3] As representing personal rights a share is an incorporeal object[4] and is regarded as movable property.[5] It is submitted that the same applies in respect of a member's interest in a close corporation. Thus a member's interest can be described as a personal right as against the corporation entitling the holder to a *pro rata* share in the aggregate of members' interests and to participate in a distribution of profits and on liquidation in the remaining assets after all creditors have been paid.

1 *Stellenbosch Farmers' Winery v Distillers Corp* 1962 1 SA 458 (A) 485 *et seq.*
2 S 1 of the Companies Act.
3 See Cilliers & Benade *Corporate Law* 88 (hereafter Cilliers & Benade); *Moosa v Lalloo* 1956 2
SA 237 (D) and 1957 4 SA 207 (D) 222.
4 *Standard Bank of SA Ltd v Ocean Commodities Inc* 1980 2 SA 175 (T) and Cilliers & Benade 88.
5 S 91 of the Companies Act.

Acquisition of member's interest

3.12 A member's interest can be acquired directly from the corporation or from an existing member or his estate.[1]

1 S 33(1).

Acquisition of interest from corporation (founding members)

3.13 A founding member of a corporation must make an initial contribution to the corporation in pursuance whereof he receives a member's interest. The contribution may consist of money, corporeal or incorporeal property or of services rendered in connection with and for the purpose of the formation and incorporation of the corporation. Particulars of the contribution must be stated in the founding statement and if it is a non-monetary contribution a description and statement of the fair value thereof must be included.[1] By agreement among all the members the contribution of any member may be increased or reduced, provided details are furnished in an amended founding statement.[2]

The initial contribution must be paid, delivered or transferred to the corporation within 90 days after the date of registration or within 90 days after the registration of the amended founding statement in the case of an increase in the contribution.[3] An undertaking to make a contribution or to increase a contribution is enforceable by the corporation in legal proceedings.[4] Failure to make a promised contribution may lead to the personal liability of members.[5]

1 S 12(f) read with s 24. In the case of partnerships any type of service rendered by partners in connection with partnership business is regarded as a valid contribution.
2 S 24(2) and (3).

3 S 24(4); note that membership is not dependent on the delivery of the contribution (See Oosthuizen 23 *et seq*).
4 S 24(5).
5 S 63(b) and see 6.02.

3.14 As was stated earlier the size of a member's contribution does not necessarily have to correspond with his member's interest expressed as a percentage. However, unless otherwise stated in the association agreement the percentage of the member's interest determines the extent of his vote in the corporation and the extent of his participation in "dividend payments".[1]

1 S 46(d) and (f).

Additional members

3.15 A person who qualifies for membership may become a member by making a contribution to the corporation in pursuance of which a percentage member's interest is allotted to him. The percentage to which he is entitled is determined by agreement between him and the existing members as their members' interest will have to be reduced in order to retain the aggregate member's interest at 100%.[1]

Contributions to an existing corporation may be in the form of money or property but not in the form of services rendered or to be rendered.[2]

1 S 33(1)(b) and s 38. For a discussion of the question whether an existing member can veto the admission of a new member see   Oosthuizen 25 *et seq*.
2 S 33(2).

Acquisition of interest from existing member

3.16 A person may acquire a member's interest from an existing member. The *causa* may be a purchase, a donation, an exchange or any other transaction.[1] Every such disposition must be in accordance with the association agreement or in the absence thereof the consent of every other member of the corporation is required.[2]

1 A forced sale resultant on the insolvency or death of the erstwhile member will be discussed separately.

2 S 37. This means that any member can veto the transfer of a member's interest.

Cessation of member's interest by order of court

3.17 In terms of section 36 and section 49 the court may under certain circumstances order the cessation of a member's membership and make such order as it deems necessary in regard to the disposal of the member's interest.

Insolvency or death of member

3.18 In case of the insolvency of a member or on his death his trustee or executor is compelled to sell his member's interest. Notwithstanding any contrary provision in the association agreement the member's interest must, in case of insolvency, be sold to either the corporation, the remaining members or an outsider who qualifies for membership.[1] A sale to an outsider can only be effected after the trustee has given the remaining members and the corporation written notice of the name and address of the proposed purchaser and of the purchase price and terms of payment and has given them a 28 days option to buy the whole of the member's interest at the same price and on the same terms.[2]

1 S 34(1).
2 S 34(2). This may be termed a sale subject to a negative suspensive condition. The outsider may   acquire the interest should it appear that the corporation or its members are not interested. See Oosthuizen 28 *et seq*.

3.19 The duties of the executor of a deceased estate to dispose of the member's interest of the deceased member must be exercised subject to the provisions of the association agreement. In the absence thereof the executor of a deceased estate may only transfer the member's interest to an heir or legatee if he qualifies to become a member and if the remaining members have given their consent.[1] If they refuse to consent within 28 days the executor must sell the member's interest of the deceased member to the corporation, the remaining members or an outsider on the same terms as in the case of insolvency.[2]

1 S 35(a).
2 S 35(b) read with s 34(2). See 3.18 *supra* and Oosthuizen 28 *et seq*.

Transfer of a member's interest

3.20 Any transfer of a member's interest should be reflected in an amended founding statement.

Formalities for transfer

3.21 The Act does not in terms stipulate the method of transfer of a member's interest. There is no requirement comparable with section 133 of the Companies Act which provides that a company may not register a transfer of shares unless a transfer form ("a proper instrument of transfer") has been delivered to it.

The transfer of an individual member's interest does, however, necessitate the registration of an amended founding statement. Accordingly the transfer of a member's interest is in practice very often effected by lodging form CK2 (amended Founding statement), showing *inter alia* in part B details of the member or members who resign and the reconstituted list of members after the transfer of the particular member's interest has been effected. This list of members must also give the full names and address of each member, the size of his interest and particulars of the contributions made by him. All members, including the members who resign must sign the form either personally or by way of a nominee appointed under power of attorney.

The transferee only becomes a member and acquires the member's interest concerned on registration of form CK2.[1]

The transfer of a member's interest solely by relying on an amended founding statement (form CK2), has on occasion given rise to problems. This is mainly due to the fact that the interest in a close corporation is not as well defined as a share in an incorporated company with structured organs (board of directors and general meeting) each with its own powers and duties. In fact, in certain respects the internal relations between members of a close corporation may resemble a partnership with some degree of limited liability. Care should thus be taken that reliance solely on a CK2 form does not, as has happened in practice, lead to the following situations:

– Where there are several members, an imbalance in the relative interests of members may occur (as result of the sale of his interest by a resigning member to a remaining member so that the remaining member concerned, with his resultant increased interest, is able to vote for increased benefits for himself such as an increased salary and/or other allowances).

– A member who has not yet signed the CK2 blocks transfer of the particular member's interest in order to obtain increased benefit for himself; thus the selling member who has not yet signed may negotiate for a more favourable consideration.

To ensure that the transfer of a member's interest takes place without any untoward problems, the agreement in regard to the sale of the interest should be embodied in a contract. The essential components of the contract are:

– The parties to the contract. (In view of the semi-partnership nature of a close corporation the parties include not only the seller and purchaser of the interest but also the other remaining members).

- The percentage member's interest being sold and the respective percentage of each member's interest after the sale and transfer.
- The selling price. Where the consideration is other than cash it should be fully described.
- The date of payment of the purchase price as well as the date of transfer of the member's interest, that is the date of lodgment of form CK2.
- An undertaking by the seller (transferor) that he guarantees signature of form CK2 by all parties.

1 S 15(1).

Restrictions on transfer

3.22 The association agreement may well contain provisions restricting the transfer of interests in any of the numerous ways commonly found in the articles of companies (for example that it may not be transferred to any non-member as long as there are existing members wishing to acquire the interest).

3.23 In the light of what was stated earlier a transferee only becomes a member on registration of the amended founding statement.[1] However, a member's interest is a right of action, a *jus in persona*, which is transferred by cession. Although there exists some doubt as to whether transfer of the necessary certificates and documents evidencing the title are necessary to complete the cession,[2] it is clear that the effectiveness of the cession itself is not dependent on the registration of the member's name in the founding statement. This is further borne out by the fact that section 29(2) states that a person qualifies for membership the moment he is entitled to a member's interest. The question therefore arises whether such a cession can be effected against the wishes of the other members. For instance where they refuse their permission to a disposition and refuse to sign the amended founding statement.[3] (In the case of a company a new "shareholder" becomes entitled to the rights attaching to the shares despite the fact that the company may have refused registration. He will, however, have to exercise his rights through the seller).[4] In the light of the underlying intention of the legislature to provide for a corporate form characterised by the close relationship between the members *inter se* and the fact that section 37 requires the consent of every member for the disposition of an *interest or a portion thereof* it is submitted that cessions not substantiated by the necessary consent are ineffective.

1 See 3.06 *supra*.
2 See e g *Labuschagne v Denny* 1963 3 SA 538 (A); *Nezar v Die Meester* 1982 2 SA 430 (T); *Standard Bank of SA Ltd v Ocean Commodities* 1983 1 SA 276 (A). See in general Malan *Collective Securities Depositories and The Transfer of Secu-*
rities (1984) 165.
3 See s 37(b) and s 15(1).
4 See e g *Standard Bank of SA Ltd v Ocean Commodities Inc* 1980 2 SA 175 (T) and Cilliers & Benade 134.

Signature of amended founding statement

3.24 The transfer of an interest necessitates the registration of an amending founding statement in terms of section 15. The amending founding statement has to be signed "by or on behalf of every member" and by or on behalf of any person who will become a member on such registration.[1] To prevent the recording of an incorrect amended founding statement unbeknown to a member whose interest is fraudulently or erroneously left out, the prescribed form for the amending founding statement (CK2) has been amended to provide for signatures of both continuing and resigning members.

1 S 2 Close Corporations Amendment Act 81 of 1992.

Security by means of member's interest

3.25 Rights of action can be used as security for debts.[1] It has become common practice to cede a shareholding in a company as security for a debt. This type of security is known as a cession *in securitatem debiti*. Nevertheless some uncertainty exists as to the legal nature of the security involved as it is seen by some as a pledge of an incorporeal and by others as an out-and-out cession.[2] In *Alexander NO v Standard Merchant Bank*[3] it was stated by Viljoen J:

> It is clear that a right being an incorporeal can be transferred only by means of a cession. But in my view a cession *in securitatem debiti* can be constituted in two ways. It can take the form of what appears on the face of it to be an out-and-out cession subject to the *pactum fiduciae* . . . or it can take the form of a pledge of the incorporeal. This latter form of cession may not be very sound dogmatically but . . . mercantile practice demands it.[4]

1 See in general Scott *The Law of Cession* 2ed 233 *et seq* and Benade 1964 *THRHR* 279.
2 See Cilliers & Benade 135 for a discussion of the various authorities. See also Malan *Beslote Korporasiereg* (1986) 55 *et seq*.
3 1978 4 SA 730 (W).
4 739 *et seq*. See also *Spendiff NO v JAJ Distributors (Pty) Ltd* 1989 4 SA 126 (C); *Incledon (Welkom) (Pty) Ltd v Qwaqwa Development Corporation Ltd* 1990 4 SA 798 (A).

3.26 As a member's interest is an incorporeal it ought likewise to lend itself to this type of security. Indeed it would be as advantageous to corporation members as it is to shareholders to use their interest in the corporate body as security. The type of security which is used will depend on the intention of the parties. If the cession to secure a debt is intended to be a pledge, the ordinary rules of pledge would apply. If the parties regard their transaction as an out-and-out cession, the cession is subject to a so-called *pactum fiduciae*. A discussion of these two situations follows.

Pledge of incorporeals

3.27 Where the cession is intended to be a pledge of incorporeals, the member pledges his member's interest as security for a debt – probably by handing over his membership certificate accompanied by a transfer form signed in blank coupled with the intention that the pledgee will retain the certificate until payment is made. In the case of non-payment the member's interest can in certain cases be sold by the pledgee in order to settle the outstanding debt. However, the pledgor remains the nominal "owner" of the member's interest whilst the pledgee obtains a "real" right therein. On the insolvency of the pledgor the interest vests in his insolvent estate but the pledgee is regarded as a secured creditor.

The Close Corporations Act, however, presents some problems in this regard. Any disposition of a member's interest is dependent on the consent of all the members – given at the time of the disposition or in advance in the association agreement.[1] Although the pledge itself would probably not be regarded as a disposition, this provision may seriously hamper the pledgee's right to effect registration in his name or to sell it to an outsider on non-payment.[2] Furthermore it should be remembered that a juristic person may not directly or indirectly hold a member's interest in a close corporation. A bank or similar financial institution as pledgee will consequently not be entitled to obtain registration in its name in the case of non-payment and neither can the interest be sold to any other body corporate.[3]

1 S 37.
2 The existing members may not be in a financial position to buy the member's interest or may offer
a deflated price.
3 See Oosthuizen 33 and Malan *Beslote Korporasiereg* 56.

Out-and-out security cession

3.28 In the case of an out-and-out cession coupled with a *pactum fiduciae* in terms of which the cessionary undertakes to cede the interest back to the cedent once the "secured" debt has been satisfied, the cessionary can only obtain registration in his name or sell the interest if the cedent has defaulted.[1] Although delivery of the certificate is not required to constitute a valid security this would be necessary to perfect the cession in the event of there being several claimants to the member's interest.[2] As this is an out-and-out cession the member's interest passes to the cessionary and will not be an asset in the estate of the cedent.

1 Cilliers & Benade 136.
2 See Cilliers & Benade 136 for the position in respect of shares.

3.29 It is doubtful whether this type of cession provides effective security in respect of close corporations. As an out-and-out cession, it amounts to a disposition of a member's interest which requires the consent of all members, unless other provision is made in the association agreement.[1] For the same reason this type of cession cannot be used where the creditor (cessionary) is a body corporate (for example a bank) as juristic persons may not directly or indirectly hold a member's interest in a corporation. It is not even permissible to make use of nominees in place of the body corporate as real creditor.[2]

1 S 37.
2 S 29(1). In terms of s 63(d) this may even lead to the personal liability of the juristic person and the nominee for all debts of the corporation incurred
during the time of the contravention. See also Oosthuizen 33 *et seq* and Malan *Beslote Korporasiereg* 55 *et seq*.

Cessation of membership

3.30   A member may cease to be a member under one of the following circumstances:

☐ Voluntary disposal of his member's interest.[1]

☐ Forced disposal of his member's interest due to his insolvency.[2]

☐ Disposal of a deceased member's interest in terms of his will.[3]

☐ On the deregistration[4] or liquidation and consequent dissolution of the close corporation.[5]

☐ By an order of the court.[6] On application by any member the court may, on one of the following grounds, order that a member shall cease to be a member of the close corporation:

    − permanent incapability to perform his part in the carrying on of the business;

    − being guilty of conduct which is likely to have a prejudicial effect on the carrying on of the business;

    − conduct making it reasonably impractical for the other members to associate with him in the carrying on of the business;

    − it being just and equitable in the view of the court that he should cease to be a member.

1 S 37. A close corporation may grant financial assistance in the acquisition of a member's interest (s 40) and may, subject to certain safeguards itself buy the member's interest (s 39). As the corporation cannot be a member of itself and as there must be at least one member, the interest so acquired must be added to the respective interests of the remaining members (s 38(c))

and a buying back by the corporation is not permissible when the seller is the sole member of the corporation.

2 S 34.
3 S 35.
4 S 26.
5 See s 66.
6 S 36.

4

Internal relations between members and the close corporation

The object of an association agreement

4.01 An association agreement may be described as a written agreement between members of a close corporation regulating the internal relations between them *inter se* and between them and the close corporation. Although it is advisable to enter into an association agreement it is not a prerequisite for the formation or running of a close corporation. By utilising an association agreement the necessary flexibility, tailored to the needs of the particular undertaking, can be obtained. In the absence of such an agreement the provisions of the act regarding internal relationships and management would apply.[1]

1 See eg Geach and Schoeman *Guide to the Close Corporations Act and Regulations* (1984) 547.

General principles applicable in absence of an association agreement

4.02 In terms of the Act the following principles apply unless altered or varied by an association agreement:

☐ Every member shall be entitled to participate in the carrying on of the business.[1]

☐ Members shall have equal rights in regard to the management of the business and in representing the corporation.[2]

☐ Differences between members in connection with the corporation's business shall be decided by majority vote.[3]

☐ A member shall have the number of votes corresponding with his percentage interest.[4]

☐ A member shall be indemnified in respect of expenditure incurred in connection with the conduct of the business and the preservation of the assets of the close corporation.[5]

☐ Payments by the corporation to its members shall be in proportion to their respective interests in the corporation.[6]

1 S 46(a).
2 S 46(b). See further Henning 3 *Tran LCB* 26-32.
3 S 46(c).
4 S 46(d).
5 S 46(e).
6 S 46(f).

The function of an association agreement

4.03 The association agreement should be seen as a document performing the following functions:

☐ It serves the purpose which the articles of association normally serves in the private company, namely to state the procedures to be adopted in the administration of the corporate body.

☐ It deals with matters normally dealt with in a partnership agreement, particularly matters relating to financing the business, grounds for terminating membership, taking over of the interests of a retiring member, restraints on retiring members, valuation of a retiring member's interest, etcetera.

☐ It deals with matters which are dealt with in shareholders' agreements, such as the division of powers in the corporation, the designation of representatives of the corporation, the percentage profit sharing and matters of policy.

Entering into an association agreement

4.04 When a close corporation has two or more members they can enter into a written association agreement. It must be signed by or on behalf of each member. The agreement may regulate any matter regarding the internal relationship between the members or the members and the close corporation as long as it is not inconsistent with the Act[1] or other provisions of the law. A copy of the agreement must be kept at the registered office where it may be inspected by any member.[2] A person who is not a member is not entitled to inspect the agreement and a person doing business with the corporation shall not be deemed to be acquainted with its contents.[3]

1 S 44(1).   3 S 45.
2 S 44(2).

Other agreements between members

4.05 Whether or not an association agreement exists, any other agreement between the parties on any matter that may be regulated by an association agreement shall be equally valid insofar as it is not inconsistent with the association agreement or the provisions of the Act.[1] However, such other agreement does not affect any person other than the corporation or a member thereof and ceases to have effect when any party to it ceases to be a member.[2]

1 S 44(3).
2 *Ibid*. It is submitted that the agreement remains valid between the remaining members. As to
problems iro other agreements between members, see also 4.06 below and Henning 1984 *JJS* 155, 170-171.

Contract constituted by association agreement

4.06 The association agreement and any other such agreement constitute a contract between the corporation and the members and as between members themselves.[1] There are, however, some important differences between the formal association agreement and the other type of agreement. The latter need not be in writing, signed by the parties thereto or be kept available at the registered office. It binds the parties thereto only as long as they remain members of the corporation. Therefore new members or members ceasing to be such are not bound thereby. New members automatically become bound by a formal association agreement without having to sign it[2] and remain bound even after they have ceased to be members. Furthermore an "informal" agreement is subordinate to the formal association agreement in case of inconsistency between the two.[3] The provisions of section 46[4] apply unless it has been superseded by an association agreement.

The definition of an association agreement does not include "informal" agreements and therefore it is submitted that in spite of informal agreements the members will still be obliged to adhere to the provisions of section 46 in the absence of a formal association agreement. Amendments to and cancellation of an association agreement must be in writing and signed by or on behalf of every member including a new member. Probably the same does not apply in respect of other agreements.[5]

Although such "informal" agreements are in line with the flexibility envisaged by the legislature members would be well advised to adhere to the formal association agreement as far as possible.

1 S 44(4).
2 S 44(5).
3 S 44(3).

4 See 4.02 *supra*.
5 See further Henning 1984 *JJS* 155, 170-171.

Matters that may be regulated by association agreement

4.07 An association agreement may for example regulate the following matters:

☐ participation of members in the management;

☐ settling of differences between members;

☐ voting at meetings and proxy votes;

☐ repayment of contributions;

☐ procedure at meetings;

☐ sale or transfer of a member's interest by a member;

☐ financing the corporation;

☐ any other matter which could have been dealt with in a shareholders agreement in respect of a limited company.[1]

1 In Part 2 a draft association agreement is set out.
See also Hyman *Close Corporation Agreements* (1985).

Unalterable provisions

4.08 The following matters cannot, however, be altered by an association agreement:

☐ the manner in which an insolvent member's interest may be disposed of;[1]

☐ members who are disqualified from taking part in the management of the corporation;[2]

☐ the power of a member to call a meeting of members.[3]

1 S 34.
2 S 47.

3 S 48(1).

Written consent of each member

4.09 For certain matters the written consent of each member is required. These include the following:

☐ acquisition of a member's interest in terms of section 39;

☐ financial assistance in respect of the acquisition of a member's interest in terms of section 40;[1]

☐ the granting of loans and furnishing of security in terms of section 52;

☐ the ratification of pre-incorporation contracts in terms of section 53;

☐ the ratification of a breach of fiduciary duties or of a breach of the duty to act with the necessary care and skill in terms of sections 42 and 43.

☐ the appointment of an accounting officer in terms of section 60(3).

1 See Lessing 1990 *SA Merc LJ* 49, 57-8; Trichard,
   Organ & Cilliers 10 *Tran CBL* (1989).

4.10 The first three categories require the previously obtained written consent of each member. These categories relate to the maintenance of capital and personal liability may follow if financial assistance jeopardise the solvency and liquidity of the corporation. Although this consent may be granted in the association agreement it may prove risky to the members as it would be impossible to gauge the financial position of the corporation at the time of entering into the association agreement. The ratification of pre-incorporation contracts and the appointment of an accounting officer are less problematic and in principle it could form part of an association agreement. However, the ratification of breaches in terms of sections 42 and 43 presupposes an appraisal of the facts at the time of the ratification and therefore it is submitted that a blanket approval given in advance in the association agreement will not suffice.

Management of the close corporation

4.11 The members may elect whether to conduct the management of the corporation in accordance with the provisions of the Act or within the formal frame-work of an association agreement.[1] The Act contains the following provisions in regard to the management of the corporation which apply unless varied or altered by an association agreement.

(a) Every member is entitled to participate in the carrying on of the business of the corporation, to exercise equal rights in regard to the management of its business and to represent the corporation in the carrying on of its business.[2] Certain members are, however, disqualified from participation in the management of the corporation. These include (a) people under legal disability with the exception of married women as well as minors over the age of 18 years who have obtained the written consent of their guardians[3] and (b) persons who have been disqualified by the court in terms of the Companies Act from appointment as director.[4] The following persons can only take part in the management of the corporation if authorised by the court: (a) an unrehabilitated insolvent; (b) persons removed from an office of trust on account of misconduct and (c) persons convicted of certain crimes involving dishonesty or in connection with the formation or management of a company or corporation and who have been sentenced to imprisonment therefor for at least six months.[5]

(b) Unless the association agreement provides otherwise matters are decided at meetings of the corporation by majority vote, each member having the number of votes that corresponds with the percentage of his interest in the corporation. The following matters, however, require the consent in writing of a member, or of members together holding at least 75% of the total members' interest in the corporation:

☐ a change in the principal business carried on by the corporation;

☐ a disposal of the whole, or substantially the whole, undertaking of the corporation;

☐ a disposal of all or the greater portion of the assets of the corporation;

☐ any acquisition or disposal of immovable property by the corporation.[6]

(c) Any member of a corporation may, in terms of section 48(1), by notice to every other member and every other person entitled to attend a meeting of members, call a meeting of members for any purpose disclosed in the notice. Unless an association agreement provides otherwise

☐ such notice must, as regards the date, time and venue of the meeting, fix a reasonable date and time, and a venue which is reasonably suitable for all persons entitled to attend the particular meeting;

☐ three-fourths of the members present in person at the meeting, constitute a quorum; and

☐ only members present in person at the meeting may vote at that meeting.[7]

(d) A corporation must minute the proceedings at a meeting of its members in a minute book which must be kept at the registered office of the corporation, within 14 days after the date on which the meeting was held.[8]

(e) A resolution in writing, signed by all the members and entered into the minute book, is as valid and effective as if it were passed at a meeting of the members duly convened and held.[9]

1 It is submitted that members cannot agree informally to depart from the provisions of s 46. See 4.05 *supra*.
2 S 46(a) and (b).
3 S 47(1).
4 S 47(1)(c).
5 S 47(1)(b). See *Marpro Trawling (Pty) Ltd v Cencelli* 1992 1 SA 407 (C) according to which a sentence of 200 days imprisonment suspended for five years qualifies as such a sentence which does not have the option of a fine.
6 S 46(b).
7 S 48(2).
8 S 48(3)(a).
9 S 48(3)(b).

4.12 By way of overview it may be stated that the close corporation has no structured set of organs such as those through which the limited company operates.

There is no board of directors and consequently no division of powers between the directors and the general meeting. The management of the close corporation is in the hands of the members and as can be seen from the few statutory requirements dealt with above, the members are able to carry on the day-to-day business of the corporation with the minimum of functional formalities. It is significant that a proxy may only be utilised if an association agreement providing therefor has been entered into.

Fiduciary position of members

4.13 Although members stand in a close relationship towards each other and in this respect are akin to partners, they owe their fiduciary duties to the corporation as a separate legal persona and not to each other as in the case of partners.[1] As the Act does not make provision for directors it is clear that each member owes his fiduciary duties to the corporation.[2]

1 S 42(1). It should be possible to state in the association agreement that members also owe fiduciary duties towards each other. See also Ribbens *The Personal Fiduciary Character of Members' inter se Relations in the Incorporated Partnership* (1982); Ribbens 1985 *MB* 132.
2 Certain members are excluded from the manage-

ment of the corporation (s 47) and the association agreement may contain further provisions in this regard. As long as these members do not take part in the management it is submitted that they owe no fiduciary duties to the corporation *in their capacity as managers.*

4.14 The exact scope of the fiduciary duties owed by partners *inter se* and by directors to their company is not clearly settled and opinions differ as to the exact extent of these duties.[1] In the case of close corporations principles of company law and partnership law come into play. As the Close Corporations Act was conceived to simplify matters and to avoid uncertainty it sets out to define some of these fiduciary duties of members ''without prejudice to the generality of the expression *fiduciary relationship''.* These provisions are largely based on the principles enunciated by the courts in relation to the fiduciary duties of directors. It is therefore submitted that in the interpretation of these sections and in considering other possible breaches of duty the courts will have regard to the principles as developed in company law but at the same time keeping in mind that the close corporation is not characterised by a separation of ownership from control.

1 See eg Naudé *Die Regsposisie van die Maatskappydirekteur* 106 *et seq*; Blackman (PhD thesis University of Cape Town 1970); Sealy *CLJ* 83; McLennan 1983 *SALJ* 417 and 644; Du Plessis

Maatskappyregtelike grondslae van die regsposisie van direkteure en besturende direkteure LLD thesis UOVS 1991.

4.15 Each member must act honestly and in good faith and must exercise the powers he has regarding its management and of representing the corporation in its interests and for its benefit and should not exceed his powers. He must avoid a conflict between his interests and those of the corporation, and in particular may not derive unwarranted personal economic benefit from the corporation, nor compete with it in its business activities. Where a member fails in his duty to disclose a material interest in any contract of the corporation to every other member, the contract is voidable at the option of the corporation. Where the corporation elects not to be bound by the contract the court may, on application by an interested party, if the court is of the opinion that it is equitable in the circumstances, order that the contract be nonetheless binding.[1]

1 S 42(2) and (3). See also Brooks 1988 *MB* 46.

4.16 A member who has breached his fiduciary duty is liable to the corporation for any loss suffered as a result thereof or for any economic benefit derived by him as the result of the breach. However, breaches may be ratified by the written approval of all the members provided they are fully cognisant of all the material facts.[1] Approval may even be granted in advance.[2]

1 S 42(3) and (4). As all breaches can be ratified and as the consent of each member is required problems relating to the so-called derivative action are avoided. See in this regard Cilliers & Benade 408 *et seq*.

2 As to the possibility and consequences of "puppet" membership, see Lessing 1989 *SA Merc LJ* 242.

Duties of care and skill

4.17 A member shall be liable to the corporation for loss caused by his failure in the carrying on of the business to act with the degree of care and skill that may reasonably be expected from a person of his knowledge and experience. Likewise breaches of this duty may be ratified by the written approval of all members.[1]

1 S 43.

Redress by court

4.18 Members of a close corporation may have recourse to the courts in the circumstances set out below.

4.19 *Unfairly prejudicial conduct*. Any member of a corporation who alleges that any particular act or omission of the corporation or of one or more other members is unfairly prejudicial, unjust or inequitable to him, or that the affairs of the corporation are being conducted in a manner unfairly prejudicial, unjust or inequitable to him, or to some members including him, may apply to a court for an order to rectify the matter. If the court considers it just and equitable, the court may with a view to settling the dispute make such order as it thinks fit, whether for regulating the future conduct of the affairs of the corporation or for the purchase of the interest of any member of the corporation by other members thereof or by the corporation.[1]

1 S 49. This remedy corresponds to a large degree with s 252 of the Companies Act. See Cilliers & Benade 421 *et seq*; Oosthuizen 53 *et seq*.

Proceedings against fellow members

4.20 Where a member or a former member of a corporation is liable to the corporation

☐ to make an initial contribution or any additional contribution as agreed upon by the members, or

☐ on account of –

- the breach of a duty arising from his fiduciary relationship with the corporation; or

- negligence in carrying on the affairs of the corporation,

any other member of the corporation may institute proceedings in respect of any such liability on behalf of the corporation against such member or former member after notifying all other members of the corporation of his intention to do so.[1]

1 S 50.

4.21 The remedy of instituting proceedings against fellow members was devised to avoid the uncertainty inherent in the common law derivative action[1] and the time-consuming and risky procedure envisaged by section 266 of the Companies Act.[2] Should it appear that the proceedings have been instituted without *prima facie* grounds the member may be ordered to pay the cost of the corporation and of the defendant in question.[3] In order to avoid "strike suits" the court's permission is required for a withdrawal of the proceedings or a settlement of the claim.[4]

1 See Cilliers & Benade 402 *et seq.*   3 S 50(3).
2 See Cilliers & Benade 408 *et seq.*   4 S 50(2).

4.22 The member institutes the action on behalf of the corporation. Therefore judgment is in favour of the corporation and the corporation is liable for costs and not the member acting on its behalf.

There is nothing in the Act prohibiting the corporation itself from instituting the action if the majority is in favour.

As any member is entitled to institute action on behalf of the corporation and as the consent of all members is required before the conduct giving rise to the action can be ratified there is no danger of the majority abusing their position and thereby stifling action against them.

4.23 This section differs from section 49 in that the latter section refers to the situation where the member's own rights are affected whereas section 50 relates to situations where the corporation's own rights are at issue.[1]

1 See Oosthuizen 58.

Restrictions on payments to members – maintenance of solvency

4.24 The following rules govern payments to members in order to maintain solvency:

(a) Any payment by a corporation to any member by reason of his membership – including a distribution (of income) or a repayment of any contribution or part thereof – may be made only

☐ if, after such payment is made, the corporation's assets fairly valued, exceed all its liabilities (the solvency criterion);

☐ if the corporation is able to pay its debts as they become due in the ordinary course of its business (the liquidity criterion); and

☐ if such payment will in the particular circumstances not in fact render the corporation unable to pay its debts as they become due in the ordinary course of its business.

A member is liable to a corporation for any payment received contrary to these requirements.

(b) However, any payment to a member in his capacity as a creditor of the particular corporation, and in particular, a payment as remuneration for services rendered as an employee or officer of the corporation, as well as a repayment of a loan or of interest thereon or a payment of rental, does not fall under these restrictions.

(c) The term "payment" includes the delivery or transfer of any property.[1]

1 S 51. See also ss 70 and 71 in connection with possible liability to repay amounts thus received   in the event of the corporation being wound-up within 2 years of such payment.

Prohibition on loans to or security on behalf of members

4.25 Without the prior express consent in writing of all its members, a corporation may not, directly or indirectly, make a loan

☐ to any of its members;

☐ to any other corporation in which one or more of its members together hold more than a 50 percent interest; or

☐ to any company or other juristic person (except a corporation) controlled by one or more members of the corporation;

and may not provide any security to any persons in connection with any obligation of any such member, or other corporation, company or other juristic person.[1]

1 S 52. This provision corresponds to similar restraints on companies set out in s 226 of the Companies Act. See Oosthuizen 64 for a discussion. Note, however, that only prior written consent of all members will suffice. Consequently ratification or *ex post facto* consent is in terms of the Act not sufficient to validate the loan. In *Standard Bank Ltd v Neugarten* 1987 3 SA 695 (W) and 1988 1 SA 652 (W) it was held that ratification was permissible in respect of the similar provisions of s 226 of the Companies Act. This was expressly rejected by majority decision of the Appellate Division (*Standard Bank Ltd v Neugarten* 1989 1 SA 797 (A)). See further Henning 1989 *JJS* 65.

5

External relations

Pre-incorporation contracts

Statutory arrangement

5.01 In effect section 53 of the Close Corporations Act 69 of 1984 is a simplified version[1] of section 35 of the Companies Act 61 of 1973.[2] Hence it also constitutes an exception to the common law principle that there can be no representation of a person not yet in existence.[3] Section 53 allows a close corporation to ratify a pre-incorporation contract concluded by an agent, if certain requirements are met.[4]

1 See Henning 1984 *JJS* 172; *Henegan v Joachim* 1988 4 SA 361 (D).
2 For a discussion of s 35, see Cilliers Benade Henning and Du Plessis *Corporate Law* (1992) 5.04 – 5.10 (hereafter Cilliers *et al*); *Sentrale*
Kunsmis Korporasie (Edms) Bpk v NKP Kunsmis-versreiders (Edms) Bpk 1970 3 SA 367 (A) 396.
3 See Cilliers *et al* 5.02.
4 See Henning 1984 *JJS* 172.

5.02 In terms of section 53 a corporation can ratify or adopt as its own, after its incorporation, a written contract entered into by someone purporting to act as the corporation's agent or trustee before its incorporation, as if the corporation had been duly incorporated at the time the contract was entered into. Such a provisional contract can only become binding on the corporation if the following requirements are complied with:[1] the contract must be in writing; it must have been entered into by a person who professed to act as agent or trustee of a corporation not yet incorporated; the corporation must duly ratify or adopt the contract after its incorporation. The specific requirements are discussed in more detail below.[2]

1 See Cilliers *et al* 5.04 fn 10.
2 As far as formalities in respect of contracts of sale of land are concerned, see Cilliers *et al* 5.04 fn 12.

5.03 *The contract must be in writing.* This requirement is wide enough to embrace oral contracts subsequently reduced to writing, for example a sale by auction concluded orally at the fall of the hammer and later reduced to writing.[1]

1 See Cilliers *et al* 5.05; *Pledge Investments v Kramer: In re Estate Selesnik* 1975 3 SA 696 (A) 702-703.

5.04 *The contract must have been entered into by a person professing to act as an agent or trustee for a corporation not yet formed.* The expression "a person professing to act as an agent or trustee" is taken from section 35 of the Companies Act. Viewed in this perspective, it seems that "trustee" in this context can be equated with "agent". It can also bear its ordinary meaning of principal, thus enabling the parties to make use of the *stipulatio alteri*[1] within the context of section 53. Compliance with the prescribed requirements is only imperative if the person contracted as agent, whether he depicted himself as agent or trustee. Hence the capacity in which the person acted is decisive and not the description he used.[2]

1 See Cilliers *et al* 5.06.
2 For further discussion, see Cilliers *et al* 5.06; *Sen-*
trale Kunsmis Korporasie (Edms) Bpk v NKP Kunsmisverspreiders (Edms) Bpk supra 397.

5.05 *The contract must be duly ratified or adopted by the corporation after its incorporation.* This must be done by the consent in writing of all the members of the corporation within the time specified in the contract. If no time is specified, the consent must be given within a reasonable time after incorporation. What is considered to be a reasonable time depends upon the circumstances of each case.[1] If all the requirements are complied with the contract comes into existence between the corporation and the other party. The corporation is, however, under no obligation to ratify or adopt the contract. If the corporation does not ratify timeously, the contract lapses. In principle the agent incurs no personal liability. However, the contract may provide that in such event the agent will be liable in his personal capacity for the due performance of the contract.[2]

1 See *Bagradi v Cavendish Transport Co (Pty) Ltd*   2 For detailed discussion, see Cilliers *et al* 5.10.
1959 1 SA 663 (D) 669.

Alternative arrangements

5.06 Like section 35 of the Companies Act, section 53 is permissive and not peremptory.[1] It was not introduced as a codification of the law relating to pre-incorporation contracts. Other arrangements may therefore also be used, such as a contract in favour of a third party (*stipulatio alteri*). Since the third party need not be in existence at the time the agreement is concluded between the *stipulans* and the *promittens*, the *stipulatio alteri* can conveniently be used in the case of a corporation not yet incorporated.[2]

1 See Cilliers *et al* 5.11; Henning 1984 *JJS* 172.
2 For detailed discussion, see Cilliers *et al* 5.11 – 5.12.

5.07 Section 53 is also not applicable if a person contracts in his personal capacity before the incorporation of the close corporation and then after its incorporation, for example, cedes his rights under the contract to the corporation, or nominates the corporation as purchaser, or transfers assets he acquired to the corporation, or cedes his rights under an option which he acquired on the basis that he can either exercise it himself or transfer it to another, to the corporation which can then exercise the option.[1]

1 Cf Cilliers *et al* 5.13. For the retrospective effect of the various arrangements, see Cilliers *et al* 5.14.

Capacity and representation – Background[1]

Common law doctrines inapplicable

5.08 The ordinary rules of agency provide the foundation for the representation of a juristic person, but have not been able to supply solutions in all cases.[2] Consequently a special or characteristic branch of agency has developed with specific common law doctrines such as the doctrine of constructive notice and the *ultra vires* doctrine.

The common law requirements[3] for a juristic person to be bound by a contract on its behalf are that –

(a) the juristic person must have the necessary capacity and powers to perform the particular act; and

(b) the juristic person's representative must have the necessary authority to bind the juristic person in respect of the particular contract.[4]

The legislature has considered it unwise to burden a close corporation, its members and third parties with the accumulated learning on the *ultra vires* doctrine and the doctrine of constructive notice. Stated generally, the Act in effect provides that these doctrines have no application and are not relevant to the question of whether or not a close corporation is bound by a particular contract made on its behalf.[5]

As far as the representation of a close corporation is concerned, the power of a member to bind the corporation is dealt with in section 54. The basic arrangement of powers in this section has its ultimate statutory origin in a number of provisions of the English Partnership Act of 1890.[6]

Attention will now be given first to the capacity and powers of the close corporation and thereafter to its representation.

1 For detailed discussion, see Henning 1984 *JJS* 166-172; Henning 1985 *De Rebus* 641 and 1986 *De Rebus* 73; Henning 3 *Transactions of the Centre for Business Law* (1986) 25; McLennan 1985 *SALJ* 322; Oosthuizen *Beslote Korporasies* (1986) 48-53. See also *S v Finance & Trust International BK 1990 3 SA 810 (N); Höltz v Douglas & Associates (OFS) CC* 1991 2 SA 797 (O); *Paterson Exhibitions CC v Knights Advertising and Marketing CC* 1991 3 SA 523 (A).

2 See Cilliers *et al* 12.01.

3 In the absence of statutory provisions to the contrary.

4 See further Cilliers *et al* 12.01, especially fn 1-4.

5 Ss 2(4), 17 and 45. See Henning 1984 *JJS* 155.

6 *Via* clause 14 of the Incorporated Private Partnership Bill drafted by Prof LCB Gower for Ghana and published in 1961. It was enacted in 1962. For detailed discussion and comparison of the various provisions, see Henning 1984 *JJS* 166-172; Henning 1985 *De Rebus* 641 and 1986 *De Rebus* 73.

Capacity and powers of a close corporation

5.09 A close corporation has the capacity and powers of a natural person of full capacity in so far as a juristic person is capable of having such capacity or exercising such powers.[1] For this reason the *ultra vires* doctrine has no application in respect of close corporations and there is no need for an equivalent of section 36 of the Companies Act. The statement of the principal business of the corporation[2] in the founding statement does not affect the corporation's capacity and powers. There is no constructive notice of any particulars stated in a founding statement.[3]

1 S 2(4).
2 S 12(b).

3 S 17.

5.10 For most practical purposes the legal capacity of a close corporation is unlimited and does not form any hindrance to its participation in business. Those having dealings with a close corporation do not run any risk of finding the validity of transactions being affected by internal limitations on the corporation's legal capacity.[1]

1 Determined with reference to the contents of its
  founding statement or other public documents.

5.11 This does not imply that a close corporation's capacity and powers are, in all respects, totally unlimited. A close corporation is incapable of acts intimately associated with the physical being of a natural person, such as contracting a marriage or making a will.[1]

1 See Cilliers and Benade *Company Law* (1982)
  103.

5.12 It should also be kept in mind that there are various restrictions limiting a corporation from participating freely in commercial transactions. Examples are a close corporation's inability to act as trustee of a unit trust scheme[1] or to practise as a medical doctor or advocate. While a private company may conduct the practice of a chartered accountant, attorney, notary and conveyancer, a close corporation may not. On the other hand a close corporation may, if the relevant statutory requirements are met, carry on business for instance as a pharmacist,[2] estate agent,[3] or commission agent selling agricultural produce,[4] or practise as a quantity surveyor in private professional practice,[5] a veterinarian,[6] an architect,[7] or render a security service.[8]

1 S 20 of the Unit Trusts Control Act 54 of 1981.
2 See Pharmacy Act 53 of 1974.
3 See Estate Agents Act 112 of 1976.
4 See Agricultural Produce Agency Sales Act 12
  of 1975.

5 See Quantity Surveyors' Act 36 of 1970.
6 See Veterinary and Para-Veterinary Professions
  Act 19 of 1982.
7 See Architects Act 35 of 1970.
8 See Security Service Act 92 of 1987.

Representation of a close corporation

Members as agents

Summary and application of section 54

5.13 The power of a member to bind the corporation is set out in section 54. Stated briefly[1] the effect is that each member is an agent of the corporation for the purposes of the corporation's business. If a member's power to represent the corporation in carrying on its business is restricted or excluded, he will still bind the corporation in respect of an outsider, unless the outsider has, or ought reasonably to have, knowledge of the restriction. Since there is no constructive notice of the provisions of an association agreement,[2] knowledge of such internal restrictions on members' powers is not imputed to outsiders. They are entitled to assume that each member has the necessary authority to act on behalf of the corporation in transactions falling within the scope of the corporation's business.[3] As in the law of partnership the *bona fide* outsider who does not know of internal restrictions of power is in principle not affected by it.[4] The corporation is, however, not bound to contracts not apparently falling within its scope of business unless they were authorised or ratified by the corporation.

1 Cf Naudé 1984 *JJS* 130.

2 S 45.

3 See Naudé 1984 *JJS* 130.

4 *Ibid.*

5.14 Section 54 deals only with the power of a member to bind the corporation in relation to a person who is not a member of the corporation and who is dealing with the corporation. It follows that section 54 does not apply, for example, in the event of a non-member's acting as agent of the corporation, or where the person dealing with the corporation is not an outsider but a member, or where the outsider does not know of the existence of the corporation at the time of the conclusion of the contract, or where the outsider knows of the existence of the corporation but deals with the member in his personal capacity and not as agent of the corporation.[1]

1 See Henning 1986 *De Rebus* 73-75 and especially fn 11.

5.15 It is submitted that section 54 should not be interpreted so as to exclude the operation of the doctrine of estoppel.[1]

1 See Henning 1986 *De Rebus* 75 especially fn 26; Malan *Beslote Korporasiereg* (1986) 95; Delport and Pretorius *Introduction to the Close Corporations Act* (1989) 49.

General rule

5.16 True to its partnership origins, section 54(1) provides that in relation to outsiders dealing with a close corporation, any member is an agent of the corporation for the purposes of the business stated in its founding statement (the "stated business") or actually carried on (the "actual business"). This general rule is subject to the provisions of section 54(2)-(5) discussed below.

5.17 It should be kept in mind throughout that no person is deemed to be acquainted with the contents of the corporation's public documents, including its association agreement, merely because such documents are registered by the registrar or lodged with him, or are kept at the registered office of the corporation.[1] This exclusion of constructive notice provides further protection to an outsider dealing with the corporation.

1 Ss 17 and 45.

Acts actually or ostensibly authorised or ratified

5.18 An act of a member binds the corporation, irrespective of whether or not it is within the scope of either the actual or the stated business of the corporation, if the act is expressly or impliedly authorised by the corporation,[1] or if it subsequently ratifies the act,[2] or if it is precluded from denying authority or ratification by virtue of the doctrine of estoppel.[3]

1 S 54(2)(a).

2 S 54(2)(a).

3 For further discussion, see Henning 1986 *De Rebus* 73-75.

Acts within scope of business

5.19 An act of a member performed for carrying on in the usual way the stated or actual business of the corporation, is binding on the corporation, unless the member has in fact no authority to act for the corporation in the particular matter, *and* the outsider has, or ought reasonably to have, knowledge of the member's lack of authority.[1] In other words, unless the outsider knew, or ought reasonably to have known, of the member's lack of authority, the corporation is bound in spite of the fact that the member had exceeded his actual authority, provided that the particular act did in fact fall within the scope of either the corporation's actual or its stated business.

1 S 54(2)(b).

Acts apparently outside scope of business

5.20 An act of a member performed for a purpose not apparently[1] connected with the ordinary course of the corporation's stated or actual business is not binding on the corporation, unless the corporation has in fact expressly or impliedly authorised[2] or subsequently ratified the act,[3] or the corporation is precluded from denying authority or ratification by virtue of the doctrine of estoppel.[4]

1 Cf s 7 of the English Partnership Act 1890, and see in particular Scamell and Banks *Lindley on Partnership* (1984): "It follows . . . that actual notice of excess of authority becomes important only where the firm seeks to escape liability for an act done by one of its members with the apparent but without the real authority of others. So long as one partner does nothing beyond the scope of his apparent authority, . . . so long is the firm responsible for his conduct, although he may have acted beyond or in direct violation of the authority within which his co-partners may have attempted to confine him."

2 S 54(3).
3 S 54(3).
4 See Henning 1986 *De Rebus* 73-75.

Restrictions on authority

5.21 If an association agreement restricts the power of a member to represent the corporation, no act in contravention of the restriction is binding on the corporation with respect to any person who has, or ought reasonably to have, knowledge of such restriction.[1] In this case knowledge of the specific contravention of the restriction is not required, merely knowledge of the existence of the restriction.

1 S 54(4).

5.22 If in terms of the proviso to section 46(b)[1] the written consent of a member or members is required in the particular case, no act in contravention of the requirement is binding on the corporation with respect to a person who has, or ought reasonably to have, knowledge of the fact that the particular act is performed in contravention of the requirement.[2] In this case knowledge of the mere existence of the particular requirement is not sufficient. The corporation will have to prove that the outsider also knew, or reasonably ought to have known, that the specific requirement was contravened by the particular act.

1 S 46(b) requires the written consent of a member or members holding at least 75% of the members' interests in the corporation for a change in the principal business of the corporation; or a disposal of the whole, or substantially the whole, undertaking of the corporation; or a disposal of all, or the greater portion of, the assets of the corporation; or any acquisition or disposal of immovable property by the corporation.

2 S 54(5).

5.23 An act of a member disqualified under section 47 from participating in the management of the corporation is not binding on the corporation with respect to any person who has, or reasonably ought to have, knowledge of such disqualification.[1]

1 S 54(4). For a detailed discussion of the provisions
  of s 47, see 4.11.

Non-members as agents

5.24 It is trite law that a close corporation may authorise a person who is not a member to act as its agent, either generally or in a particular matter. In such event section 54 is not applicable.

5.25 On the basis of the general principles of representation, the close corporation will be bound by an agreement entered into on its behalf by a non-member, if the non-member had express or implied authority from the close corporation to enter into the agreement on the close corporation's behalf, or if the close corporation subsequently ratified the agreement, or if the close corporation is precluded from denying authority or ratification by virtue of the doctrine of estoppel.[1]

1 See *Inter-Continental Finance v Stands 56 and
  57 Industria* 1979 3 SA 740 (W).

Contracts with members

5.26 A contract between a member and a close corporation, falls outside the scope of section 54. Again the general principles of representation should apply, but it should be kept in mind that a member will normally be fully conversant with internal limitations on and requirements for authority. In any event the contract will be voidable at the option of the corporation by reason of a breach of the member's fiduciary duties, if the member failed to disclose his interest in the contract at the earliest opportunity.[1] In addition, without the prior written consent of all the members, loans and the provision of security by a close corporation to its members or to juristic persons controlled by them are prohibited and invalid.[2]

1 See s 42(3)(b).
2 S 52.

Transactions in a group and the regulation of loans and the provision of security[1]

General

5.27 In general, juristic persons are excluded from membership of a close corporation.[2] As a consequence of the exclusion of corporate membership, companies are precluded from doing business through the instrumentality of close corporation subsidiaries, and such group formation is avoided. A natural person may well have several cose corporations, but in principle none of these may be a member of any of the other close corporations.[3]

1 For a detailed discussion of these complex provisions of the Companies Act and Close Corporations Act, see Henning 3 *Transactions of the Centre for Business Law* (1986) 36-40; Henning 1989 *JJS* 65-88; Henning 1992 *THRHR* 286-296.
2 Ss 29(1) and 63(d).

3 In view of the general restriction of membership of close corporations to natural persons, such a corporation cannot become the "holding" or "subsidiary" corporation of another close corporation.

5.28 Although a company may not be a member of a close corporation, the latter may be a member and shareholder of a company and may even control a company. It is clear that it would be undesirable to allow a close corporation to control companies free from the restraints imposed by company law on holding companies.

5.29 Section 55 of the Close Corporations Act is designed specifically to prevent evasion of the "abuse of control" provisions of the Companies Act, which could be effected by simply putting a close corporation on top of one or more companies in a pyramid. It provides for the application of sections 37 and 226 of the Companies Act where the relationship between a company and a close corporation is such that the corporation (the "holding corporation") if it were a company, would be a holding company of that company (the "subsidiary company").

5.30 In the absence of prior consent of members, section 52 of the Close Corporations Act prohibits loans and the provision of security by a close corporation to its members and juristic persons controlled by them. Although this provision is also dealt with in the chapter on internal relations, it should be kept in mind that it is in effect a simplified version of the prohibition in section 226 of the Companies Act on loans and the provision of security by a company to its directors or managers or to bodies corporate controlled by them. Hence section 52 is relevant to this discussion to give a more complete picture of the statutory regulation of loans and the provision of security by and to close corporations, especially as various anomalies between sections 52 and 55 of the Close Corporations Act and sections 37 and 226 of the Companies Act can be identified when the regulation of various transactions in a specific group situation is subjected to a detailed analysis.[1]

1 For detailed discussion, see Henning 1989 *JJS* 85-88; Henning 1992 *THRHR* 286-296.

Loans or security furnished to a holding corporation or fellow subsidiary company

5.31 To prevent the abuse by a holding corporation of its control over a subsidiary company by using the company's funds for loans to itself or to another subsidiary company at unfairly advantageous terms, section 55(1) of the Close Corporations Act provides for the *mutatis mutandis* application of the provisions of section 37 of the Companies Act to the employment of funds of a subsidiary company in a loan to its holding corporation or fellow subsidiary company, or the provision of security by a subsidiary company to another person in connection with an obligation of its holding corporation or fellow subsidiary.

5.32 Where a subsidiary company makes such an "upward" or "sideward" loan, or provides "upward" or "sideward" security, the subsidiary company must furnish detailed particulars of the loan or security in its annual financial statements for every year during which the loan or security is in operation. This does not apply to *bona fide* transactions by the subsidiary company in the ordinary course of carrying on a business of making loans and providing security.[1]

In addition, the directors and officers of the subsidiary company and the members and officers of the holding corporation who authorise or permit or are party to the transaction, are personally liable to the subsidiary for damages, should the terms of the loan or security be unfair to the subsidiary or not provide reasonable protection for its business interests and as a result the subsidiary suffers loss.[2]

1 S 37(1) of the Companies Act; s 55(1) of the Close Corporations Act.

2 S 37(3) of the Companies Act; s 55(2) of the Close Corporations Act.

5.33 The provisions relating to disclosure and personal liability do not apply to anything done by a subsidiary company with the consent of all its members. In the case of a *wholly owned* subsidiary company the consent of its holding corporation will be sufficient, if it is the only member of the company. In addition, these provisions do not apply to a "downward" loan or provision of security by the subsidiary company, for example a loan to a fellow subsidiary company which is also a subsidiary of the lending company itself.

Prohibition on loans and security furnished to certain members, officers, directors and controlled bodies corporate

5.34 Subject to a number of detailed exemptions, some conditional some unconditional,[1] section 226(1) of the Companies Act as applied by section 55(3) of the Act prohibits loans or the provision of security by a subsidiary company to

☐ a member or officer of its holding corporation, or

☐ a director or officer of its fellow subsidiary company, or

☐ a close corporation, company or other body corporate controlled by one or more of the members or officers[2] of its holding corporation, or

☐ a close corporation, company or other body corporate controlled by one or more of the directors or managers[3] of its fellow subsidiary company.

A loan or provision of security contrary to the prohibition is fatal to the validity of the transaction.[4]

A director or officer of the subsidiary company or a member or officer of its holding corporation who authorises, permits or is a party to a loan or security contrary to the prohibition, is guilty of an offence and is liable to indemnify the company and any person having no actual knowledge of the contravention, against any loss resulting directly from the invalidity of the loan or security.[5]

1 See Cilliers *et al* 25.24. It should be noted in particular that this prohibition does not apply if the specific company to which the loan is made or the security provided, is the holding *company* or a fellow subsidiary or the own subsidiary of the company making the loan or providing the security, see s 226(1B). For a detailed discussion of the ambit of s 226(1B) of the Companies Act in this regard, see Henning 1992 *THRHR* 286-296.

2 Cf the inconsistent use of the terms "officer" and "manager" in s 55(3)(i) and s 55(3)(ii) respectively.

3 *Ibid.*

4 *Neugarten v Standard Bank of South Africa Ltd* 1989 1 SA 717 (A).

5 S 226(4) of the Companies Act; s 55(4) of the Close Corporations Act.

Further prohibitions on loans and the provision of security involving close corporations

5.35 Subject to a number of detailed exemptions, some conditional, some unconditional,[1] section 226(1) of the Companies Act prohibits loans or the provision of security

(a) by a company to or for the benefit of a close corporation or other body corporate controlled by one or more directors or managers of the company;

(b) by a subsidiary to a close corporation or other body corporate controlled by one or more directors or managers of the company's holding company, or one or more directors or managers of the company's fellow subsidiary.

1 See 5.34 *supra*.

5.36 Unless the express prior consent in writing of all members to the particular transaction is obtained, loans[1] and the provision of security[2] by a close corporation to another corporation in which one or more of its members hold more than a 50% interest, or to a company or other juristic persons controlled[3] by one or more members of the corporation, are prohibited.[4]

1 See the definition of loan in s 52(4)(a).
2 See the definition of security in s 52(4)(c).

3 See the definition of control in s 52(4)(b).
4 S 52(1) and (2). For further discussion, see 4.25.

Deficiencies in prohibition rectified

5.37 The reasons for the "deficiency in the prohibition in respect of loans and security" which could be "exploited by directors or managers"[1] were twofold. Firstly, the strict delimitation of "control" in section 226(1A) of the Companies Act excluded "controlled" close corporations from the ambit of the prohibition in section 226 itself. Hence "controlled" close corporations were also excluded from the ambit of the *mutatis mutandis* application of the prohibition in section 226 by section 55(3) of the Close Corporations Act. Secondly, section 55(3)(b) and 55(3)(ii) expressly referred to only a "controlled" company and not to a "controlled" close corporation or other "controlled" juristic person.

1 Memorandum on the Companies Amendment Bill, 1985.

5.38 Section 226 was amended in 1985 to include "controlled" close corporations. Unfortunately section 55(3) was not amended accordingly at the same time. One of the main reasons for the deficiency in the prohibition concerning loans to or security for close corporations controlled by members of a holding corporation or by directors and managers of a fellow subsidiary, remained in existence until its removal by the Close Corporations Amendment Act 17 of 1990. Implementing the recommendation of the Standing Advisory Committee on Company Law,[1] section 2 of that Act inserted the words "or another juristic person" after "company" in both section 55(3)(b) and section 55(3)(ii).

1 See Henning 1989 *JJS* 84.

Some caveats concerning close corporations in group context

5.39 The mere fact that section 55 provides for the application of certain provision of the Companies Act to prevent abuse of control by holding corporations, does not mean that the legal position of "holding corporations" and their "subsidiary companies" can to all intents and purposes and in all circumstances be equated to that of holding companies and their subsidiaries.

5.40 For instance, there is no prohibition on a subsidiary company's providing financial assistance for the purchase of a member's interest in its holding corporation.[1] In addition, exemptions in the Companies Act concerning wholly owned subsidiaries[2] are not applicable in the case of a holding corporation.[3] It should also be noted that there is no general statutory obligation, such as that contained in section 288 of the Companies Act, on a holding corporation to prepare group annual financial statements. However, in accordance with generally accepted accounting practice it may be necessary in particular circumstances for the corporation to prepare consolidated financial statements in order to achieve fair presentation and which will be meaningful and useful to its members.[4]

1 S 38 of the Companies Act does, however, prohibit financial assistance by a subsidiary for the purchase or subscription of shares of its holding *company*. For further discussion, see Henning 1992 *THRHR* 286-296.

2 See ss 66, 117(4), 190, 288(1), 299(1), 303 and 304 of the Companies Act.

3 For further discussion, see Henning 1992 *THRHR* 286-296.

4 *Ibid*.

Personal liability for debts of the corporation

Personal liability as a sanction

6.01 The Act contains virtually no criminal sanctions and seeks to be self-regulatory. The main instrument towards self-regulation is the imposition of personal liability for members and certain other persons for the debts of the corporation in the event of contravention of certain of the provisions of the Act.[1] The provisions concerned relate mainly to the correct use of the name of the corporation, qualification for membership, management and, in particular, the maintenance of the solvency and liquidity of the corporation.

1 See De Koker *13 Tran CBL* (1990) 124-206.

Liability of members and others for corporate debts

6.02 Members of a close corporation are in principle not liable for the debts of the corporation but in the following circumstances liability, jointly and severally with the corporation, may arise:

(a) If the name of the corporation is used without joining the abbreviation CC in English or BK in Afrikaans[1] the members will be so liable for debts resulting from a transaction with a person who can show that he was unaware that he was dealing with a close corporation.[2]

(b) If a member fails to contribute his initial or additional agreed contribution to the corporation,[3] he will be so liable for every debt of the corporation incurred from registration to date of actual contribution.[4] In addition any other member of the corporation may institute action to recover such contribution after notifying the other members of his proposed action.[5]

(c) If the number of members exceeds ten[6] for a period of six months every member shall be so liable for debts incurred while the number of members so exceeded the maximum.[7]

(d) If a juristic person or a trustee of a trust *inter vivos* purports to hold a member's interest in circumstances other than those provided for in section 29, the juristic person or trustee of a trust *inter vivos* or their nominee will be so liable for the debts of the corporation incurred during the time of purported membership and the membership shall be invalid.[8]

(e) If a corporation acquires a member's interest in exchange for payment or property in contravention with the requirements of section 39 (the consent of every member to such acquisition and the maintenance of solvency and liquidity of the corporation) every member at the time of acquisition who was aware of the payment, including any member or former member who received such payment, shall be so liable for every debt incurred prior to such acquisition. A member who can prove that he took all reasonable steps to prevent payment will escape liability.[9]

(f) If the corporation gives financial assistance for the acquisition by a member of his interest in contravention with the requirements of section 40 (the previous consent of every member and maintenance of the solvency and liquidity of the corporation) every member at the time of the giving of the assistance who was aware of such assistance being given, including the person who received such assistance, shall be liable for every debt incurred prior to the giving of such assistance. A member who can prove that he took all reasonable steps to prevent the assistance will not be liable.[10]

(g) If a person disqualified from taking part in the management of the corporation as provided for in section 46 nevertheless does so, such person shall be so liable for every debt incurred as a result of his participation in the management.[11]

(h) If the office of accounting officer is vacant for a period of six months every member who at any time during that period was aware of the vacancy and who at the expiration of that period was still a member shall be so liable for every debt of the corporation incurred during the existence of the vacancy, as well as for every debt incurred thereafter while the vacancy and his membership continues.[12]

1 As required by s 22. See in general De Koker 13 *Tran CBL* (1990).
2 S 63(a).
3 In the form of money or property as required by s 24.
4 S 63(b).
5 S 50.
6 As required by s 28.
7 S 63(c).
8 S 63(d).
9 S 63(e). In company law such an acquisition is not possible without a formal reduction of capital. See also Lessing 1990 *SA Merc LJ* 49, 57-8.
10 S 63(f). In company law such assistance is normally prohibited in terms of s 38 of the Companies Act. See also Lessing 1990 *SA Merc LJ* 49, 57-8.
11 S 63(g). See also *Marpro Trawling (Pty) Ltd v Cencelli* 1992 1 SA 407 (C).
12 S 63(h).

Reckless or fraudulent carrying on of business

6.03 Section 64 makes provision for special liability where the corporate form is abused. It provides that if at any time it appears that any business of a corporation was carried on recklessly, with gross negligence or fraudulently, the court may declare that any person who was knowingly a party to the carrying on of the business in such a manner shall be personally liable for such of the debts or other liabilities of the corporation as the court may direct. The section also provides that the court may give such further orders as it considers proper for giving effect to and enforcing such liability. The application may be brought by the Master, any creditor, member or the liquidator of the corporation. The carrying on of business in such a manner is also declared a criminal offence, apart from any other criminal liability resulting from such conduct.

The significant difference in practice between this provision and the related provision in section 424 of the Companies Act is that in a close corporation its *members* are subjected to personal liability, while in a company its *directors* (and not its shareholders) are so at risk. The explanation is that the members of the close corporation are responsible for the carrying on of the business of the close corporation, while the directors carry that responsibility in a company.[1]

1 The case law in respect of section 424 of the Companies Act is instructive and can serve as authority in applying s 64 of the Close Corporations Act. See Cilliers & Benade 31.70; De Koker 13 *Tran CBL* (1990).

Abuse of corporate juristic personality

6.04 In section 65 the Close Corporations Act creates a useful remedy which has no counterpart in the Companies Act. The court may be called upon to find that the incorporation of the corporation or any act by or on behalf of it constitutes a gross abuse of its juristic personality as a separate entity. The application to court may be made "by an interested person, or in any proceedings in which a corporation is involved". How wide the remedy extends time will have to tell. The much more accessible forum of the magistrates' court should in time contribute to its increased utilisation but at present no known precedents are available.

If such abuse is found, the court may declare that the corporation is deemed not to be a juristic person as regards the rights, obligations or liabilities of the corporation or of any of its members or of any person specifically referred to in such an order. The court may also give such further orders as it may deem fit so as to give effect to its declaration.

In company law the court may in appropriate circumstances rely on its judicial discretion to disregard the separate corporate existence of a company.[1]

1 See Cilliers & Benade 1.20 – 1.22. See in general, regarding company law, Larkin 1989 *SA Merc LJ* 283. See also De Koker 13 *Tran CBL* (1990).

Improper distribution of income

6.05 A corporation may distribute net income to its members only if it is solvent and sufficiently liquid. A distribution in breach of these requirements may be recovered from members. This aspect is dealt with more fully in 4.24 and 7.02.

Other possibilities of personal liability

6.06 Under the following circumstances, members can either be held liable personally for the debts of the corporation, or they can be compelled to compensate the corporation:

☐ If a corporation is deregistered while having outstanding liabilities, persons who are members at the time of deregistration are liable jointly and severally for such liabilities.[1]

☐ If a member breaches a fiduciary duty or his duty of care and skill towards the corporation, he can be held liable by the corporation, except if this right has been waived by other members on behalf of the corporation. Members do not in this instance become liable towards creditors for the debts of the corporation.[2]

☐ If loans are made or security is given by the corporation in contravention of s 52, any member who authorizes, permits or is a party to the transaction can be held liable to indemnify the corporation as well as other persons who may have suffered loss directly resulting from the invalidity of the loan or security.[3]

1 S 26(5).
2 Ss 42(3), 43(1). See further 4.13 to 4.17.

3 S 52(3)(a). See further 4.25.

Liability of members, employees, etcetera

6.07 Members as well as employees or any other person acting on behalf of a corporation, can be held liable personally where for instance orders are placed or cheques signed and the cheque, notice, invoice, receipt or other document issued on behalf of the corporation does not state both the name and registration number of the corporation. Such persons are liable only if the corporation fails to pay.[1]

1 See s 23(2); par 2.10; *Bouwer v Andrews* 1988
   4 SA 337 (E); Nagel 1989 *De Jure* 183.

Distribution of net income

Member's interest in a close corporation and shareholders' equity in a limited company contrasted

7.01 A comparison of the concepts of "members' interest in a close corporation" and "shareholders' equity in a limited company" is desirable in order to provide a meaningful background for the discussion of the distribution of net income.

7.02 Members' interest in a close corporation can comprise the following:

(a) Contributions by members.[1]

(b) Surplus on the revaluation of fixed assets.[2]

(c) Undistributed (retained) income – termed "undrawn profits" in the Act.[3]

1 S 24: see 8.25
2 See 7.09 below on the distribution of a surplus on the revaluation of assets.

3 S 58(2)(c) and see 8.14 for a discussion of the anachronistic term "undrawn profits".

7.03 Shareholders' equity in a limited company is more formally structured and may comprise:

☐ Issued share capital
- – Shares at nominal value[1]
- – Share premium account

☐ Non-distributable reserves
- – Capital redemption reserve fund

☐ Distributable reserves
- – General reserve
- – Reserve for increased replacement cost of plant
- – Unappropriated (retained) income.

1 In the interests of lucidity no par value shares are omitted.

7.04 The capital maintenance rule which applies to a limited company is founded on the basic approach followed by the courts that the issued share capital (being total proceeds of shares issued, that is nominal value *plus* share premium account) of a limited company constitutes the capital fund on which creditors of the company can rely for the satisfaction of their claims.[1] In other words this capital fund consists of *contributed or paid-in* shareholders' equity as contrasted with *accumulated* shareholders' equity comprising both *non-distributable* and *distributable* reserves.[2]

1 See Cilliers *et al Corporate Law* (1992) 20.01 *et seq.*

2 See Cilliers *et al Corporate Law* (1992) 13.12 – 13.13.

7.05 The component of *members' contributions* forming part of members' interest in a close corporation is accordingly the approximate equivalent of *contributed or paid-in shareholders' equity* in the context of a company.

Payment of dividends by a limited company

7.06 A limited company declares and pays dividends to its shareholders out of the net income (profit) available for dividend distribution.[1] Only divisible income, that is profits which the law allows the company to distribute to shareholders, may be applied for dividends; the (mainly common law) rules applicable to divisible income may best be summed up "by saying that dividends cannot be paid out of capital . . . [but] only out of profits".[2] The directors generally have the power to make provision for past losses and such transfers to reserves as they deem necessary before declaring a dividend. Any balance of net profits so deemed available for dividends is shown in the annual financial statements as retained (or undistributed) income. A shareholder is entitled to a dividend only after it has been duly declared in the manner provided by the articles.

1 See Cilliers *et al Corporate Law* (1992) 22.01 *et seq Divisible profits and dividends* on the declaration and payment of dividends. "Net income" has, as an accounting term, replaced the term "net profit" traditionally used in company law.

2 *Verner v General and Commercial Investment Trust* [1894] 2 Ch 239 at 266 per LINDLEY LJ.

Distribution of net income by a close corporation

Solvency and liquidity criteria replace capital maintenance rule

7.07 Sections 39, 40 and 51 respectively state that the following actions can only be undertaken provided that the solvency and liquidity of the corporation is unimpaired:

☐ Payment by the corporation for the acquisition of members' interests.

☐ Financial assistance by the corporation in respect of the acquisition of a member's interest.

☐ Any payment by the corporation to a member (by reason only of his membership) whether by way of a *distribution (of net income)*, or a repayment (wholly or in part) of the member's contribution.[1]

1 See 4.24 for restrictions on payments to members.

7.08 These solvency and liquidity requirements impose stricter restraints than the *maintenance of capital rule* applicable to a limited company, also as regards the distribution of net income:

☐ The *solvency criterion* postulates that after any such payment to members is made, the assets of the corporation fairly valued must exceed its liabilities.

☐ The *liquidity criterion* imposes two further strict constraints, in that after such payment to members is made
  – the corporation must be able to pay its debts as they become due in the ordinary course of business, and
  – conversely, such payment must in the particular circumstances not in fact render the corporation unable to pay its debts as they become due in the ordinary course of business.[1]

In the case of a limited company, on the other hand, the only basic legal requirement is that dividends may not be paid out of issued share capital.[2]

A member of a close corporation is liable to the corporation for any payment received contrary to the provisions in regard to the maintenance of solvency and of liquidity in section 51(1).[3]

1 S 51(1).
2 See 7.06 above.

3 S 51(2).

Distribution of a capital profit

7.09 The distribution of available net proceeds out of a realised capital profit poses no legal problem. Unrealised capital profit resulting from a revaluation should only be distributed to members provided extreme care is taken that the solvency and liquidity of the corporation is not affected thereby.[1]

1 SA Institute of Chartered Accountants *Close Corporations Auditing and Accounting Guide* (see 8.10 fn 10 on Statements and Guides of the SA Institute of Chartered Accountants) states that unrealised revaluation surpluses may be distributed to members provided the requirements of s 51 of the Act have been met, the assets of the corporation exceed its liabilities and the corporation can pay its debts when they fall due after payments have been made. Until formally distributed, the unrealised revaluation surpluses remain as reserves of the corporation (par 77).

Member's proportionate share of distributable income

7.10 The percentage of members' interest held by a member of necessity also determines his *pro rata* share in the distribution of net income.[1]

1 See 3.11.

Procedure for the payment of a net income distribution to members

Approval for payment of income distribution

7.11 The application of general principles of law and especially the persuasive authority of the dispensation in limited companies, leads to the conclusion that no member is entitled to any payment out of income available for distribution until it has been approved by a formal resolution or validated by the approval of annual financial statements, in which such distribution of income is proposed. The approval and signature by or on behalf of the holder(s) of at least 51% of total members' interest is necessary to confirm (validate) the annual financial statements.[1]

1 S 58(3) deals with the approval of financial statements. Cilliers *et al, Corporate Law* (1992). See 23.51 on the validation of annual financial statements.

7.12 An important factor to be borne in mind concerning the approval of the payment of a distribution of income to members, is that the annual financial statements do not have a constituent element equivalent to the directors' report,[1] which *inter alia* has to deal specifically with dividends paid, declared or proposed.

An appropriate manner of dealing with the approval of the distribution of income is to incorporate such approval formally in the written resolution approving the annual financial statements of the corporation.[2]

1 See Cilliers *et al, Corporate Law* (1992) 23.34 – 23.37 on the directors report.

2 The following example of such a resolution forms part of the example of annual financial statements in 8.25.

It was unanimously agreed –

  (*a*) that the sum of Rx as reflected as proposed distributions to members in the income statement for the year ended 28 February 19.6

forthwith be distributed, by way of cash payments, to members in proportion to their percentage share of total members' interest;

  (*b*) that the amount of retained income as at 28 February 19.6 be kept intact to ensure the continued liquidity of the corporation; and

  (*c*) that the annual financial statements for the year to 28 February 19.6 be approved.

Undistributed (retained) income and reserves

7.13 Any balance on income available for distribution which is in fact not distributed to members is shown in the annual financial statements as retained (undistributed) income unless prudence dictates that part thereof should be transferred to a reserve in order, *inter alia*, explicitly to conform with the solvency and liquidity requirements.[1]

1 See 8.25 on the treatment of undistributed (retained) income in the balance sheet and income statement.

"Partnership" approach to the distribution of income

7.14 Initially, after the promulgation of the Close Corporations Act in 1984, there was support for a practice which is termed the *partnership* approach of accounting for the equity elements.

Members' contributions, reserves and undrawn profits (the term used by section 58(2)(c) for income available for distribution or retained income) were allocated to each member as would be done in a partnership. This approach would appear to have stemmed from a verbalistic interpretation of specific sections such as sections 24, 56(2) and 58(2)(c).

It is trite law that the close corporation is a legal person or separate legal entity, which has the capacity to acquire legal rights and duties in its own name. These rights do *not* vest in, *nor* are the duties owed, by individual members. As stated above no member is *entitled* as of right to any payment out of net income available for distribution until it has been approved by a formal resolution or validated by the approval of the annual financial statements.

1 See Laughton 1989 *Accountancy SA* 191 *et seq*.

7.15 Regrettably vestiges of the partnership approach are still to be found in the Act itself (the English version of which was signed by the State President) which in section 58(c) used the term *undrawn* profits instead of undistributed profits (the Afrikaans counterpart of section 58(c) correctly refers to *onuitgekeerde* winste).

8

Accounting records and annual financial statements

Accounting records

8.01 The rules governing the keeping of accounting records in terms of section 56 may be summarised as follows:

☐ A close corporation must keep in one of the official languages of the Republic such accounting records as are necessary *fairly to present* the state of affairs and business of the corporation *and* to explain the transactions and financial position of the business of the corporation. The annual financial statements of the corporation are in turn based on such accounting records.

☐ The accounting records must include the following:

- Records showing its assets and liabilities, members' contributions, undrawn profits[1] (retained income), revaluations of fixed assets and amounts of loans to and from members.

- A register of fixed assets showing the respective dates of acquisition of the assets, the cost thereof, depreciation (if any), and where any of the assets have been revalued, the date of the revaluation and the revalued amount thereof, the respective dates of any disposals and the consideration received in respect thereof.[2]

- Records containing entries from day to day of all cash received and paid out, in sufficient detail to enable the nature of the transactions and, except in the case of cash sales, the names of the parties to the transactions to be identified.

- Records of all goods purchased and sold on credit and services received and rendered on credit, in sufficient detail to enable the nature of those goods or services and the parties to the transactions to be identified.

- Statements of the annual stocktaking, and records to enable the value of stock at the end of the financial year to be determined

- Vouchers supporting entries in the accounting records.

☐ The accounting records relating to the following matters must contain sufficient detail of individual transactions to enable the nature and purpose thereof to be clearly identified:

- Contributions by members.
- Loans to and from members.
- Payments to members.

☐ These accounting records must be kept in such a manner as to provide adequate precautions against falsification and to facilitate the discovery of any falsification.

☐ The accounting records must be kept at the place or places of business or at the registered office of the corporation and, wherever kept, be open at all reasonable times for inspection by a member.

☐ Any corporation which fails to comply with any of the following provisions relating to accounting records and every member thereof who is a party to such failure or who fails to take all reasonable steps to secure compliance by the corporation with any such provisions, is guilty of an offence.[3]

---

1 The Afrikaans version of the Act uses the term "onuitgekeerde winste" (undistributed profits) instead of the misleading term "undrawn profits" which is an inappropriate concept when dealing with a legal person.

2 In the case of a corporation which has been converted from a company, the existing fixed assets register of the company is deemed to be such a register in respect of the corporation.

3 In any proceedings against any member of a corporation in respect of an offence consisting of a failure to take reasonable steps to secure compliance by a corporation with any provision of s 56, it is a defence if it is proved that the accused had reasonable grounds for believing and did believe that a competent and reliable person was charged with the duty of seeing that any such provision was complied with, and that such person was in a position to discharge that duty, and that the accused had no reason to believe that such person had in any way failed to discharge that duty.

Financial year

8.02 The financial year of a corporation is governed by section 57.

☐ The financial year of a corporation is its annual accounting period. A Corporation must state the date of the end of its financial year in its founding statement.[1]

☐ In common with the other provisions in the founding statement, the date of the end of the financial year may be changed by the registration of an amended founding statement provided that the date is not changed more than once a year.[2]

☐ Subject to any alteration to the end of the financial year (causing an increase or decrease in its duration), a financial year normally consists of a period of twelve months.[3]

　－ The first financial year commences on the date of registration of the corporation and must consist of a period of not less than three months and not more than 15 months.[4]

　－ In the case of a close corporation converted from a company, the first financial year ends on the date on which the financial year of the company would have ended had it not been so converted,[5] except where such first financial year has been changed (see (b) above).

1 Ss 12 and 57(1).
2 Ss 15 and 57(2).
3 S 57(3).
4 S 57(4)(a).
5 S 57(4)(b). If a close corporation is created by conversion of a company, or *vice versa*, its financial statements should be prepared for the full financial year or period. Thus if a company is converted into a corporation, the first annual financial statements for the corporation will be prepared for the financial year including the results of the period prior to the conversion. There is no requirement for the financial information of the company and corporation to be disclosed separately (*Close Corporations: Auditing and Accounting Guide* par 57 – see 8.10 fn 1 on *Statements and Guides of the SA Institute of Chartered Accountants*).

Annual financial statements

Submission of annual financial statements

8.03 The members of a corporation must, within nine months after the end of every financial year of the corporation, cause annual financial statements in respect of that financial year to be made out in one of the official languages of the Republic.[1]

1 S 58(1).

Composition of annual financial statements

8.04 The annual financial statements of a corporation should consist of the following:[1]

☐ A balance sheet and any notes thereon.

☐ An income statement or any similar financial statement where such form is appropriate, and any notes thereon.

☐ The report of the accounting officer.[2]

☐ A cash flow statement.

The Act does not explicitly require that a cash flow statement form part of the annual financial statements. It is, however, submitted that generally accepted accounting practice[3] makes the inclusion of a cash flow statement desirable if not essential, especially where the close corporation has several members and conducts a reasonably large business.[4]

1 S 58(2).
2 Unlike the Companies Act, the Close Corporations Act does not *explicitly* require an auditor's report. The report of the accounting officer may in a very *limited sense* be regarded as fulfilling the function of the auditor's report – see 8.24 on the *duties* of the accounting officer and 8.25 on his *report* where an audit has in fact been carried out.
3 S 286(2)(bA) requires a cash flow statement as

part of the financial statements of a company. Also see GAAP AC 118.
4 The *Close Corporations: Auditing and Accounting Guide* also states that the presentation of a cash flow statement could assist members in determining the source and disposition of its liquid funds. As the management of cash is vital to the success of any business venture, the presentation of a cash flow statement is considered to be an essential feature of financial reporting (par 84).

Comparative figures

8.05 The Act contains no provision for comparative figures. It is, however, submitted that comparative figures should be shown in the interest of fair presentation.[1]

1 The illustrative examples in the *Close Corporations: Auditing and Accounting Guide* do contain comparative figures.

Fair presentation and generally accepted accounting practice

8.06 The annual financial statements must, in conformity with *generally accepted accounting practice appropriate to the business of the corporation, fairly present* the state of affairs of the corporation as at the end of the financial year concerned, and the results of its operations for that year.[1]

The two basic principles underlying the preparation of the financial statements of a close corporation are thus

(a) fair presentation, and
(b) generally accepted accounting practice.

1 S 58(2)(b).

Fair presentation

8.07 Fair presentation of the state of affairs of the corporation at the end of the financial year and of the results of its operations for the financial year is the overriding objective in the preparation of the annual financial statements of a corporation. Accordingly these statements must comply with the guidelines for the preparation of financial statements as applicable to companies.[1]

1 Cilliers *et al Corporate Law* (1992) chapter 23. Aspects of particular importance in the context of close corporations are –
(a) the fundamental accounting concepts
  – going concern concept
  – matching concept (it is doubtful whether financial statements prepared on a cash basis could fairly present the state of affairs and results of the corporation)
  – the consistency concept
  – the prudence concept.
(b) the principle that substance and reality must prevail over the legal (or contrived) form.

Generally accepted accounting practice appropriate to the business of the corporation

8.08 The Close Corporations Act does not contain a schedule setting out the requirements for financial statements (see Schedule 4 of the Companies Act). The provision that the financial statements must conform to generally accepted accounting practice appropriate to the business of the corporation, is thus of great importance in that it contains the only statutory requirement regarding the scope of the contents of such statements.

8.09 In determining what is generally accepted accounting practice appropriate to the business of the corporation, the preparer of the financial statements should have regard to the needs of the members. The primary users of financial statements of a corporation will be the members themselves. The financial statements will be used to assist them not only in determining compliance with any statutory regulations but also in managing, controlling and developing the business.[1]

1 As stated in 4.12 the close corporation has no structured set of organs such as those through which a limited company operates. There is especially no board of directors and management is in the hands of the members (although conceivably different roles may be assigned to specific members by the association agreement).

8.10 Over the years, accounting practices, structured as *Statements of Generally Accepted Accounting Practice*[1] have evolved in different economic and business environments to record and fairly present the transactions and events common to those environments. Thus, in deciding what is "appropriate to the business", consideration should also be given to the trading and operating activities of the corporation and the generally accepted accounting practices of the environment in which the corporation operates. A company that converts to a corporation does not change its economic and business environment. Most accounting practices that such company previously adopted are therefore still relevant and appropriate in its new legal form.

1 The *Member's Handbook of the South African Institute of Chartered Accountants* contains at present 19 Statements of Generally Accepted Accounting Practice (GAAP) and 8 Accounting Guidelines as well as *inter alia* 5 Audit and Accounting Guides (in booklet form) including *Close Corporations: An introduction and a guide* to some of the more important aspects of the *Close Corporations Act, No 69 of 1984 as amended (revised and issued February 1991)*, abbreviated reference used in chapters 7 and 8 by us is *Close Corporations: Auditing and Accounting Guide*. See par .70 – .75 on Generally Accepted Accounting Practice.

8.11 The main reason for the problem of determining whether compliance with the formal *Statements of Generally Accepted Accounting Practice* is in fact necessary in order to ensure that the annual financial statements do in fact, in conformity with the appropriate *generally accepted accounting practice*, fairly present the state of affairs and the results of its operations, stems from the inherent vagueness of the essential attributes of a close corporation. The most important element to which, it is submitted, not sufficient attention was paid by the legislature, is that the only limiting factor placed on the formation of a close corporation is that its *membership is limited to a maximum of ten natural persons*. No limitation is placed on the size of the corporation's financial resources or the complexity of its business.

The authoritative *Close Corporations Auditing and Accounting Guide*[1] states:

> In practice the close corporation has been used by a whole variety of businesses as their trading vehicle.[2] These businesses also vary in size from small, one-man organisations to some very large corporations.

1 Par .07. See 8.10 fn 1.
2 Afrikaans: "handelsmedium".

8.12 *Statements of Generally Accepted Accounting Practice*[1] contain measurement and disclosure standards. These standards should apply to any financial statements which purport to achieve fair presentation, including those of corporations. The disclosure requirements set down have been determined as the minimum disclosure required to achieve fair presentation and to meet the needs of the broad spectrum of users of company financial statements.

1 See 8.10 fn 1.

8.13 *Statements of Generally Accepted Accounting Practice*[1] apply to the financial statements only insofar as their effect will be material. Financial statements need not disclose information which is immaterial to fair presentation. AC 104 *Earnings and dividends per share* is the only GAAP-statement which can not apply to the financial statements of a close corporation.

1 See 8.10 fn 1

Specific disclosure of items

8.14 The annual financial statements must disclose separately the aggregate amounts, as at the end of the financial year and the movements in these amounts during the year, of the following:[1]

(a) Contributions by members.

(b) Undistributed profits (income).[2]

(c) Revaluations of fixed assets.

(d) Amounts of loans to and from members.

1 S 58(2)(c).
2 The Act uses the term "undrawn profits", an unfortunate vestigial remnant of the outdated partnership approach adopted in certain quarters in the initial implementation phase of the Close Corporations Act (see 7.14 *et seq*). The English version of the Act was signed by the State President.

Agreement with accounting records

8.15 The financial statements must be in agreement with the accounting records.[1] These records must be kept in such a manner that the financial statements can be drafted therefrom in accordance with the requirements set out above. The records must also enable the accounting officer to report to the corporation that the annual financial statements are in agreement with such financial records and to state the accounting policy applied in these statements.[2]

1 S 58(2)(d) and (e).
2 See 8.24. *Duties of accounting officer.*

Accounting officer not required to perform audit

8.16 It is not the legal duty of the accounting officer to perform any audit.[1] He must merely report to members on the annual financial statements in the manner prescribed by the Act.

1 S 58(2)(e). See 8.25 on the report of the accounting officer on the annual financial statements to
   be made to members.

Approval and signature of annual financial statements

8.17 The annual financial statements must be approved and signed by or on behalf of a member, or members, holding a member's interest of at least 51%.[1]

1 S 58(3).

Criminal liability

8.18 Any member of a corporation who fails to take all reasonable steps to comply or to secure compliance with any provision of section 58 dealing with annual financial statements, shall be guilty of an offence. In any proceedings against any member of a corporation, the defence in terms of section 56(2)(b) is available to him.[1]

1 S 58(4). See 8.01 fn 3 on the defence available
   in terms of s 56(5)(b).

Accounting officer

Appointment

8.19 Every corporation must appoint an accounting officer.[1]

☐ The appointment of the first accounting officer of a corporation referred to in the founding statement (which must be accompanied by his written consent to act as such) takes effect on the date of the registration of the corporation.

☐ If a vacancy occurs in the office of an accounting officer, whether as a result of removal, resignation or otherwise, the corporation must within 14 days appoint another accounting officer and comply with the provision in regard to the registration of an amended founding statement (again accompanied by his written consent).

1 S 59(1) to (3).

Resignation and removal

8.20 The Act regulates the resignation and removal of the accounting officer.[1]

☐ A corporation must inform its accounting officer in writing of his removal from office.

☐ An accounting officer must on resignation or removal from office forthwith inform every member of the corporation thereof in writing, and send a copy of the letter to the last known address of the registered office of the corporation; in addition he must forthwith inform the Registrar by certified post

– that he has resigned or been removed from office;

– of the date of his resignation or removal from office;

– of the date up to which he performed his duties; *and*

– that at the date of his resignation or removal from office he was not aware of any matters in the financial affairs of the corporation which are in contravention of the provisions of the Act.

☐ If an accounting officer who has been removed from office is of the opinion that he was removed for improper reasons, he must forthwith inform the Registrar thereof by certified post, and send a copy of the letter to every member.

1 S 59(4) and (5).

Qualification of accounting officer

8.21 The following provisions apply in regard to the qualification of an accounting officer:[1]

☐ No person shall be appointed as or hold the office of an accounting officer of a corporation, unless he is a member of a recognised profession which

– as a condition for membership, requires its members to have passed examinations in accounting and related fields of study which in the opinion of the Minister would qualify such members to perform the duties of an accounting officer under this Act;

– has the disciplinary power to exclude from membership those persons found guilty of negligence in the performance of their duties or of conduct which is discreditable to their profession; *and*

– has been named in a notice which the Minister may from time to time publish by notice in the *Government Gazette* stating the names of those professions whose members are qualified to perform the duties of an accounting officer.[2]

☐ A member or employee of a corporation, and a firm whose partner or employee is a member or employee of a corporation, does not qualify for appointment as an accounting officer of such corporation unless all members consent in writing to such appointment.

☐ A firm as defined in section 1 of the Public Accountants' and Auditors' Act 80 of 1991, and any other firm may be appointed as an accounting officer of a corporation, provided each partner in the latter firm is qualified to be so appointed.

1 S 60.
2 By R2488 of 16 November 1984 the Minister designated:
(a) The South African Institute of Chartered Accountants (whether in public practice or not).
(b) Accountants and auditors registered in terms of the provisions of the Public Accountants' and Auditors' Act 80 of 1991.
(c) The Southern African Institute of Chartered Secretaries and Administrators.
(d) The Institute of Cost and Management Accountants.
(e) The Institute of Accounting Technicians of Southern Africa (now the Institute of Commercial and Financial Accountants).
The list has been extended by R1234 of 7 June 1985 and R206 of 7 February 1986 to include:
(f) Those members of The Institute of Administration and Commerce of Southern Africa who have obtained the Diploma in Accountancy or the Diploma in Cost and Management Accountancy *or* the Diploma for Company Secretaries.

Right of access to accounting records and documents

8.22 An accounting officer of a corporation has a right of access to the accounting records and all the books and documents of the corporation at all times, and to require from members such information and explanations as he considers necessary for the performance of his duties as an accounting officer.[1]

1 S 61.

Remuneration

8.23 The remuneration of an accounting officer is determined by agreement with the corporation.[1]

1 See 8.22 fn 1.

Duties of accounting officer

8.24 The statutory duties of an accounting officer are as follows:[1]

☐ The accounting officer must, not later than three months after completion of the annual financial statements[2] –

(a) determine whether the annual financial statements are in agreement with the accounting records of the corporation:

The accounting records must be summarised in such a form that the accounting officer is enabled to perform this function leading up to his report without its being necessary to refer to any *subsidiary* accounting records and vouchers supporting the entries in the accounting records – his right to inspect such subsidiary accounting records and vouchers, if he deems it necessary, is not affected;[3]

(b) determine the accounting policies applied in the preparation of the annual financial statements;[4]

(c) report to members stating

- whether the annual financial statements are in agreement with the accounting records;

- the accounting policies applied in the preparation of the annual financial statements.

☐ If during the performance of his duties an accounting officer becomes aware of any contravention of a provision of the Act, he must describe the nature of such contravention in his report.

☐ Where the accounting officer is a member or employee of the corporation, or is a firm of which a partner or employee is a member or employee of the corporation, his report must state that fact.

☐ If an accounting officer of a corporation –

(a) at any time knows, or has reason to believe, that the corporation is not carrying on business or is not in operation and has no intention of resuming operations in the foreseeable future; or

(b) during the performance of his duties finds

- that any change, during a relevant financial year, in respect of any particulars mentioned in the founding statement has not been registered; or

- that the annual financial statements indicate that as at the end of the financial year concerned the corporation's liabilities exceed its assets;

- that the annual financial statements incorrectly indicate that at the end of the financial year concerned the assets of the corporation exceed its liabilities, or has reason to believe that such an incorrect indication is given,

he must forthwith by certified post report accordingly to the Registrar.[5]

1 S 62.
2 S 58(1). The members of the corporation shall cause annual financial statements to be made out within nine months after the end of the financial year.
3 S 58(2)(d).
4 See 8.08 *et seq* on the generally accepted accounting practice appropriate to the business of the corporation. Par 105 of the *Close Corporations: Auditing and Accounting Guide* states that the accounting officer has to determine, by enquiry of members, the accounting policies applied in the preparation of the annual financial statements and to be satisfied that they are appropriate to the business. The accounting officer *is not required to ensure that the accounting policies have been implemented because this would require an audit to be done.*
5 If the accounting officer finds that subsequent financial statements indicate that the situation has changed or has been rectified, he may report accordingly to the Registrar (Regulation 21A).

Example of the annual financial statements of a close corporation

Basic layout of annual financial statements

8.25 The illustrative example that follows is in broad accord with the general layout of the annual financial statements of a limited company. The present example is more in the form of an outline, containing less detail, *and* follows the pattern of presenting information in the body of the balance sheet and the income statement, thus restricting notes to the annual financial statements to a minimum. This form of presentation gives a simpler overview of the financial position of a relatively small corporation with a maximum of ten members.

This illustrative example is in general accordance with the illustrative financial statements contained in *Close Corporations: Auditing and Accounting Guide Appendix 1.*[1]

1 See 8.10 fn 10 on the *Close Corporations: Auditing and Accounting Guide.*

ZEE CLOSE CORPORATION CK 86/00001/23

ANNUAL FINANCIAL STATEMENTS FOR THE YEAR ENDED 28 FEBRUARY 19.6

Contents	Page
A Approval of annual financial statements by members	1
B Report of the accounting officer	1
C Balance sheet	2
D Income statement	3
E Notes to the annual financial statements	4
F Cash flow statement	5

APPROVAL OF ANNUAL FINANCIAL STATEMENTS

The attached annual financial statements were approved by all members on 15 May 19.6 and are signed on their behalf.

A Blue

B Orange

C Red

THE ACCOUNTING OFFICER'S REPORT WHEN NO AUDIT WAS CARRIED OUT

(a) Report of the accounting officer to Zee CC

I have performed the duties of accounting officer to Zee CC as required by section 62 of the Close Corporations Act, 69 of 1984. No audit was conducted.

The financial statements set out on pages 1 to 4 are the responsibility of the members. I have determined that the financial statements are in agreement with the accounting records and have done so by adopting such procedures and conducting such enquiries in relation to the books of account and records as I considered necessary in the circumstances. I have also reviewed the accounting policies which have been represented to me having been applied in the preparation of the annual financial statements and I consider that they are appropriate to the business.

Accounting Officer

Date:

Address:

ACCOUNTING OFFICER'S REPORT WHEN AN AUDIT HAS BEEN CARRIED OUT

(b) Report of the independent auditor to the members of Zee CC

I have performed the duties of accounting officer to Zee CC as required by section 62 of the Close Corporations Act, 69 of 1984. I have also audited the annual financial statements of Zee CC set out on pages 1 to 4. These financial statements are the responsibility of the members of the Close Corporation. My responsibility is to report on these financial statements.

I have conducted my audit in accordance with generally accepted auditing standards. These standards require that I plan and perform the audit to obtain reasonable assurance that, in all material respects, fair presentation is achieved in the financial statements. An audit includes an evaluation of the appropriateness of the accounting policies, an examination, on a test basis, of evidence that supports the amounts and disclosures included in the financial statements, as assessment of the reasonableness of significant estimates and a consideration of the appropriateness of the overall financial statement presentation. I consider that my auditing procedures were appropriate in the circumstances to express the opinion presented below.

In my opinion these financial statements fairly present the financial position of Zee CC at 28 February 19.6 and the results of its operations and cash flow information for the year then ended in conformity with generally accepted accounting practice appropriate to the business.

Auditor CA(SA)

Date:

Address:

ZEE CLOSE CORPORATION

BALANCE SHEET at 28 FEBRUARY 19.6

	Note	19.6 R	19.5 R
Capital employed			
Members' interest			
Members' contributions	2	x xxx	z zzz
Surplus on revaluation of fixed assets	4	x	z
Retained income		xx	zz
Aggregate of members' interest		x xxx	z zzz
Loans from members	5	xx	zz
Other long-term liabilities	6	xxx	zzz
		xx xxx	zz zzz

Employment of capital

		Cost or valuation	Depre- ciation	Book value	
Fixed assets					
Land and buildings	4	xxx	–	xx	zz
Plant and equipment		xx	x	xx	zz
Vehicles		xx	x	xx	zz
		x xxx	x	xxx	zzz
Investments	7			xx	zz
Shares in listed companies				x	z
Shares in unlisted companies				x	z
Loans to members	8			xx	zz
Net current assets				xxx	zzz
Current assets				xxx	zzz
Stock				xx	zz
Debtors				x	z
Cash on hand and at bank				x	z
Current liabilities				xx	zz
Creditors				x	z
Bank overdraft				x	z
Provision for taxation				x	z
				xx xxx	zz zzz

ZEE CLOSE CORPORATION
INCOME STATEMENT YEAR ENDED 28 FEBRUARY 19.6

	Note	19.6 R	19.5 R
Sales	9	x xxx	z zzz
Less: Cost of sales		x	z
Gross profit		x xxx	z zzz
Less: Expenses		xx	zz
Accounting officer's remuneration		x	z
Salaries to members		xx	zz
Interest paid on members' loans		x	z
Interest paid on other loans		x	z
Depreciation of fixed assets		x	z
Sundry expenses		x	z
Net income		xxx	zzz
Less: Taxation		xx	zz
Net income after taxation		xxx	zzz
Add: Retained income from previous year		xx	zz
		xxx	zzz
Less: Distributions to members		x	z
Undistributed (retained) income 28 February 19.6		xx	zz

Comments:

The income statement should preferably be presented so as to highlight major categories of revenue and expense important to the business of the corporation.

Note – Additional information: The relevant explanatory information on any significant items in the financial statements, including an explanation of material transactions between the corporation and its members, should be disclosed by way of notes to the statements.

Notes to the annual financial statements

1 Accounting policy

The financial statements have been prepared in accordance with generally accepted accounting practice appropriate to the business of the corporation which has been consistently applied. The principle accounting policies of the corporation are as follows:

1.1 Basis of presentation

The financial statements are presented on the historical cost basis except that certain land was revalued.

1.2 Stock

Stock is valued at the lower of cost and net realisable value.

2 Percentage interest of members, interests and contributions by members

Members' interests and the contributions made and outstanding by members are as follows:

	Members' interests	Contributions made	Contributions outstanding
A Blue	50%	xxx	—
B Orange	30%	xxx	—
C Red	20%	xx	x
Aggregate 28 February 19.6	100%	Rx xxx	Rx

3 Distribution of net income – written resolution

It was unanimously agreed:

☐ that the sum of Rx as reflected as proposed distributions to members in the income statement for the year ended 28 February 19.8 be distributed forthwith, by way of cash payments, to members in proportion to their percentage share of total members' interest;

☐ that the amount of retained income as at 28 February 19.8 be kept intact to ensure the continued liquidity of the corporation; and

☐ that the annual financial statements for the year to 28 February 19.8 be approved.

(A short-form written resolution merely approving the annual financial statements would probably suffice where the financial position of the corporation is undoubtedly sound. In formulating this resolution it should be borne in mind that the annual financial statements of a close corporation do not have a constituent part equivalent to the directors' report, which *inter alia* has to deal specifically with dividends paid, declared or proposed.)[1]

1 See Cilliers *et al Corporate Law* (1992) par 23.
  34 – 23.37 on the director's report.

4 Surplus on revaluation of fixed assets

Land and buildings of the corporation were revalued by I See, a sworn appraiser, on an open market value basis on 28 February 19.6.

5 Loans from members

The following loans at 18% interest per annum were made to members:

	Balance 1.3.19.5	Advances during year	Repayments during year	Balance 28.2.19.6
A Blue	xx	x	—	xx
B Orange	xx	—	x	x
Aggregate 28 February 19.6				Rxx

6 Other long-term liabilities

A loan of Rxx bearing interest at 20% per annum and repayable on 28 February 19.8 was made to the corporation by a supplier with the name B Reddy.

7 Investments

	R
Listed investments	
Shares at cost	x
(Market value Ry)	
Unlisted investments	x
(Valuation by members Ry)	
	xx

8 Loans to members

The following loans at 19% per annum interest were made by members:

	Balance 1.3.19.5	Advances during year	Repayments during year	Balance 28.2.19.6
C Red	Rx	Rx	—	Rxx

9 Comparative figures are in respect of the converted company and have been adapted in order to be comparable.

ZEE CC

CASH FLOW STATEMENT FOR THE YEAR ENDED 28 FEBRUARY 19.6

	Note	19.6 R	19.5 R
Cash retained from operating activities:		xx	zz
Cash generated by operations	1	xx	zz
Investment income		xx	zz
Utilised to increase working capital	2	xx	zz
Cash generated by operating activities		xx	zz
Finance costs		(xx)	(zz)
Taxation paid	3	(xx)	(zz)
Cash available from operating activities		xx	zz
Distribution during the year	4	(xx)	(zz)
Cash utilised in investing activities:		(xx)	(zz)
Investment to maintain operations		(xx)	(zz)
Replacement of fixed assets	5	(xx)	(zz)
Proceeds of disposal of fixed assets	6	xx	zz
Investment to expand operations		(xx)	(zz)
Addition to fixed assets	7	(xx)	(zz)
Purchase of a subsidiary	8	(xx)	(zz)
		xx	zz
Cash effects of financing activities:			
Decrease in long-term borrowings	9	(xx)	(zz)
Increase/(Decrease)			
in short-term borrowings	10	xx	zz
		(xx)	(zz)

Comments The cash flow statement should refer to appropriate notes.

1 See Cilliers *et al Corporate Law* (1992) par
 13.30.4(c) for example of cash flow statement and
 the notes thereto.

Basic accounting aspects relating to taxation of a close corporation[1]

General rules applicable to the taxation of close corporations

8.26 The main elements in the taxation of a close corporation are as follows:

☐ (a) In terms of the definition of the Income Tax Act a close corporation is taxed as if it were a company. It is also deemed to be a private company so that the close corporation is not exempt from donations tax (section 38(1)).

(b) A close corporation must make provisional tax payments in the same way as a company. All income is taxed in the hands of the close corporation in the year that it is earned and it is not subject to undistributed profits tax.

(c) A close corporation is also taxed at the rate applicable to limited companies (presently 48%).

☐ (a) A member of a close corporation is included in the definition of "shareholder" in terms of section 1 of the Income Tax Act. Accordingly a member who is active in the affairs of a close corporation may be deemed to be a "holder of an office" and be subject as an employee to the fringe benefits tax provisions; he will correspondingly be entitled to the concessions granted in respect of retirement gratuities (section 7A(4) and (4A) and section 10(1)(x)).

(b) Profits distributed to members of a close corporation rank as dividends. As in the case of dividends received by shareholders of a limited company no such "dividends" are taxed in the hands of resident members.

(c) Non-resident members are, however, subject to non-resident shareholders' tax on dividends, currently 15%.

(d) Ordinary expenses are deductible in the determination of the taxable income of the corporation. Salaries paid to members are regarded as expenses and not taxable in the hands of the corporation unless excessive.

Tax avoidance schemes are subject to the same sanctions imposed on companies by section 103. It is submitted that the mere fact that a member's effective tax rate is less than 48% and he accordingly draws his income as remuneration (so that it is not taxed in the hands of the corporation at 48%), would not in the spirit of the Act constitute an avoidance scheme unless excessive.

(e) A *member* of a close corporation is a provisional taxpayer, unless the Commissioner in particular circumstances determines otherwise. In the case of a company only the *directors*, and not all the shareholders *per se*, are provisional taxpayers. (Definition of shareholder in section 1, definition of provisional taxpayer in Part I Schedule 4.)

☐ Assessed losses incurred by a close corporation in a particular year are *not* apportioned to its members but may be carried forward by the corporation to the following year.

1 NB: References are to sections of the Income Tax
Act 58 of 1962.

Taxation on the conversion of a limited company into a close corporation

8.27 On the conversion of a company to a close corporation the main tax considerations are as follows:

☐ The *persona* of the company is not affected by the conversion. The close corporation thus succeeds to the company's wear and tear allowances, value of trading stock, etcetera (section 40A(1)).

☐ Assessed losses carried forward in the converted company are available to the close corporation as such (section 103(2)).

☐ Changes from the shareholding in the company to the member's interest in the corporation should be embodied in writing and the consideration, or conversion factor, clearly stated. In the unlikely event of there being no consideration or if the consideration is inadequate or not fair, the transfer may constitute a donation and be subject to donations tax.

Taxation on the conversion of a close corporation into a limited company

8.28 The converted company is regarded for all purposes by the Income Tax Act as the same tax entity as its predecessor corporation. Once more the same wear and tear allowance, value of trading stock, etcetera, will remain undisturbed (section 40A(1)).

9

Taxation

Taxation of a close corporation: general principles

Close corporation taxed as a company

9.01 A 'close corporation' is defined in section 1 of the Income Tax Act[1] as a 'close corporation within the meaning of the Close Corporations Act 69 of 1984'. Further, it is included in the definition of 'company' in terms of paragraph (f) of the definition of 'company' in section 1. Since it is a company for tax purposes, a close corporation pays tax at the corporate rate of tax, which is 48 percent for the 1992/93 year of assessment.[2]

With a single exception a close corporation is taxed in the same manner as a company, the exception being that public companies are exempted from donations tax.

All references to sections in this chapter are references to sections of the Income Tax Act 1962[1] unless otherwise stated.

1 Income Tax Act 58 of 1962. The Income Tax Act 121 of 1984 amended the Income Tax Act of 1962 to provide for the taxation of close corporations.

2 The corporate rate of tax is 48 percent for the 1992/93 year of assessment for companies that are not gold mining or diamond mining companies.

A close corporation and dividends

9.02 The following rules apply:

Dividends received by a close corporation

Whereas a company is exempt from normal tax in respect of dividends received or accrued under section 10(1)(k), a close corporation was before the 1991 year of assessment not so exempt. Dividends received by or accrued to any limited company, *which during any portion of the year of assessment before 1991 was a close corporation*, are taxed in the hands of the close corporation (section 10(1)(k)(i)(ee)), subject to a deduction of one-third thereof (section 19(3)(b)). From the 1991 year of assessment, both companies and a close corporation (which are also companies for tax purposes) are exempt from tax on dividend income.

Dividends paid by a close corporation

Any distribution by a close corporation to its members is exempt from normal tax in their hands, whether the distribution consists of capital, capital profits or revenue profits (section 10(1)(kA)). However, the dividends distributed by a company that converts to a close corporation during a year of assessment prior to the 1991 year of assessment will be exempt only if they are distributed during the specified period in relation to that year.

Shareholders of companies which are not close corporations were, prior to the 1991 year of assessment, taxed on their dividend income, subject to a minimum exemption of one third. From the 1991 year of assessment dividends distributed by both limited companies and companies which are close corporations are exempted from normal tax. It no longer makes any difference whether the dividend was paid by a company or a close corporation. The need therefore to convert a company to a close corporation solely for the purposes of dividend exemption has fallen away.

Conversion of a company to a close corporation

9.03 The tax status is not affected by conversion of a company to a close corporation. The Close Corporations Act allows for the conversion of a company to a close corporation (section 27). Where a company has been converted to a close corporation the tax status of the entity is not affected. The company and the close corporation are deemed to be and to have been one and the same company for the purposes of the Act (section 40A(1)). The effect of this is to identify completely for tax purposes the two bodies and to provide for the continuation of taxation as if there had been no conversion. A company converting to a close corporation will, therefore, maintain existing tax values of assets, scrapping allowances, any assessed loss, the valuation of trading stock and recoupments as if there had been no conversion.[1]

---

1 In other words the *persona* of the company is not affected by the conversion. However, changes from the shareholding in the company to the member's interest in the corporation should be embodied in writing *and* the consideration, or conversion factor, clearly stated. In the unlikely event of there being no consideration or if the consideration is inadequate or not fair, the transfer may constitute a donation and be subject to donations tax (see 9.09).

Undistributed reserves on conversion

9.04 Where, prior to the 1991 year of assessment, a company had been converted to a close corporation, the undistributed reserves of the company at the end of the company's financial year which ended immediately prior to the conversion were deemed to have been distributed by the company to the close corporation on the date of conversion and in terms of section 40A(2), to be taxable income accruing to the close corporation on that date. Section 40A(2) has since the 1991 year of assessment been repealed, and since then no conversion tax has been payable.

Non-resident shareholders' tax

9.05 A close corporation is a company for tax purposes (see 9.01) and the members of a close corporation are deemed to be shareholders, as the definition of 'shareholder' in section 1 of the Act includes a member of a close corporation. Distributions by a close corporation to its members are thus governed by the definition of 'dividend' in section 1, and although such dividends are exempt from normal tax in the hands of the members (section 10(1)(kA)) there is no exemption in respect of non-resident shareholders' tax.

In consequence where non-resident shareholders' tax of 15 percent is payable under section 42 in respect of dividends declared by a company, it will be equally payable in respect of distributions by a close corporation in similar circumstances. It follows that there is no advantage to a non-resident in being a member of a close corporation as opposed to a shareholder of a company. In fact, where a close corporation was in receipt of dividend income before the 1991 year of assessment the non-resident member would have been in a worse tax position, the reason being that the dividend income was, prior to the 1991 year of assessment, partially subject to normal tax in the hands of the close corporation. This disparity has fallen away with the total exemption of dividends from normal tax.

Assessed losses

9.06 Section 103(2) was introduced to prevent a specific type of tax avoidance, namely trafficking in assessed losses of companies. It provides that whenever the Commissioner is satisfied that any agreement affecting any company or any change in the shareholding in any limited company or in the members' interests in any company which is a close corporation, and as a direct or indirect result of which income has been received by, or has accrued to, that company during any year of assessment, and which has at any time before or after the commencement of the Income Tax Act of 1946 been entered into or effected by any person – solely or mainly for the purpose of utilising any assessed loss or any balance of assessed loss incurred by the company, in order to avoid liability on the part of that company or any other person for the payment of any tax, duty or levy on income, or to reduce the amount thereof, the setting off of any such assessed loss or balance of assessed loss against any such income, he may disallow such agreement.

Thus section 103(2) brings within its ambit any changes in members' interests within a close corporation where entered into solely or mainly for the purpose of utilising any assessed loss.

Moreover, an assessed loss of a close corporation is not attributable to its members and in circumstances where a close corporation is likely to incur a tax loss while the members have taxable income, the members will be prejudiced.

It is also worth noting that if, in any year of assessment a company or a close corporation does not carry on a trade, it is not permitted to carry forward to that year any balance of assessed loss established in the year of assessment immediately preceding it (section 20(1)(a)).[1] Under these circumstances a close corporation may lose its right to carry forward such an assessed loss for ever. The possibility that it may commence a trade in a later year of assessment is irrelevant. So, for example, if Ajax CC has an assessed loss of R10 000 in year 1 and did not carry on a trade in year 2, but commenced trading in year 3 when it derived a taxable income of R15 000, the position would be as follows:

Year 1   Assessed loss R10 000

Year 2   Nil assessment, that is no taxable income or assessed loss (the assessed loss of R10 000 established in year 1 cannot be carried forward because no trade was carried on in year 2).

Year 3   Taxable income of R15 000

1 *SA Bazaars (Pty) Ltd v CIR* 1952 4 SA 505(A);
   18 SATC 240.

Provisional tax

9.07 Since the close corporation is a company for tax purposes, it is also a provisional taxpayer and must pay a provisional tax in the same way as any other company.

As far as a member of a close corporation is concerned, paragraph (bA) of the definition of a provisional taxpayer in paragraph 1 of the Fourth Schedule to the Act provides that every member of a close corporation who is ordinarily resident in the Republic will be a provisional taxpayer (except where such a member has received that payment from the corporation which is subject to SITE (Standard Income Tax for Employees).

Relationship between close corporation and members

9.08 The legislature has enacted detailed provision in the Act for the tax treatment of directors, employees and the holders of office.

The term 'director' is defined in section 1 in relation to a close corporation as meaning any person who in respect of the close corporation holds any office or peforms any functions similar to the office or functions of a director of a company. It is submitted that in the absence of an agreement to the contrary between members of a close corporation, all of them are entitled to participate in the management of the close corporation and consequently each member of the close corporation will fall within the definition of 'director'.

For provisional tax purposes a member of a close corporation is a provisional taxpayer if he is ordinarily resident in the Republic, unless the Commissioner directs otherwise (paragraph (bA) of the definition of a 'provisional taxpayer' in paragraph 1 of the Fourth Schedule). Unless the Commissioner so directs otherwise, directors' emoluments are included in the definition of 'remuneration' in paragraph 1 of the Fourth Schedule, and consequently subject to the payment of employees tax.

In other words where a working member's remuneration can be quantified before the end of February his remuneration is subject to PAYE.

A further consequence is that a member of a close corporation who is entitled to participate in the carrying on of the business and has equal rights with regard to the management of the close corporation, is liable for the payment of provisional tax on all benefits derived from the close corporation including the so-called fringe benefits.[1] This will be the case where his remuneration and benefits cannot be separately ascertained before February; for example, his remuneration consists partially of a basic salary plus a bonus calculated as a percentage of profits which can only be quantified after the financial year end.

Where, however, a member is excluded from the management of the close corporation in terms of the association agreement, he is not a 'director' and it follows that his salary and other benefits, if he is employed by the close corporation, constitute remuneration which are therefore subject to employees' tax.

The word 'employment' has not been exhaustively defined by our courts, but the dominant criterion in the determination of whether any situation constitutes employment for this purpose is that of control of the employee (servant) by the employer (master).[2] 'Employment' may be taken to signify the situation 'where an employee is employed by an employer, analogous but not necessarily coinciding with the position of master and servant'.[3] In other words, the employer must have control of the conduct of the work in which the employee is employed, and a duty must rest on the employee to carry out that work in accordance with the instructions of the employer given from time to time.

The meaning assigned to the term 'holder of office' by the courts can be described as 'a position which generally carries with it some remuneration and which is "a substantive position which has an existence independent of the person who fills it", and which will, in the ordinary course, be filled by successive holders'.[4] A director of a company thus clearly holds an office.[5]

It is submitted that a member of a close corporation will not automatically be its employee. His status as an employee will be a question of fact and law. The importance of this issue is reflected by the following examples:

(a) Only where a member was an employee would the close corporation be able to include him in its pension or provident fund.[6] In turn, the member's status as an employee or holder of office will be of importance in determining his 'retirement-funding employment' income, which will affect his deductions in respect of contributions to pension funds (section 11(k)) and retirement annuity funds (section 11(n)).

(b) If a member is not an employee he cannot be paid an 'ante-dated salary or pension' by the close corporation and benefit from section 7A(2).

(c) Unless the member of a close corporation is an employee or the holder of an office, he cannot enjoy the exemption of R30 000 offered by section 10(1)(x) or the concessional rate of tax offered by sections 5(10) and 7A(4A).

(d) Section 11(w) provides for an allowance in respect of premiums paid by the taxpayer under a policy of insurance taken out, in the case of a company, upon the life of a director or employee of the company. Unless the association agreement excludes a member from the management of the business of the close corporation every member of a corporation is a director, so that a policy on the life of a member may qualify under section 11(w) for the deduction of the premiums paid by the close corporation in respect of the policy and accordingly render the proceeds of the policy subject to tax under paragraph (m) of the definition of gross income in section 1.

1 See 'Employees Tax' and directors. Practice note 14 issued by the Commissioner for Inland Revenue on 6 December 1991.
2 *SIR v Somers Vine* 1968 2 SA 138 (A); 29 SATC 179 at 189-90.
3 Per Ingram KC, President of the Special Court for Hearing Income Tax Appeals, in ITC 566 (1944)

13 SATC 332 at 334. See also *SIR v Somers Vine* 1968 2 SA 138 (A); 29 SATC 179 at 189, where this definition was not unreservedly approved. See also *ITC* 544 (1943) 13 SATC 191.
4 Per Ogilvie Thompson JA, as he then was, in *SIR v Somers Vine* 1968 2 SA 138 (A); 29 SATC 179 at 185, adopting the meaning attributed to the

word in certain English decisions. See also *ITC 570* (1944) 13 SATC 450 at 451.

5 *Taxpayer v Commissioner of Taxes, Botswana* (court of Appeal, Botswana) (April 1980); 43

SATC 118 at 122.

6 See the definitions of 'pension fund' and 'provident fund' in s 1.

Donations tax

9.09 Subject to certain exceptions, donations tax is payable on the cumulative taxable value of all property disposed of (whether directly or indirectly and whether in trust or not) under donations that take effect on or after 1 July 1962 by any person other than a company who is ordinarily resident in the Republic or by any domestic company (section 54). The word 'property' is defined as any right in or to property wherever situated and whether movable or immovable, corporeal or incorporeal (section 55(1)(v)). Thus an interest in a close corporation is clearly 'property' for the purposes of donations tax. A close corporation is also a 'body corporate' for the purposes of section 57(2) of the Act. To protect the fiscus against attempts by taxpayers to donate property through their companies and thus avoid the payment of donations tax, section 57(2) provides that donations made by a body corporate at the instance of any person are deemed to be donations by that person and will therefore be included in the value of his taxable donations.

Trading realities of the close corporation

9.10 Despite the dividend parity between a limited company and a company which has been a close corporation since the 1991 year of assessment, there is still a continuous stream of conversion to close corporations. One of the reasons for conversion seems to be the reduction in legal and administration requirements applicable to close corporations. The Close Corporation Act is less prescriptive as far as disclosure requirements, audit requirements and secretarial practice are concerned. In fact, a close corporation need not have an auditor or a secretary.

From a taxation point of view the only other form of business undertaking which hitherto could be compared with the close corporation is the business trust. This form of undertaking has been very popular in property syndications. Since the trust is taxed at tax rates applicable to single persons it affords substantive tax savings over the corporate forms of business. Savings in transfer duty and stamp duty were obtained in using the business trust. Where no companies were involved transfer of property could be taken at rates applicable to individuals. Transfer of property could also be effected by merely changing the beneficiaries by filing an amended trust deed at the Master's office. Inland Revenue has caught up with this tax freeway and from the 1993 year of assessment a business trust will be taxed as a company.

Stamp duty

9.11 The following aspects should be borne in mind in regard to utilising a close corporation for stamp duty purposes.

The close corporation affords a substantial saving in stamp duties where a members' interest is sold, compared to where shares are sold in a private company. There are no stamp duties payable with a change in members' interest. The only requirement is that the new and old members sign an amended founding statement which is lodged with the Registrar. Stamp duties are, however, payable on share transfers.

Stamp duty can accordingly be saved by converting a private company to a close corporation before the sale is concluded provided that there are no problems inherent in such conversion as appeal from the following example.

XYZ CC is the owner of a property free from any mortgage bond. The members of XYZ CC intend selling their members' interest and loans in XYZ CC to B who intends to raise finance from a bank to settle the purchase price. B cannot negotiate with the bank, thereby encumbering the assets of XYZ CC before he becomes a member which would enable him to contract on behalf of XYZ CC. The old members are at risk since they have to sign off as members before being paid. The only security they would have to rely on under these circumstances would be a banker's guarantee. In the case of a private company they could resign as directors, appoint B as sole director and B could make his own arrangements. The old directors being also the shareholders would still retain their shares. Once all conditions were fulfilled they could sign their shares off in return for a bank cheque. For the sake of this lack in security it may at times be advisable to convert a close corporation back to a private company. Note that stamp duty will in this circumstance have to be paid on the difference between the selling price and the nominal value the shareholders' loans sold.

Dividends may be used as an instrument to reduce stamp duty, since dividends received from a limited company have since the 1991 tax year, also been exempt from tax in the hands of the shareholders. There is in certain circumstances no longer any need for a tax strategy to convert to a close corporation where shares in a private company are to be sold in an arm's length transaction at a premium over the net book value of the assets. The relative assets can merely be revalued at the selling price and the difference credited to a revaluation reserve. A dividend declared out of this reserve and credit to shareholders will convert the reserve to loan capital. The loans will now represent the major portion of the selling price, thereby reducing both the price paid for the shares and also stamp duty. Obviously the application of this technique should be applied with care and due consideration should be paid the circumstances in each case.

Where, however, high leverage financing forms part of the financial structure of the company or close corporation, care should be taken that any initial saving in stamp duty is not outweighed by future income tax liabilities. Higher tax liabilities could arise from the fact that the portion of the interest on loans would not be allowed as a deduction for normal tax. This part of the interest is regarded by the Commissioner of Inland Revenue as unproductive and not incurred in the production of income. In practice an allocation is made in which the financial structure before and after the dividend declaration is taken into account. This apportionment can be avoided by distinguishing clearly between interest bearing and interest free loans. Future net income can then first be applied in repaying the interest free loans.

Transfer duty and value-added tax

9.12 Where there is a relatively high interest compound in the expense structure of a close corporation it may be preferable to pay the one time transfer duty (on property) or value-added tax (on other assets) respectively. The close corporation will then reflect the assets in its books at their current market values:

– all interest paid will be tax deductible as the proceeds of the loans were used to acquire assets and not members interest;

– the close corporation will also be able to claim depreciation on assets qualifying therefore at current market value as opposed to book value where members' interest were taken over. (Note however that depreciation cannot be written off on the finance charges or input value-added tax component of the asset.)

Where the close corportion is a registered vendor for value-added tax it may in certain circumstances be advantageous to take the value-added tax route when acquiring assets or a business. The close corporation must ensure that the seller is also registered for value-added tax in order to obtain a tax invoice from him in respect of the transactions. The value-added tax paid can then be deducted from the output value-added tax generated from the close corporation's own activities.

Conversions

Conversion of a company into a close corporation

10.01 The following provisions apply to the conversion of a company into a close corporation:[1]

(a) Any company having ten or less members all of whom qualify for membership of a corporation (see 3.02) may be converted into a corporation.

(b) To effect the conversion the following must be lodged with the Registrar[2] –

☐ an *application for conversion*, on form CK4, signed by *all* the members of the company, containing a statement that every member of the company will become a member of the corporation, that upon conversion the assets of the corporation, fairly valued, will exceed its liabilities, and that after conversion the corporation will be able to pay its debts as they become due in the ordinary course of its business;

☐ a *statement in writing by the auditor* of the company that he has no reason to believe that a material irregularity contemplated in section 26(3) of the Public Accountants' and Auditors' Act has taken place or is taking place in relation to the company or, where steps have been taken in terms of that subsection, that such steps have been completed; and

☐ a *founding statement* (see 2.04).

(c) In the founding statement referred to above –

☐ the statement of the aggregate of the contributions of the members must reflect an amount not greater than the excess of the fair value of the assets to be acquired by the corporation over the liabilities to be assumed by it by reason of the conversion: provided that the corporation may treat any portion of such excess not reflected as members' contributions as an amount which may be distributed to its members; and

☐ the members' interests, expressed as a percentage need not necessarily be in proportion to the shares held by the respective members in the company at the time of the conversion.[3]

(d) Thereupon the Registrar must, if he is satisfied that the company has complied materially with the requirements of the Companies Act –

☐ register the founding statement;[4]

☐ satisfy himself that, simultaneously with the registration, the registration of the memorandum and the articles of the company is cancelled in accordance with the provisions of section 29B of the Companies Act;[5]

☐ endorse on the founding statement a certificate of incorporation stating that the corporation has been converted from a company and the name and registration number of the former company;[6] and

☐ give notice in the *Gazette* of the conversion.[7]

---

1 Ss 27 and 29.
2 Ss 12 and 13.
3 S 12(e).
4 Ss 13 and 27(4)(a).

5 S 27(4)(b).
6 Ss 14(1) and 27(4)(c).
7 Ss 27(4)(d).

10.02 Effect of conversion of a company into a close corporation

(a) On the registration of a corporation converted from a company the assets, rights, liabilities and obligations of the company vest in the corporation. Any legal proceedings instituted by or against the company before the conversion may be continued by or against the corporation, and any other thing done by or in respect of the company shall be deemed to have been done by or in respect of the corporation.

The conversion of a company into a corporation specifically does not affect –

☐ any liability of a director or officer to the company on the ground of breach of trust or negligence, or to any other person pursuant to any provision of the Companies Act; or

☐ any liability of the company, or of any other person, as surety.[1]

(b) The corporation must forthwith after its conversion from a company, give notice in writing of the conversion to all creditors of the company at the time of conversion, and to all other parties to contracts or legal proceedings in which the company was involved at the time of the conversion.[2]

(c) Upon submitting a certified copy of its founding statement to any registrar or other officer maintaining a register under any law (and on compliance with all the requirements of such law), he must make in his register all such alterations as are necessary by reason of the conversion. No transfer or stamp duties shall be payable in respect of such alterations.[3]

(d) If the accounting officer mentioned in the founding statement of a converted corporation is not the person who or firm which has acted as auditor for the company, the appointment of that person or firm lapses upon the conversion into a corporation.[4]

(e) The juristic person which used to be a company continues in existence but in the form of a close corporation.

(f) The effects of conversion as regards income tax is dealt with in Chapter 9.

1 S 27(5).
2 S 27(6). No sanction for failing to do so is imposed.
3 S 27(7).
4 S 27(8).

Conversion of a close corporation into a company

10.03 The following provisions apply to the conversion of a close corporation into a company:[1]

(a) A close corporation may with the written consent of *all* its members, apply to be converted into and be incorporated as a company, provided that every member of the close corporation becomes a member of such company.

(b) If the application is accompanied by all the documentation as required by chapter IV of the Companies Act for the registration of a company *and* the statements set out in (c), the Registrar must –

☐ register the memorandum and articles in accordance with the provisions of section 63 of the Companies Act; and

☐ satisfy himself that simultaneously with the registration, the registration of the founding statement of the corporation is cancelled in terms of section 27(9) of the Close Corporations Act.

(c) An application for conversion of a corporation into a company must be accompanied by –

☐ a statement that the paid-up share capital is an amount not greater than the excess of the fair value of the assets to be acquired by the company over the liabilities to be assumed by the company on the conversion, but the company may treat any portion of such excess not reflected as paid-up share capital, as an amount distributable as dividend; and

☐ a statement by the close corporation's accounting officer, that he is not aware of any contravention of the Close Corporations Act by the close corporation or its members or of any circumstances which may render the members of the corporation together with the corporation jointly and severally liable for the corporation's debts.

The shares or the nominal value of the shares to be held in the company by the members individually need not necessarily be in proportion to the members' interests as stated in the founding statement of the close corporation concerned.

(d) The Registrar must give notice in the *Gazette* of the conversion of a close corporation into a company.

1 S 29C of the Companies Act 1973.

Effect of conversion of a close corporation into a company

10.04 According to section 29D of the Companies Act, on the registration of a company converted from a close corporation:

(a) all the assets, liabilities, rights and obligations of the corporation vest in the company;

(b) any legal proceedings instituted before the registration by or against the corporation may be continued by or against the company, and any other thing done by or in respect of the corporation shall be deemed to have been done by or in respect of the company; and

(c) the juristic person which used to be a close corporation continues in existence but in the form of a company.

Upon submitting its certificate of incorporation to any registrar or other officer maintaining a register under any law (and on compliance with the requirements of such law) he must make in his register all such alterations as are necessary by reason of the conversion. No transfer or stamp duty shall be payable in respect of such alterations.[1]

The effects of conversion as regards income tax is dealt with in chapter 9.

1 S 29D(2) of the Companies Act.

10.05 Where a contract of sale of a member's interest in a close corporation provides that the purchaser shall not have the right to alienate or to pledge or to cede or to in any other manner dispose of his interest in that close corporation without the seller's written consent, the conversion of that close corporation into a company without such consent is prohibited. Conversion in contravention of such prohibition amounts to a breach of contract.

1 *Mörsner v Len* 1992 3 SA 626 (A).

11

Liquidation: Methods and initiation

Winding up

11.01 A corporation can be wound up[1] either voluntarily, upon the initiation of members, or by the court, upon the application of either members or creditors.[2] The winding up of corporations is regulated by Part IX of the Close Corporations Act and in part by Chapter XIV of the Companies Act[3] as well as the provisions of the law relating to insolvency.[4]

Provision is made for composition proceedings similar to the procedure to be followed in terms of the Insolvency Act 24 of 1936. No provision is made for compromise proceedings as provided for in company law;[5] nor for the judicial management of a corporation,[6] or for any similar procedure.

1 The terms "liquidation" and "winding up" are used interchangeably and have the same meaning.
2 See 11.08 below.
3 See s 66, and in general Bonnet *17 Tran CBL* (1992) on problems in regard to liquidation of close corporations.
4 S 66(1) read with s 339 of the Companies Act 61

of 1973; see also De la Rey *3 Tran LCB* (1986) 84; *Spendiff v JAJ Distributors (Pty) Ltd* 1989 4 SA 126 (C) 135.
5 However, for further discussion of the availability of a section 311 compromise, see Henning 1987 *JJS* 218; Henning and Bonnet 1991 *THRHR* 274; Bonnet and Henning 1992 *JSAL* 537.
6 For further discussion see Henning 1992 *JJS* 90.

Voluntary winding up

11.02 A voluntary winding up can only be initiated by a written resolution of all members, taken at a meeting called for this purpose. The resolution must be signed by all members and must state whether it shall be a voluntary winding up by members or by creditors.[1] After the resolution has been passed, it must be lodged with the registrar within 28 days, together with the prescribed fee.[2] Registration of the resolution, in a members' voluntary winding up, only takes place after confirmation by the Master that the necessary security has been lodged or that he has dispensed with security. If the registrar does not register the resolution within 90 days from the date on which it was passed, the resolution lapses and is void.[3] The resolution does not become effective until its registration.[4]

1 S 67(1). For the form of the resolution, see form CK6. See also reg 20.
2 S 67(2). The resolution must be lodged in duplicate. The prescribed fees are set out in Sched-

ule 1 of the Regulations.
3 S 67(3).
4 S 67(4).

Notice of winding up

11.03 Within 28 days after registration of the resolution to wind up voluntarily, the corporation must give notice of the voluntary winding up in the *Gazette*. In addition, a copy of the resolution must be sent to certain sheriffs, registrars and messengers within 14 days of registration of the resolution.[1]

1 See 11.14.

Voluntary winding up by members

11.04 A voluntary winding up by members can only take place where a corporation is liquidated for some reason other than its insolvency. When the resolution referred to in 11.03 above is lodged with the registrar, it must be accompanied by a further resolution nominating a person for appointment as liquidator.[1]

Security, to the satisfaction of the Master, for the payment of the debts of the corporation[2] within a period not exceeding 12 months from the commencement of the winding up, must be furnished[3] before registration of the resolution, unless the Master has dispensed with security.

The Master will only dispense with security if an affidavit is furnished by the members that, to the best of their knowledge and belief and according to the records of the corporation, it has no debts. The affidavit must be supported by a certificate to the same effect by the accounting officer.

Both the affidavit and the certificate must be furnished to the Master before registration of the resolution for voluntary winding up. As the resolution must be registered within 90 days of the date on which it was passed, it is possible that the resolution may lapse before registration. A resolution which has lapsed is void[4] and in such instance the whole procedure will have to be repeated; no provision is made for an application to court for condonation.

After registration of the resolution, the Master normally appoints the person nominated by members as liquidator of the corporation, although he may appoint a person of his own choice.[5] The liquidator's remuneration may be determined by a meeting of members.[6]

The liquidator must give notice of his appointment in the *Gazette*,[7] but he need not convene any meetings of creditors.[8] No claims are proved against the corporation;[9] no report is submitted to creditors[10] and no statement of affairs of the corporation need be completed.[11]

The liquidator can therefore immediately after receipt of his certificate of appointment, but subject to the consent of members, realise the assets of the corporation and lodge his account with the Master. It is not necessary that all assets be realised. The liquidator may distribute the assets *in specie* in his account, provided such distribution is strictly in proportion to the interest of every member in the corporation.

The powers of the liquidator are the same as in other types of winding up, except that he may exercise the powers granted by section 386(4) of the Companies Act only with the authority granted by a meeting of members.[12]

---

1 S 356(2) Companies Act.
2 As the Master must be able to judge the sufficiency of the security, a recent balance sheet of the corporation should be made available to him.
3 The costs of furnishing security may be recovered from the corporation: s 350(2) Companies Act.
4 S 67(3).
5 S 74(3).
6 S 384(1) Companies Act.
7 S 375(5)(b) Companies Act.

8 S 78, by implication. In the case of companies, this is implied from s 364(1) Companies Act. Although s 364 does not apply to corporations, there is no reason why the liquidator should call any meetings of creditors.
9 S 366 Companies Act, by implication.
10 S 79.
11 Form CM100. This is implied from s 363 Companies Act.
12 See 12.19.

Voluntary winding up by creditors

11.05   Although somewhat inappropriately termed a voluntary winding up by creditors, this type of winding up is initiated solely by a resolution of members.[1] No application to court is involved and it can be a more economical and faster method of reaching the same result as an application to court by the corporation itself.

Where a voluntary winding up by creditors is envisaged, the members of the corporation must make out a statement of affairs of the corporation in the prescribed form.[2] This statement must be submitted to the meeting of members convened for the passing of the winding up resolution.[3]

After registration of the necessary resolution, the rest of the procedure in a voluntary winding up by creditors is similar to that of a winding up by the court.

As from the commencement of a voluntary winding up by creditors, all the powers of the members of the corporation shall cease except in so far as their continuance is sanctioned by the liquidator or by the creditors.[4]

1 See 11.03 above.
2 CM100.

3 S 363(1), (4) Companies Act. See 11.03 above.
4 S 353(2) Companies Act.

Intervention by the court

11.06   In the case of a corporation being wound up voluntarily, an application for the winding up of that corporation by the court can be brought by the Master or any creditor or member of that corporation.[1] The court may also, at any time after the commencement of the winding up, on application of any liquidator, creditor or member, and on proof to the satisfaction of the court that all proceedings in relation to the winding up should be stayed or set aside, make an order staying or setting aside the proceedings or for the continuance of any voluntary winding up on such terms and conditions as it thinks fit.[2]

1 S 346(1)(e) Companies Act.
2 S 354(1) Companies Act.

Winding up by the court

11.07   A corporation may be wound up by the court if:[1]

(a) members having more than one half of the total number of members' votes so resolve and sign a resolution to the effect that the corporation is to be wound up by the court;

(b) the corporation has not commenced business within a year of its registration, or has suspended its business for a whole year;

(c) the corporation is unable to pay its debts; or

(d) it appears, on application to the court, that it would be just and equitable that the corporation be wound up.[2]

A corporation is deemed to be unable to pay its debts if:

(a) a creditor to whom the corporation is indebted in a sum of not less than R200 has served on the corporation a demand requiring it to pay the sum so due, and the corporation has for 21 days thereafter neglected to pay the sum or to secure or compound for it to the reasonable satisfaction of the creditor; or

(b) any process issued on a judgment, or order of any court in favour of a creditor of the corporation is returned by a sheriff or a messenger with an endorsement stating that he has not found sufficient disposable property to satisfy the judgment, decree or order, or that any disposal property found did not upon sale satisfy such process; or

(c) it is proved to the satisfaction of the court that the corporation is unable to pay its debts.[3]

1 See 2.13 as to the jurisdiction of the court to wind up a corporation.
2 S 68; see also *Tjospomie Boerdery (Pty) Ltd v*
   Drakensberg Botteliers (Pty) Ltd 1989 4 SA 31 (T), which dealt with a company.
3 S 69(1).

The applicant

11.08 The application to the court can be brought by the corporation, a creditor, member, or the Master.[1]

Where the corporation applies to court for winding up, a written resolution signed by members having more than one half of the total number of votes of members is required.[2] Where individual members apply, there is no requirement as to minimum length of membership and no restriction as to the grounds on which the member may apply.[3]

Winding up by the court is most frequently ordered on the application of a creditor of the corporation. The ordinary meaning of 'creditor' has specifically been extended to include a contingent or prospective creditor.[4] The amount of a creditor's claim cannot disqualify him from applying for winding up; it is only when liquidation is sought on the ground that the corporation is unable to satisfy a debt after a demand was made in terms of section 69(1)(a), that the creditor's claim must amount to at least R200.

The Master cannot initiate proceedings for the winding up of a corporation; his *locus standi* is limited to making an application for the conversion of a voluntary winding up to a winding up by the court. Such application may be made at any stage prior to the dissolution of a corporation.

1 S 346(1) Companies Act. The corporation, a creditor or a member, or any of them, may also apply jointly – s 346(1)(d) Companies Act.
2 S 68(a).
3 See in contrast s 346(2) Companies Act.
4 S 346(1)(b) Companies Act. See *Spendiff NO v JAJ Distributors (Pty) Ltd* 1989 4 SA 126 (C).

The application for winding up

11.09 The application, consisting of a notice of motion and supporting affidavits,[1] is filed with the court and must be accompanied by a certificate by the Master, issued not more than ten days before the date of the application, to the effect that sufficient security has been given for the payment of all fees, charges and administration costs until appointment of a provisional liquidator, or if no such liquidator is appointed, of all fees and charges necessary for the discharge of the corporation from winding up.[2] A copy of the application and of every affidavit confirming the facts stated therein must also be lodged with the Master. The Master may report to the court any facts which would justify the court in postponing the hearing or dismissing the application; a copy of such report must be transmitted to both the applicant and the corporation.[3]

1 For a specimen application, see Part 2.   3 S 346(4) Companies Act.
2 S 346(3) Companies Act.

The powers of the court

11.10 The court may grant or dismiss any application for winding up of a corporation, or adjourn the hearing thereof conditionally or unconditionally, or make any interim order or any other order it may deem just.[1] In sequestration proceedings, it has sometimes been doubted whether a secured creditor has *locus standi* to apply for sequestration, but in the case of a corporation, it is clear that the court may not refuse to make a winding up order only because the assets of the corporation have been mortgaged to an amount equal to or in excess of those assets, or because the corporation has no assets.[2]

Where the applicants for winding up are members of the corporation and it appears to the court that they are entitled to relief, the court may make a winding up order, but it may refuse to make such order if it is satisfied that some other remedy is available to the applicants and that they are acting unreasonably in pursuing the winding up of the corporation instead of that other remedy.[3]

1 S 347(1) Companies Act.   79 ("Mars *Insolvency*"); De la Rey 1990 *SA Merc*
2 S 347(1) Companies Act. See De la Rey *Mars The*   *LJ* 95.
  Law of Insolvency in South Africa 8 ed (1988)   3 S 347(2) Companies Act.

11.11 If the court finds that the applicant has made out a *prima facie* case it customarily issues a provisional winding up order with a rule *nisi* in terms of which interested parties are called upon to show cause on the return day why the corporation should not be placed under final liquidation. The Act does not specifically require the issuing of a provisional order, so that this is left to the discretion of the court.

On the return day of the rule *nisi* the applicant usually asks the court to confirm the winding up order.

11.12 On proof that it is expedient, the court may, at any time after the commencement of the winding up,[1] on the application of any liquidator, creditor or member, order that any or all proceedings in relation to the winding up be stayed or that any voluntary winding up be continued on such terms and conditions as the court deems fit.[2] The reason for the application for such an order is usually that a compromise has been entered into with creditors.

Once a winding up order has been granted, the winding up is deemed to have commenced at the time of the presentation of the application to court.[3]

1 Ie the time of presentation to the court of the application for the winding up (s 348 Companies Act).
2 S 354(1) Companies Act. In the case of companies, the court has stated that the setting aside of a winding up order is an extraordinary step

which will only rarely be granted. The applicant will also have to satisfy the common law requirements relating to the recision of a judgment (*Herbst v Hessels* 1978 2 SA 105 (T) 109).
3 S 348 Companies Act.

Publication of the winding up order or resolution

11.13 Once the winding up of a corporation has commenced, it is important that it be brought to the attention of certain officials and the public.

A copy of every provisional and final winding up order and any order of court staying, amending or setting such order aside, must be sent forthwith by the registrar of the court to the persons mentioned hereafter. In the case of a voluntary winding up, the copy of the resolution must be forwarded by the corporation.[1]

The officials who must be notified, are:

☐ the sheriff of the province in which the registered office of the corporation is situated and the sheriff of every province in which it appears that the corporation owns property;

☐ every registrar or other officer charged with the maintenance of any register under any act in respect of any property in the Republic which appears to be an asset of the corporation;

☐ the messenger of every magistrate's court by the order whereof it appears that property of the corporation is under attachment.[2]

After receipt of a winding up order the Master must give notice of the winding up in the *Gazette*.[3]

1 See 11.04 above.   3 S 356(1) Companies Act.
2 S 357(1) Companies Act.

Consequences of the winding up order

11.14 As soon as the winding up order is made, the corporation is no longer under the control of its members but control passes initially to the Master and then, upon the appointment of a liquidator, into his hands.[1] Unlike the sequestration of an individual, which results in the assets vesting in the trustee, the corporation is not divested of its assets. The corporation continues to exist while being under the control of a liquidator for winding up and the distribution of its assets in satisfaction of the debts of its creditors, as well as the division of any surplus assets amongst members.

1 S 361(1) Companies Act.

11.15 Other consequences are:

☐ Every transfer of a member's interest in the corporation being wound up made after the commencement of the winding up without the sanction of the liquidator is void.[1]

☐ Every disposition of its property (including rights of action) made after commencement of the winding up by a corporation being wound up and unable to pay its debts, is void unless the court orders otherwise.[2]

☐ All civil proceedings by or against the corporation concerned are automatically suspended until a liquidator is appointed.[3]

☐ Any attachment or execution put into force against the estate or assets of the corporation after the commencement of the winding up is void.[4]

1 S 341(1) Companies Act.   3 S 359(1)(a) Companies Act.
2 S 341(2) Companies Act.   4 S 359(1)(b) Companies Act.

12

Liquidation: Administrative procedure

Introduction

12.01 Although a liquidation by the court and a creditors' voluntary liquidation are initiated in different ways, the two procedures are virtually identical as from the first meeting of creditors. The two procedures are therefore discussed together.

Statement of affairs

12.02 Within 14 days after an order for the winding up of a corporation has been granted[1] or within 28 days after a resolution for the voluntary winding up of a corporation by creditors has been registered, two certified copies of the statement of affairs of the corporation must be lodged with the Master.[2] Upon appointment of a liquidator, the Master must send a copy of the statement of affairs which has been lodged with him, to the liquidator.[3]

In a winding up by the court, the statement of affairs must be drawn up by the persons who were members and managers of the corporation as at date of the winding up order.[4]

The statement of affairs must contain, in the prescribed form,[5] *inter alia* particulars of the corporation's assets, debts, liabilities (including contingent and prospective liabilities); any pending legal proceedings by or against it; the names, addresses and nature of the business of its creditors, the security held by each of them and the date on which each security was given; and, generally, such further information as the Master may require.[6] The statement of affairs must be verified by affidavit by each person obliged to make it out and those affidavits must be annexed to the statement.[7]

1 Or within such extended time as the Master or the court may for special reasons appoint (s 363(2) Companies Act).
2 S 363(2) and s 356(2)(a)(ii) Companies Act.
3 S 363(5) Companies Act.
4 S 363(2)(a) Companies Act.

5 CM100 Companies Act.
6 S 363(4)(a) Companies Act. Those concerned should ascertain from the Master beforehand what further information he requires.
7 S 363(4)(b) Companies Act.

The liquidator

12.03 The Master must appoint a suitable natural person as a liquidator as soon as is practicable after a provisional winding up order has been granted or a copy of a resolution for a voluntary winding up has been registered.[1] No provisional liquidator is appointed. In a voluntary winding up by members, the Master must consider the appointment of the person nominated by a resolution of members, as liquidator.[2] Where the winding up is not a voluntary winding up by members, creditors may at the first meeting nominate a person for appointment as joint or co-liquidator and the Master is then obliged to make such an appointment, subject to his right in terms of section 76 of the Act to refuse to appoint a specific person.[3]

A person nominated as liquidator must give security to the satisfaction of the Master for the proper performance of his duties.[4]

1 See *Krumm v The Master* 1989 3 SA 944 (D) 947-8 regarding certain guidelines laid down by the Master.

2 S 74(3).
3 S 74(4).
4 S 375(1) Companies Act.

Persons who may not be appointed as liquidator

12.04 The following persons are disqualified from being nominated or appointed as liquidator:[1]

(a) an insolvent;

(b) a minor or a person under legal disability;

(c) a person declared by the court to be incapable of appointment as a liquidator while such incapacity lasts;[2]

(d) a person removed from an office of trust by the court on account of misconduct or a person who is the subject of any order disqualifying him as director;[3]

(e) a corporate body;

(f) a person who has been convicted of theft, fraud, forgery or uttering a forged document or perjury and has been sentenced to imprisonment without the option of a fine or to a fine exceeding R20;

(g) a person who has by means of misrepresentation or reward attempted to procure his appointment as liquidator;[4]

(h) a person who does not reside in the Republic;

(i) a person who at any time during the 12 months immediately preceding its winding up, was a member, manager or accounting officer of that corporation;[5]

(j) any agent authorised to vote for or on behalf of a creditor at a meeting of creditors of the corporation concerned and acting or purporting to act under that authority.

1 S 372 Companies Act.
2 See s 373 Companies Act.
3 In terms of s 219 of the Companies Act.
4 In terms of s 365(1) Companies Act it is an offence to offer any reward to a member or creditor to secure or prevent the nomination of a person as liquidator.
5 Excluding, in a members' voluntary winding up, the accounting officer.

12.05 The court may, on the application of any interested party declare a person disqualified for appointment as liquidator or remove a liquidator from office and, if it deems fit, declare him incapable of being appointed liquidator during the period of his life, or for such other period as it may determine, on the grounds:[1]

(a) that he attempted to obtain a share in the commission or any other benefit of any auctioneer, agent or other person acting on behalf of the corporation being liquidated;

(b) that he canvassed for the votes of creditors or members or attempted to procure his nomination as liquidator by –

– wrongfully inserting or omitting the name of any person in or from any statutory list or schedule;

– giving or offering consideration in a direct or indirect manner;

– offering or agreeing to abstain from investigating any transactions relating to the corporation or its members or managers; or

– being a party to the splitting of claims for the purpose of increasing the number of votes.

1 S 373 Companies Act.

12.06 Where a vacancy occurs in the office of liquidator, the Master can instruct a remaining liquidator to convene a meeting of creditors or members to elect a substitute. If the person who vacated office was originally appointed by the Master without any nomination by creditors or members, the Master may appoint the remaining liquidator to fill the vacancy. Where only one liquidator was appointed, the Master may appoint another suitable person to fill the vacancy.[1]

1 S 76.

Termination of office of liquidator

12.07 The liquidator normally holds office until the winding up process has been completed. Provision is however made for the resignation[1] and removal[2] of a liquidator.

A liquidator may not be absent from the Republic for more than 60 days without the prior permission of the Master in writing.[3] The Master may require the liquidator to give notice of his intended absence in the *Gazette* and to appoint a suitable person to wind up the corporation in terms of a power of attorney.[4]

1 S 77(1).
2 S 379 Companies Act.
3 S 77(2).

4 S 77(2)(b) empowers the Master to lay down conditions for the leave of absence of the liquidator.

General duties of the liquidator

12.08 As soon as the liquidator is appointed, the Master shall send him a copy of the statement of affairs.[1] The information contained in this statement serves as the basis for the liquidator in the performance of his duties.

1 S 363(5) Companies Act. See 12.02 above as to
   the statement of affairs.

12.09 The liquidator takes control of the affairs of the corporation and must forthwith take possession of all assets belonging to the corporation. He must investigate the affairs of the corporation prior to winding up, report to creditors, realise the assets as instructed, collect outstanding debts and then account to the Master before paying the costs incurred in connection with the liquidation and distributing the surplus amongst creditors and members.[1]

1 S 391 Companies Act.

The position of the liquidator

12.10 The liquidator must liquidate the corporation for the benefit of the creditors and members of the corporation. He occupies a fiduciary position and may receive no benefit for himself from this position apart from his fixed remuneration.[1] The legal position of a liquidator corresponds to that of an agent.[2] It is wrong to regard him as a trustee charged with the care of trust property since ownership of the corporation's assets does not pass to him; until it is dissolved, the corporation in liquidation continues to exist and when the liquidator enters into an agreement he does so in the name of the corporation.[3] The liquidator is expected to show a high degree of care and diligence and to be impartial in his actions.

1 S 384(3); *Symington NO v Die Meester* 1960 4 SA 70 (O).

2 *Terrace Bay Holdings (Pty) Ltd v Strathmore Diamonds (Pty) Ltd* 1976 3 SA 664 (SWA) 667.

3 See *R v Heyne* (3) 1958 1 SA 614 (W); *Letsitele Stores (Pty) Ltd v Roets* 1958 2 SA 224 (T). Both cases deal with companies.

12.11 The Master exercises control over liquidators to the extent that he, either *mero motu* or on complaints being made to him by any creditor or member, must investigate any apparent dereliction of duty on the part of the liquidator.[1] The Master may require a liquidator to answer any enquiries, examine him or any other person under oath concerning the winding up and appoint a person to investigate the books and vouchers of the liquidator.

The liquidator must also assist the Master to perform his duties under the Act and in particular must furnish any information required and give the Master access to the books and documents of the corporation.[2]

1 S 381 Companies Act.
2 S 392 Companies Act.

Some specific duties of the liquidator

12.12 Immediately after his appointment the liquidator must open a book or other record in which he must enter from time to time statements of all moneys, goods, books, accounts and other documents received by him on behalf of the corporation.[1] The Master may at any time direct the liquidator to produce such book or record to him and any creditor is entitled to inspect it at all reasonable times.[2]

1 S 393(1) Companies Act.
2 S 393(2), (3) Companies Act.

12.13 The liquidator must open a current banking account in the name of the corporation in liquidation[1] and must at the earliest opportunity[2] deposit in that account all moneys received on behalf of the corporation. The liquidator may also open a savings account for the corporation and effect interest-bearing deposits with a bank or building society.[3]

1 S 394(1)(a) as amended by s 6 of the Companies Amendment Act 63 of 1988, requires that amounts must be withdrawable from the account by cheque. The account must be opened with a banking institution registered under the Banks Act 23 of 1965.

2 S 394(1) Companies Act. Delay in depositing any amount over R40 on the earliest possible day after receipt thereof renders the liquidator liable to pay to the corporation double the amount in question. The same penalty applies where assets of the cor-

poration are used unlawfully (s 394(7) Companies Act).

3 S 394(1) Companies Act, as amended by s 6 of the Companies Amendment Act 63 of 1988. The building society can be a mutual building society registered under the Mutual Building Societies Act 24 of 1965 or a building society registered under the Building Societies Act 82 of 1986. Money withdrawn from the savings account or other deposit must first be transferred back to the banking account.

Report on offences

12.14 The liquidator is obliged to examine the affairs and transactions of the corporation before its winding up to determine whether any of the present or past members and managers of the corporation have or appear to have contravened any provision of the Act or have committed any other offence.[1]

1 S 400 Companies Act.

Powers of the liquidator

12.15 In a voluntary winding up by creditors the liquidator may, unless the Act otherwise provides, without the sanction of the court, exercise all the powers given by the Act to the liquidator in a winding up by the court. This is subject to such directions as may be given by the creditors.[1]

1 S 351(2) Companies Act. See *Albert v Windsor
    Hotel (Pty) Ltd* 1963 2 SA 237 (E).

12.16 The powers of a liquidator in any winding up may be divided into three categories:

(a) powers which he can exercise on his own;

(b) powers for which the authority granted by meetings of creditors and members is required; and

(c) powers which can only be exercised with the leave of the court.

12.17 The liquidator on his own has the power:[1]

(a) to sign all deeds, receipts and documents in the name of the corporation;

(b) to prove a claim against the estate of a debtor;

(c) to draw, accept, make or endorse any bill of exchange or promissory note on behalf of the corporation provided no additional liability is placed on the corporation;[2]

(d) to summon any meetings of creditors and members for the purpose of obtaining their authority or sanction for any matter or purpose as he might consider necessary;

(e) to take, subject to the other provisions relating to the exercise of his powers,[3] such measures for the protection and better administration of the affairs and property of the corporation as the trustee of an insolvent estate may take of his own account.[4]

1 S 386(1) Companies Act.
2 Additional liabilities may only be imposed (a) with
    the leave of the court or (b) with the authority
    granted by meetings of creditors and members
    or (c) to carry on the business of the corporation
    under s 386(4)(f) – s 386(1)(c) Companies Act.
3 I e s 386(3), (4), (5).

4 S 386(1)(e) Companies Act. A trustee may, for
    example, continue the business of the insolvent
    until he obtains the necessary authority of the creditors or the Master – s 80(1) Insolvency Act 24
    of 1936; Smith *The Law of Insolvency* 3 ed (1988)
    195-196 ("Smith *Insolvency*"); Mars *Insolvency*
    268.

12.18 The liquidator enjoys certain powers before a general meeting is convened for the first time:[1]

(a) He may terminate any lease in terms of which the corporation is the lessee of movable or immovable property, subject to the consent of the Master.

(b) The liquidator shall, if satisfied that any movable or immovable property of the corporation ought to be sold forthwith, make such written recommendation to the Master, who may then authorise the sale of the property.

1 S 386(2) and (2A) Companies Act.

12.19 The liquidator has, if authorised thereto:

(a) in the case of a winding up by the court, by meetings of creditors and members; and

(b) in a creditor's voluntary winding up, by a meeting of creditors;
the powers mentioned in section 386(4) of the Companies Act.[1]

These provisions authorise the liquidator

— to bring or defend either civil or criminal legal proceedings in the name of and on behalf of the corporation;

— to agree to any reasonable offer of composition made by any debtor;

— to compromise or admit any claim or demand against the corporation, including an unliquidated claim;

— to make an arrangement with creditors, including creditors in respect of unliquidated claims, provided the corporation is able to pay its debts;

— to submit to arbitration any dispute concerning the corporation or any claim or demand by or upon the corporation;

— to carry on or discontinue any part of the business of the corporation in so far as may be necessary for the beneficial winding up thereof;

— to exercise the same powers as are conferred upon a trustee by sections 35 and 37 of the Insolvency Act, 1936, subject thereto that the powers conferred by section 35 can only be exercised if the corporation is unable to pay its debts. The application of section 35 serves to authorise the liquidator to enforce or abandon a contract for the purchase of immovable property which has not been transferred to the corporation.[2] The provisions of section 37 authorise the liquidator to confirm[3] or terminate contracts of lease entered into by the corporation in respect of both movable and immovable property;[4]

— to sell any movable and immovable property of the company as a whole[5] or separately by public auction, public tender or private contract and to give delivery thereof;[6]

— to perform any act or exercise any power for which the leave of the court is not expressly required by the Act.

1 S 386(3) Companies Act.
2 See Smith *Insolvency* 149-152; Mars *Insolvency* 145-146.
3 *Durban City Council v Liquidators Durban City Icedromes Ltd* 1965 1 SA 600 (A).
4 *Montelindo Compania Naviera SA v Bank of Lisbon & SA Ltd* 1969 2 SA 127 (W) 135. See however also s 386(2) and 12.18 above. See further Smith *Insolvency* 161-163; Mars *Insolvency* 156-158.
5 *Stern NO v Standard Trading Co (Pty) Ltd* 1955 3 SA 423 (A).
6 See *Jacobson v Boyes NO* 1966 3 SA 90 (W).

Uncompleted or executory contracts

12.20 In regard to executory or partly performed contracts of a corporation which is placed in liquidation, other than those referred to above and which are dealt with in the Insolvency Act, the following principles have been evolved by the courts.[1] Liquidation of the corporation does not terminate an executory contract lying outside the categories specifically covered by the Insolvency Act, but the liquidator cannot be forced to render specific performance in terms of the contract. He may repudiate the contract, in which event he may not insist on further performance by the other party and is not expected to fulfil the corporation's outstanding obligations under it. The other party is in the position of any creditor owed an ordinary debt by the corporation: he has a concurrent claim for damages against the estate, entitling him to share in the free residue.[2] If the liquidator chooses to continue the contract, it remains fully in force. The other party must perform all his contractual obligations and the liquidator is bound to fulfil in their entirety all the corporation's undischarged contractual obligations, including any which ought to have been carried out before liquidation. The other party's claim is now not directed against the free residue of the estate, but against the liquidator, who must meet it as an expense of administration, as the liquidator's decision to continue the contract is reached in the course of, and for the purposes of, the administration of the estate.[3]

1 *Bryant & Flanagan (Pty) Ltd v Muller* 1977 1 SA 800 (N) (which was confirmed on appeal at 1978 2 SA 807 (A)) and the cases therein cited (at 804); *Ex parte Venter* 1976 3 SA 267 (O) 281, 282; *Montelindo Compania Naviera SA v Bank of Lisbon & SA Ltd* 1969 2 SA 127 (W) 141, 142; *Noord-Westelike Ko-operatiewe Landboumaatskappy Bpk v Die Meester* 1982 4 SA 486 (NC); *Cohen NO v Verwoerdburg Town Council* 1983 1 SA 334 (A) 352; *Somchem (Pty) Ltd v Federated*

Insurance Co Ltd 1983 4 SA 609 (C) 615; *Porteous v Strydom NO* 1984 2 SA 489 (D); *Thomas Construction (Pty) Ltd (in liquidation) v Grafton Furniture Manufacturers (Pty) Ltd* 1988 2 SA 546 (A). See also Smith *Insolvency* 172-4; Mars *Insolvency* 143-145.

2 *Bryant & Flanagan* case *supra* 804.

3 *Bryant & Flanagan* case *supra* 805; *Montelindo Compania Naviera* case *supra* 141, 142.

Consultation with creditors and members

12.21 The process of winding up a corporation is carried out subject to the directions and with due consideration for the rights of interested parties as the winding up is done for their benefit. Such interested parties are the creditors of the corporation whose interests, particularly in the case of a corporation which is unable to pay its debts, are of paramount importance, and its members. The Act makes provision for these groups of interested parties to be consulted and their directions to be obtained at meetings convened and held in the prescribed manner.

First meetings of creditors and members

12.22 The liquidator must, as soon as possible and, except with the consent of the Master, not later than one month after a final winding up order[1] has been granted by the court or a resolution of a creditors' voluntary winding up has been registered, summon a meeting of the creditors of the corporation.[2] This meeting is summoned for the purpose of:

(a) considering the statement of affairs of the corporation lodged with the Master;

(b) the proof of claims;

(c) deciding whether a co-liquidator should be appointed and, if so, nominating a person for appointment; and

(d) receiving directions or authorisation in respect of any matter regarding the liquidation.

It would therefore seem that the liquidator can report to creditors at the first meeting and immediately be authorised to realise assets.[3]

The liquidator must also summon a meeting of members of the corporation.[4] This meeting is summoned for the purpose of:

(a) considering the statement as to the affairs of the corporation, unless the meeting of members when passing a resolution for the voluntary winding up of the corporation has already considered the said statement;

(b) receiving or obtaining directions or authorisation in respect of any matter regarding the liquidation.

No provision is made for resolving any conflict which may arise between the directions given by creditors and those given by members.[5]

1 The first meeting can only be summoned after the final winding up order has been granted: *De Wit v Boathavens CC (King Intervening)* 1989 1 SA 606 (C).
2 S 78.
3 See De la Rey 3 *Transactions Luyt Centre For Business Law* 84, 101.
4 S 78(1)(b).
5 Contrast s 387 Companies Act which does not however apply to corporations.

The liquidator's report

12.23 Except in the case of a member's voluntary winding up a liquidator must, as soon as practicable and except with the consent of the Master, not later than three months after the date of his appointment, submit a report on the following matters to a general meeting of creditors and members:[1]

(a) the estimated amounts of the corporation's assets and liabilities;

(b) the causes of the corporation's failure, if it has failed;

(c) whether he has submitted or intends to submit to the Master a report under section 400(2) of the Companies Act. This report must contain full particulars of any contraventions or offences or suspected contraventions or offences by members;

(d) whether any member or former member appears to be liable to the corporation on the ground of breach of trust or negligence, or to make repayments as set out in sections 70 and 71;[2] or whether such member or former member appears to be liable to a creditor of the corporation or the corporation itself for the debts of the corporation under Part VIII of the Act;

(e) any legal proceedings by or against the corporation;

(f) whether or not further enquiry is desirable in regard to any matter relating to the formation or failure of the corporation or the conduct of its business;

(g) whether or not the corporation has kept the required accounting records;

(h) the progress and prospects in respect of the winding up; and

(i) any other matter which he may consider fit, or in connection with which he may require the directions of the creditors.

1 S 79. On the wording of s 78(1)(a)(iv) it would appear that this report may be submitted to the   first meeting of creditors.
2 See 12.53 and 12.54 below.

Second meeting of creditors

12.24 After the first meeting of creditors, a second meeting may be convened for the proof of claims. If the report of the liquidator was not submitted to the first meeting, the report must now be considered by creditors. Thereafter creditors may give directions to the liquidator in connection with the liquidation of the corporation.[1]

1 S 40(3)(a) Insolvency Act.

Special and general meetings

12.25 After the second meeting of creditors the liquidator must convene a special meeting of creditors if requested to do so by an interested party who tenders payment of all costs in connection with such meeting. A special meeting is held for the further proof of claims. The liquidator may in his discretion convene general meetings of creditors to obtain instructions concerning the liquidation; he must convene such a meeting if requested to do so by the Master or creditors representing one-fourth of the value of proved claims.[1]

1 S 41 Insolvency Act. Witnesses may be interrogated at a general meeting, but such a meeting may not be convened for the sole purpose of interrogation – *Essop v The Master* 1983 1 SA 926 (C) 932B. There is some difference of opinion as to whether claims may be proved – see Smith *Insolvency* 206-207; Mars *Insolvency* 321-322, 341. S 44(3) Insolvency Act states that claims must be proved 'at a meeting of the creditors'.

Attendance at meetings

12.26 Where the corporation being wound up is unable to pay its debts, every member and manager of the corporation is obliged to attend the first and second meetings of creditors, as well as any subsequent or adjourned meeting of creditors which the liquidator has in writing required him to attend.[1] The Master may also subpoena other persons to appear at those meetings.[2] Such members and other persons can then be examined under oath, concerning the business affairs of the corporation, by the presiding officer and, *inter alia*, any creditor or his agent.[3]

1 S 414(1) Companies Act.
2 S 414(2) Companies Act. See further *Levin v Ensor* 1975 2 SA 118 (D); *Cox v Swanepoel* 1977 4 SA 260 (W) 266-268.
3 S 415 Companies Act; s 416 provides that ss 65, 66, 67 and 68 of the Insolvency Act apply to persons required or subpoenaed to attend those meetings and the production of books or

documents by and interrogation of such persons under s 415 (see Smith *Insolvency* 212-215; Mars *Insolvency* 357-363). As to possible liability for defamatory statements made during such an enquiry, see *Zwiegelaar v Botha* 1989 3 SA 351 (C).

Voting by creditors

12.27 The wishes of the creditors as a group are ascertained by means of resolutions which are passed by general vote at a meeting of creditors. The general rule is that every creditor who has proved his claim against the corporation is entitled to vote.[1] Each creditor can vote either personally or through an agent, provided that the agent is not the liquidator, his employer, employee or co-employee, a member of his family or a person having a direct or indirect pecuniary interest in his remuneration as liquidator.[2] The vote of a creditor must be reckoned according to the value of his claim, unless the Insolvency Act provides that votes are to be reckoned in number,[3] in which event only a creditor with a claim of at least R100 can vote.[4] A creditor is also not permitted to vote in respect of any claim which was ceded to him after commencement of the winding up proceedings.[5]

1 S 52(1) Insolvency Act. On voting by conditional and secured creditors, see ss 48 and 52(5) Insolvency Act.
2 S 53(2) Insolvency Act; Smith *Insolvency* 209-211; Mars *Insolvency* 323-326.
3 S 52(2) Insolvency Act.
4 S 52(3) Insolvency Act. For the nomination of a liquidator a majority in value and number of creditors' votes is required (s 54 Insolvency Act).
5 S 52(4) Insolvency Act.

12.28 Creditors may vote at a meeting of creditors on all matters relating to the administration of the estate of the corporation, but not those concerning the distribution of the corporation's assets, except to direct the liquidator to contest, compromise or admit any claim against the corporation.[1]

1 S 53(1) Insolvency Act.

Meetings convened by the court

12.29 The court may direct meetings of the creditors or members to be called, held and conducted in the manner it directs for the purpose of ascertaining the wishes of such group.[1]

1 See ss 354(2) and 413 Companies Act.

Proof of claims by creditors

12.30 In a winding up by the court the Master on the application of the liquidator may fix a time within which the creditors of the corporation must prove their claims.[1] Should a creditor fail to prove his claim, he is excluded from the benefits of any distribution under an account lodged with the Master before the claim in question is proved.[2]

1 S 366(2) Companies Act.
2 *Ibid*; *Trans-Drakensberg Bank Ltd v The Master, Pietermaritzburg* 1966 1 SA 821 (N).

12.31 In a winding up by the court and in a creditor's voluntary winding up all claims must be proved against the corporation at a meeting of creditors in accordance with the provisions of the Insolvency Act.[1] Each claim must be proved by an affidavit in the prescribed form, in which is set out the nature of the claim and any security held. This affidavit with any documents in support of the claim must be lodged with the presiding officer and lie for the inspection of the liquidator and creditors for 24 hours before the commencement of the meeting of creditors.[2] The presiding officer must examine each claim carefully and decide whether it can be admitted.[3]

1 S 366(1)(a) Companies Act. The provisions of the Insolvency Act with regard to secured and unsecured creditors and the order of preference in which creditors must be paid out thus apply also to a winding up by the court. See Smith *Insolvency* 217 *et seq* and Mars *Insolvency* 332-356 as to proof of claims generally.
2 A power of attorney intended to be used at the meeting, must be lodged with the presiding officer at least 24 hours before the advertised time of the meeting (reg 12(2), Winding Up Regulations).
3 S 44 Insolvency Act; see Smith *Insolvency* 221-222; Mars *Insolvency* 349-350). On the disputing of claims by the liquidator, reg 3 Insolvency Regulations.

12.32 In each liquidation a secured creditor[1] has the same duty to place a value on his security as if he were proving a claim against an insolvent estate.[2] When proving his claim such a creditor may state that he relies on the proceeds of the property constituting his security for the satisfaction of his claim and by so doing may limit his liability to contribute to any shortfall.[3] The provisions of the Insolvency Act concerning movable property in the possession of the creditor as security for his claim apply to the winding up of a corporation unable to pay its debts both as regards the realisation of the security by the creditor and the taking over thereof by the creditor or the liquidator.[4]

1 A secured creditor is a person who has a preferent right to *particular assets* of the corporation by virtue of a special mortgage, landlord's legal hypothec, pledge or right of retention (see s 2 Insolvency Act).
2 S 366(1)(b) Companies Act; See Smith *Insolvency* 220; Mars *Insolvency* 391.
3 S 89(2) Insolvency Act.
4 S 366(1)(c) Companies Act. See s 83 Insolvency Act; if the security consists of marketable securities or bills of exchange the creditor may sell them before the second meeting of creditors after notice to the Master or liquidator, and then prove his claim with a statement of the proceeds of his security; if the security consists of any other sort of movable property the liquidator may take it over at an agreed value or at the value of the claim – if he does not do so the creditor may realise the property himself; such creditor is, however, entitled to prove his claim in the usual way and place a valuation on his security. See Smith *Insolvency* 236-238; Mars *Insolvency* 390-395; *Spendiff v JAJ Distributors (Pty) Ltd* 1989 4 SA 126 (C) 135.

Gathering information

12.33 The Act contains a number of provisions designed to enable information with regard to the affairs of a corporation which is unable to pay its debts to be obtained by the liquidator, members and creditors of the corporation.

This information is essential to assist the liquidator in his collection of assets of the corporation, for example in regard to setting aside voidable transactions,[1] and his administration of the winding up for the benefit of all the creditors in accordance with the law of insolvency. The information relating to the affairs of the corporation is also fundamental to the application of the provisions of the Act to counteract fraud.[2]

1 See 12.39 *et seq* below.
2 See 12.52 *et seq* below.

12.34 Section 363A of the Companies Act facilitates the task of the liquidator to contact members and secretaries of the corporation who may be able to assist him with information by obliging them to notify him of changes of their addresses.

12.35 The procedures provided by the Act for obtaining information, which are to be dealt with here, are:

(a) the inspection of the books etcetera of a corporation by a member or creditor; and

(b) interrogation of members and others at meetings of creditors.

Inspection of books, etcetera of a corporation by a member or creditor

12.36 On application by any member or creditor of a corporation unable to pay its debts and which is being wound up, the court may authorise him to inspect all or any of the books and papers of that corporation, whether in the possession of the corporation or the liquidator.[1] This section is not intended to be used to obtain information on which to decide whether the winding up order should be opposed or not.[2]

1 S 360 Companies Act.
2 *Blom v Promit Beleggings (Edms) Bpk* 1970 2 SA
   774 (E) 777.

Interrogation of members and others at meetings of creditors

12.37 In every winding up of a corporation unable to pay its debts, every member and manager must attend the first and second meetings of creditors unless previous written permission to absent himself has been granted to any of them by the Master after consultation with the liquidator.[1] The duty imposed on a member or manager to attend those meetings is an absolute duty and lack of personal, individual notice to the member or manager is no defence in a prosecution for non-attendance, as he is deemed to know of a meeting by virtue of its being convened by publication in the *Gazette*.[2] Members and managers of the corporation must also attend any subsequent or adjourned meetings of creditors if required to do so by written notice of the liquidator.[3]

1 S 414(1)(a) Companies Act.
2 *S v Di Stefano* 1977 1 SA 770 (C).
3 S 414(1)(b) Companies Act. If they attend meetings held after the second meeting or an adjournment thereof, they are entitled to an expense allowance out of the funds of the corporation (s 415(8) Companies Act).

12.38 The presiding officer may also subpoena any other person[1] who is known or on reasonable ground believed to be in possession of any property of the corporation or indebted to the corporation or who has any material information regarding the corporation, to be interrogated at the meeting of creditors.[2] Any one of these persons may be interrogated under oath; the interrogation must be relevant and may relate to any matters concerning the corporation or its affairs or property belonging to the corporation.[3]

1 "Any person" does not include the liquidator himself (*Scott-Hayward NO v Queensland Insurance Co Ltd* 1961 4 SA 540 (W)).
2 S 414(2)(a) Companies Act. As to the subject-matter and nature of the meeting, see *Pretorius v Marais* 1981 1 SA 1051 (A) 1062.
3 S 415(1) Companies Act. As to the ambit of the protection afforded to a witness making defamatory statements at an enquiry, see *Zwiegelaar v Botha* 1989 3 SA 351 (C).

Following-up and collecting property

12.39 The Act contains a number of provisions to protect the creditors of a corporation which is unable to pay its debts and is being wound up, against the prejudicial consequences of certain dispositions of property by the corporation and also provides the liquidator with a summary remedy to obtain the restoration of property of the corporation. Clearly the effective utilisation of these provisions will usually be founded on information as to the affairs of the corporation obtained by the liquidator through interrogations or examinations of members and managers of the corporation.[1]

1 See 12.30 above.

Dispositions which can be set aside

12.40 If a corporation which cannot pay all its debts is wound up,[1] the provisions of the Insolvency Act[2] regarding voidable dispositions of property apply.[3]

1 Regardless of whether it is a winding up by the court or a creditor's voluntary winding up (*In re Hardwood Timber Co Ltd (in liquidation)* 1932 NLR 170).
2 Act 24 of 1936, ss 26, 29, 30, 31, 32 and 34.
3 S 340 Companies Act; *Dally v Galaxie Melodies (Pty) Ltd* 1975 2 SA 337 (C); confirmed on appeal 1975 4 SA 736 (A).

12.41 To facilitate the application of those provisions of the Insolvency Act, it is provided that the event which is deemed to correspond with the sequestration order in the case of an individual is:

(a) the presentation of the application for winding up to the court (unless that winding up supersedes a voluntary winding up,[1] in which case the registration of the resolution to wind up the corporation is the determining moment);

(b) in the case of a creditors' voluntary winding up, the registration of the resolution to wind up.[2]

1 Ss 346(1)(e), 347 Companies Act.
2 S 340(2) Companies Act.

What a "disposition" is

12.42 In section 2 of the Insolvency Act the term "disposition" is defined in extremely wide terms as meaning any transfer or abandonment of rights to property and includes a sale, lease, mortgage, pledge, delivery, payment, release, compromise, donation or any contract therefor, but does not include a dispostion in compliance with an order of court. This definition is not exhaustive and contracts or transactions not specifically mentioned therein may nevertheless be included, for example a suretyship by a subsidiary for debts of its holding company.[1]

Dispositions of this nature which are made by a corporation before its winding up can be set aside either because creditors are prejudiced thereby or because assets are not distributed equally amongst creditors or because one or more of the creditors is given an undue preference. The liquidator may accordingly apply to the court to have the disputed transaction set aside.[2]

For the purposes of easy reference the voidable transactions are set out briefly.[3]

1 *Langeberg Koöperasie Bpk v Inverdoorn Farming & Trading Co Ltd* 1965 2 SA 597 (A) 602. See also *Muller v John Thompson Africa (Pty) Ltd* 1982 2 SA 86 (D).

2 S 32(1) Insolvency Act; see Smith *Insolvency* 139-142; Mars *Insolvency* 236-243.

3 For a full discussion of the subject, see Smith *Insolvency* 119-148; Mars *Insolvency* 206-243.

Disposition without value

12.43 A disposition by a corporation of its property not for value may be declared void if the disposition was made within two years of winding up and the person benefited cannot prove that immediately after the disposition the assets of the corporation exceeded its liabilities. If the disposition was made more than two years before winding up, it is voidable only if the liquidator can prove that immediately after the disposition the liabilities of the corporation exceeded its assets. If the value of the property disposed of exceeds the amount whereby the liabilities exceed the assets, the disposition can only be set aside to the extent of the excess.[1] For the purposes of such a disposition "property" has been held to include the undertaking of a suretyship by a corporation, while "value" is not necessarily confined to money.[2]

1 S 26(1) Insolvency Act. See Smith *Insolvency* 121-125; Mars *Insolvency* 207-215.

2 *Langeberg Koöperasie Bpk v Inverdoorn Farm-*

ing & Trading Co Ltd 1965 2 SA 597 (A); *South African Fabrics Ltd v Millman NO* 1972 4 SA 592 (A) 601; *Swadif v Dyke* 1978 1 SA 928 (A) 939.

Voidable preference

12.44 Every disposition of its property made by a corporation within six months of winding up which has the effect of preferring one of its creditors above another, may be set aside by the court, if immediately after the disposition the liabilities of the corporation exceed its assets. The person benefited can, however, raise the defence that the disposition was made in the ordinary course of business and that it was not intended to prefer one creditor above another.[1]

1 S 29(1) Insolvency Act; see Smith *Insolvency* 125-136; Mars *Insolvency* 215-227. See also *Illings (Acceptances) Co (Pty) Ltd v Ensor NO* 1982

1 SA 570 (A); *Meyer NO v Transvaalse Lewendehawe Koöperasie Bpk* 1982 4 SA 746 (A).

Undue preference to creditors

12.45 In this case every disposition, regardless of when it was made, may be set aside if, at the time when the disposition was made, the liabilities of the corporation exceeded its assets and it was intended to prefer one creditor above another.[1]

1 S 30(1) Insolvency Act; see Smith *Insolvency*
136-138; Mars *Insolvency* 227-228.

Collusive dealings before winding up

12.46 Where the corporation and another person at any time before liquidation *knowingly* colluded to dispose of the property of the corporation with the intention of prejudicing creditors or of preferring one creditor above another, such disposition may be set aside by the court.[1]

1 S 31(1) Insolvency Act; see Smith *Insolvency*
138-139; Mars *Insolvency* 228-229.

Voidable sale of business by a trading corporation

12.47 If a trading corporation disposes of its business or the goodwill of such business or any of its property (except stock in trade in the ordinary course of business) and is wound up within six months thereafter, then such disposition is void as against the liquidator unless the corporation published a notice of the intended disposition in the *Gazette* and in two issues of an Afrikaans newspaper and two issues of an English newspaper circulating in the district where the business is carried on, within a period of not less than 30 days and not more than 60 days before the date of such disposition.[1]

1 S 34 Insolvency Act; *Galaxie Melodies (Pty) Ltd
v Dally NO* 1975 4 SA 736 (A); see Smith *Insolvency* 143-145; Mars *Insolvency* 229-233.

Alienations in fraud of creditors under common law

12.48 In addition to the remedies which creditors have under the Insolvency Act, they also have the right under our common law to attack alienations which have been made to defraud them and have those transactions set aside.[1]

1 *Fenhalls v Ebrahim* 1956 4 SA 723 (D) 727; see
Smith *Insolvency* 145-147; Mars *Insolvency*
233-236.

12.49 Any person who parted with any property or security or lost any right in consideration for any disposition which can be set aside, is not obliged to restore any property or benefit he received under that disposition, if he acted in good faith, unless the liquidator indemnifies him for parting with his property or losing his right.[1] The rights of persons who acquire property in good faith and for value from anyone other than a corporation which is subsequently wound up, are not affected by the provisions of the Insolvency Act relating to voidable dispositions.[2]

1 S 33(1) Insolvency Act; *Ruskin NO v Barclays Bank DCO* 1959 1 SA 577 (W).

2 S 33(2) Insolvency Act; see Smith *Insolvency* 142; Mars *Insolvency* 241.

Disposition after commencement of winding up

12.50 Every disposition of a corporation's property (including rights of action) by any corporation being wound up and unable to pay its debts, made after the commencement of the winding up, shall be void unless the court otherwise orders.[1]

1 S 341(2) Companies Act. In *Herrigel v Bon Roads Construction (Pty) Ltd* 1980 4 SA 669 (SWA), a cheque in favour of B was paid on the day after the liquidation of Q, but without either B or the bank being aware of the liquidation. The liquidator of Q succeeded with a claim for repayment of this amount, based on the provisions of s 341(2) Companies Act.

Warrant to search for and take possession of goods

12.51 Should the liquidator upon reasonable grounds suspect that any property, book or document belonging to the corporation, is concealed on any person or on or in any place, vehicle, vessel or receptacle of whatever nature, or is otherwise unlawfully withheld from him, he may apply for a warrant to search for and take possession of the specific goods.[1]

1 S 69(3) Insolvency Act. See Smith *Insolvency* 187; Mars *Insolvency* 267.

Repayments by members

12.52 The liquidator of a corporation unable to pay its debts must ascertain whether members or former members of the corporation are liable to make repayments.[1] He must also ascertain whether circumstances justify an approach to the Master for a direction that members or former members make repayments. The liquidator may enforce such repayments and, in the event of the death of a member or former member or the insolvency of his estate, claim the amount due from the estate concerned.

Liability for repayments may arise from payment made by reason of membership, or from payment of salary or other remuneration.

1 S 80.

Repayments arising from membership

12.53 No member of a corporation which is being wound up is liable for the repayment of any payment made by the corporation to him only by reason of his membership, if such payment complies with the following requirements:

(a) after such payment is made, the corporation's assets, fairly valued, exceed all its liabilities;

(b) the corporation is able to pay its debts as they become due in the ordinary course of business; and

(c) such payment will not render the corporation unable to pay its debts as they become due in the ordinary course of business.[1]

In the winding up of a corporation unable to pay its debts, any such payment made to a member by reason of his membership only within a period of two years before the commencement of the winding up of the corporation, must be repaid to the corporation by the member unless he can prove that:[2]

(a) after such payment was made the corporation's assets, fairly valued, exceeded all its liabilities; and

(b) such payment was made while the corporation was able to pay its debts as they became due in the ordinary course of its business; and

(c) such payment, in the particular circumstances did not in fact render the corporation unable to pay its debts as they became due in the ordinary course of its business.

A person who has ceased to be a member of the corporation concerned within the said period of two years is also liable for any repayment referred to in the preceding paragraph if and to the extent that repayments by present members, together with all other available assets, are insufficient for paying all debts of the corporation.[3]

1 S 70 read with s 51(1).
2 S 70(2).
3 S 70(3).

Repayment of salary or remuneration

12.54 If a corporation being wound up is unable to pay its debts and:

(a) any payment of salary or remuneration was made by the corporation within a period of two years before the commencement of its winding up, to a member in his capacity as an officer or employee of such corporation; and

(b) such payment was, in the opinion of the Master, not *bona fide* or reasonable in the circumstances,

the Master must direct that such payment, or such part thereof as he may determine, be repaid by such member to the corporation.[1]

Any person who has, within the two-year period, ceased to be a member of a corporation may, under the circumstances referred to in (a) above, be directed by the Master to make a repayment if, and to the extent that, any such repayments by present members are, together with all other available assets, insufficient for paying all the debts of the corporation.[2]

1 S 71(1).
2 S 71(2).

Enforcement of repayments

12.55 In both types of repayment, the liquidator may forward a certificate by the Master as to the amount payable by a member or former member to the clerk of the magistrate's court having jurisdiction, who must record it. The notice then has the effect of a civil judgment. The normal steps of issuing summons and taking judgment in a court have been dispensed with.[1]

1 S 70(4). This is a very drastic and rather contentious remedy viewed against normal procedures. Provision is made in s 70(5) for the court in question, on application by a member or former member, to make any order that it deems fit in regard to the Master's certificate.

Repayments, payments of damages and restoration of property by members and others

12.56 Where in the course of any winding up it appears that any person who took part in the formation of the corporation, or any former or present member, officer or accounting officer of the corporation has misapplied or retained or become liable or accountable for any money or property of the corporation, or has been guilty of any breach of trust in relation to the corporation a court may, on the application of the Master, liquidator or any creditor or member enquire into the conduct of such person, member, officer or accounting officer, and may order him to repay or restore the money or property or to contribute such sum to the assets of the corporation by way of compensation or damages in respect of the misapplication, retention or breach of trust, as the court considers just.[1]

1 S 73(1).

13

The liquidator's account and finalisation of liquidation

Application of the proceeds of the corporation's assets

13.01 The order of preference in terms of the Insolvency Act applies as nearly as possible to the application of the proceeds of the assets of a corporation in liquidation.[1]

1 S 342(1) Companies Act. See also s 339 Companies Act read with s 66 Close Corporations Act for the general application of the Insolvency Act to a corporation unable to pay all its debts as well as the Insolvency Act ss 95-103; Smith *Insolvency* 253-262; Mars *Insolvency* 410-412.

13.02 For the purposes of the distribution of the proceeds, the assets of the corporation are divided into encumbered assets and free residue. An encumbered asset is one which is subject to a special mortgage, landlord's legal hypothec, pledge or right of retention;[1] all other assets constitute the free residue.

1 S 95 Insolvency Act.

Application of the proceeds of encumbered assets

13.03 The proceeds of the encumbered assets are applied in payment of costs and claims, namely:

(a) The cost of maintaining, conserving and realising such assets.[1] The costs of realisation include the liquidator's remuneration in respect of such assets,[2] a proportionate share of the liquidator's costs incurred in giving security and of the Master's fees and, where necessary, arrear property taxes which are due for a period not exceeding two years prior to the date of winding up. Should the proceeds of such assets be insufficient to cover the aforementioned costs, the secured creditor(s) who have a preferent right over those assets must pay the deficiency.[3]

(b) The claim(s) of the creditor(s)[4] which were secured by the asset in question.[5] Interest up to the date of winding up is an integral part of the secured creditor's claim; where the proceeds of the encumbered asset permit it, the secured creditor also receives interest, usually at eight percent, from the date of winding up to the date of payment.[6]

1 S 89(1) Insolvency Act.
2 The liquidator's remuneration consists of a certain percentage on the proceeds of the different kinds of assets.
3 S 89(1) Insolvency Act.
4 Where more than one claim is secured by a particular asset, the order of their preferences amongst each other applies, for example the holder of an enrichment lien over immovable property enjoys a preference over the bondholder (*United Building Society v Smookler's Trustee* 1906 TS 623).
5 S 95(1) Insolvency Act; Smith *Insolvency* 253-255; Mars *Insolvency* 407-409.
6 Ss 95(1) and 103(2) Insolvency Act; where the claim carries a higher rate of interest by virtue of a written stipulation, that rate applies.

13.04 Any income from an encumbered asset – for example, rent received in respect of fixed property subject to a special bond – after the date of winding up, forms part of the proceeds of that encumbered asset.

Application of the free residue

13.05 If there is a surplus of the proceeds of the encumbered assets after payment of the items set out in the preceding paragraph, that surplus together with the proceeds of the unencumbered assets and of the demands made on contributories form the free residue. The free residue is, broadly speaking,[1] applied in the following order of preference.[2]

(a) the payment of the costs of winding up;

(b) the payment of the claims of creditors; and

(c) the division of any surplus amongst the members.

1 If the corporation cannot pay its debts the ranking of preferences of the Insolvency Act (ss 97-103) in so far relevant must be applied *seriatim.*

2 Ss 391 and 342(1) Companies Act.

Costs of winding up

13.06 Costs of winding up[1] include:

☐ the prescribed fees payable to the Master;[2]

☐ the costs of the successful applicant as taxed by the taxing master; the court may also direct that the costs of reasonable opposition to the application may be regarded as liquidation costs;[3]

☐ costs in connection with the drafting of the statement of affairs;[4]

☐ the remuneration of the liquidator as taxed by the Master.[5]

☐ all other costs in connection with the maintenance, conservation and realisation of the assets, including the costs of giving security by the liquidator;[6]

☐ bank charges, postages and other small disbursements;

☐ costs of advertisements incurred in regard to the convening of meetings of creditors and members;

☐ costs or expenditure incurred by the liquidator as a consequence of a decision taken by him in the control and liquidation of the insolvent estate, such as an obligation to pay endowment on property to a local authority in order to be able to pass transfer thereof in terms of a sale;[7]

☐ costs of the sheriff incurred since liquidation;[8] and

☐ the salary or wages of a person employed by the liquidator in regard to the finalisation of the liquidation.[9]

1 S 97 Insolvency Act; Smith *Insolvency* 257-259 s v "costs of sequestration"; Mars *Insolvency* 400-403.

2 R 23, Winding Up Regulations and CM103. See *Ensor v The Master* 1983 1 SA 843 (A); *The Master v IL Back & Co Ltd* 1983 1 SA 986 (A).

3 S 97(3) Insolvency Act. All legal costs must have been taxed before they can be paid by the liquidator, except in a members' voluntary winding up (r 22, Winding Up Regulations), *Rivoy Investments (Pty) Ltd v Wemmer Trust (Pty) Ltd* 1939 WLD 151; *Abelson v Abelris Products Ltd* 1948 2 SA 991 (O).

4 S 363(7) Companies Act.

5 S 384(1) Companies Act.

6 S 383(1) Companies Act. Costs of realisation of assets include commission paid to an auctioneer or agent, as well as advertising costs of sales. Maintenance costs include costs of insurance, safeguarding (e g hiring a nightwatchman), costs of removal and storage in a warehouse, costs of feed for livestock etc.

7 *De Wet v Stadsraad van Verwoerdburg* 1978 2 SA 86 (T) 98.

8 S 97(2)(a) Insolvency Act. An example of such costs is fees for an attachment, on instructions from the Master, in accordance with r 2, Winding Up Regulations.

9 S 97(2)(c) Insolvency Act.

Remuneration of the liquidator

13.07 The liquidator in a *winding up by the court* or a *creditors' voluntary winding up* is entitled to a reasonable remuneration for his services which must be taxed by the Master in accordance with the prescribed tariff.[1] The liquidator's remuneration is only payable after the liquidation account in which the proceeds and application of the assets is set out, is confirmed.[2] The remuneration in terms of the tariff is exhaustive: neither the liquidator nor his partner, his employee or his fellow employee is entitled to any additional remuneration, for example, for services rendered in his capacity as auctioneer, accountant or attorney.[3] Where there are co-liquidators, the prescribed remuneration must be divided between them.[4]

1 S 384(1) Companies Act; r 24 Winding Up Regulations and CM104.
2 Because his remuneration is calculated as a percentage on the proceeds of the different assets (*Abbott v Bryant* (1910) 20 CTR 943; *R v Macleod* 1935 EDL 284); apparently the Master or the court may approve payment in advance.
3 S 384(3) Companies Act; *De Jager's Trustee v The Master* 1918 CPD 535; *In re Insolvent Estate Raw & Wilkinson* (1885) 6 NLR 149; *Nieuwoudt v Estate Van der Merwe* 1928 CPD 486.
4 *Buyskes v SA Association* (1885) 3 SC 204.

13.08 In a *members' voluntary winding up*, a meeting of members of the corporation may determine the liquidator's remuneration.[1] If the corporation does not thus determine his remuneration the liquidator is still entitled to a reasonable remuneration for his services.[2]

1 S 384(1) Companies Act.
2 S 384 Companies Act.

Costs of execution

13.09 Any balance of the free residue must then be applied in defraying the taxed fees of the sheriff or messenger in connection with any execution on the property of the corporation and any proceedings which resulted in that execution.[1]

1 S 98 Insolvency Act.

Preferent creditors

13.10 The claims of ordinary creditors are subordinate to the following preferent rights:[1]

☐ any amount due in terms of the Workmen's Compensation Act 1941 by the corporation in its capacity as an employer;

☐ any amount due in terms of the Income Tax Act 1962 which the corporation has withheld in respect of another person's obligation to pay taxation, but did not pay to the Secretary for Inland Revenue prior to liquidation;

☐ any amount due in terms of the Occupational Diseases in Mines and Works Act 78 of 1973 by the corporation in its capacity as the owner or former owner of a mine;

☐ any amount of customs, excise or sales duty or interest, fine or penalty due in terms of the Customs and Excise Act 1964;[2]

☐ the amount of any sales tax, interest, penalty or fine due by the corporation, immediately prior to liquidation, in terms of the Sales Tax Act 1978;

☐ any amount due in terms of the Unemployment Insurance Act 1966 by the corporation in its capacity as an employer;

☐ any other contributions due under any law by the corporation in its capacity as an employer (including those payable in respect of its employees) to any pension, sick, medical, unemployment, holiday, provident or other insurance fund.[3]

All the abovementioned claims rank *pari passu*, and abate in equal proportion, if necessary.[4]

1 See Smith *Insolvency* 260-261; Mars *Insolvency* 404-405.
2 The State has a lien over goods and property in terms of s 114 of the Customs and Excise Act 91

of 1964, and its claims have priority over the claims of all other persons.
3 S 99(1) Insolvency Act.
4 S 99(2) Insolvency Act.

Wages and salaries

13.11 Thereafter the free residue must be applied to pay arrear wages and salaries, for a period not exceeding two months prior to the winding up of the corporation, due to its employees and any fees due to a registered[1] accountant or auditor for keeping, writing up or auditing the books of the corporation,[2] as well as any leave pay or leave bonus for any period, not exceeding 21 days, then due to an employee.[3]

1 Ie registered in terms of the Public Accountants' and Auditors' Act 51 of 1951.
2 S 100(1) Insolvency Act; the amount payable to

any person must not exceed R2 000.
3 S 100(2) Insolvency Act; such bonus is subject to a maximum of R1 000.

13.12 Any balance remaining of the free residue must next be applied in paying any arrear income tax payable in respect of any period prior to winding up whether or not it has become payable since that date.[1]

1 S 101 Insolvency Act.

13.13 After payment of the above the free residue is applied to payment of claims secured by a notarial bond over movables, with interest to date of payment.[1] A notarial bond confers a preference above concurrent claims as far as the proceeds of the assets secured by the bond are concerned, to the extent that those proceeds fall into the free residue.

1 S 102 Insolvency Act.

13.14 Thereafter concurrent claims, if any, are paid on a *pro rata* basis; if the free residue is sufficient, concurrent creditors are awarded interest to the date of payment.[1]

In those cases where only a part of the creditor's claim is preferent, the remaining part constitutes a concurrent claim, for example where R3 000 is owing in respect of three months' salary, R1 000 of that amount will be a concurrent claim.

1 S 103 Insolvency Act; interest is calculated at 8% pa unless stipulated otherwise in writing; see Smith *Insolvency* 262; Mars *Insolvency* 412.

Contributions by creditors

13.15 The provisions of the law of insolvency in respect of contributions by creditors towards any costs apply to every winding up of a corporation.[1] If the free residue is insufficient to pay the costs of winding up, all creditors who have proved claims against the corporation as well as the creditor who applied for winding up (whether he proved a claim or not), are liable to make good the deficiency; non-preferent creditors each in proportion to the amount of his claim and secured creditors each in proportion to the amount which otherwise would have been awarded to him on a distribution of the free residue.[2] A secured creditor who has stated in his affidavit in proof of claim that he relies solely on his security for the payment of his claim is accordingly not liable to contribute.[3] Should, however, there be no creditors entitled to share in the free residue, the secured creditors are liable to make good the entire shortfall each in proportion to his claim, notwithstanding the fact that they may not have ranked upon the surplus of the free residue.[4]

1 S 342(2) Companies Act.
2 S 106 and s 14(3) Insolvency Act; see Smith *Insolvency* 264; Mars *Insolvency* 413-415.
3 If the proceeds of the security are however insufficient to cover the costs of maintaining, conserving and realising the assets, the secured creditor(s) concerned is liable for such shortfall (s 89(1) Insolvency Act).
4 S 106 Insolvency Act. A preferent creditor who did not apply for winding up, is not liable to contribute: *Ongevallekommissaris v Die Meester* 1989 4 SA 69 (T); De la Rey 1990 *SA Merc LJ* 95.

Dividends to members

13.16 Any surplus assets available after payment of the costs incurred in the winding up and the various claims of creditors must be distributed among the members according to their interest in the corporation.[1]

1 S 342(1) Companies Act.

Function and submission of the liquidator's account

13.17 The liquidator's account fulfils an important function in the winding up process as it is the instrument by means of which the liquidator accounts for his actions in the winding up of a corporation. The liquidator must lay a liquidation and distribution account before the Master within six months of his appointment,[1] unless the Master or the court grants an extension.[2] If a liquidator is unable to lodge an account within the prescribed period, he must, before expiration of that period:[3]

(a) lodge an affidavit with the Master setting out the reasons for his inability to lodge the account, the funds in hand available for distribution, a summary of the position of the winding up and whether he has applied for an extension of time;

(b) send a copy of that affidavit to each creditor of the corporation;

(c) lodge with the Master written reasons for his inability to lodge the accounts as well as the grounds upon which he claims an extension of time to lodge the account.[4]

1 S 403(1)(a) Companies Act.
2 S 404 Companies Act.

3 S 404(1) Companies Act.
4 See further ss 404 and 405 Companies Act.

The liquidator's account

13.18 The liquidator must lodge with the Master:

(a) an account of his receipts and payments (a *liquidation account*) and

(b) (i) a plan of distribution (a *distribution account*) for the distribution of any surplus assets to members of the corporation, *or* (ii) a plan of contribution (a *contribution account*), if there is a liability among creditors to contribute to the costs of winding up, apportioning their liability. It is also possible that both a distribution and a contribution account may be needed, as for example where a distribution is made to secured creditors while a contribution is collected from concurrent creditors.[1]

1 S 403(1) Companies Act. The account must be submitted in duplicate in the prescribed form   (CM101) and be verified by an affidavit by the liquidator (CM102).

Inspection of liquidator's account and objections thereto

13.19 The liquidator's account must lie for inspection by creditors, members or contributories and other interested parties at the office of the Master for a period of at least 14 days.[1] When the account is lodged the liquidator must give notice in the *Gazette* of the place where and the period during which the account will lie for inspection and he must post or deliver a similar notice to each creditor who has proved a claim.[2]

1 S 406(1) Companies Act; where the office of the Master and the registered office of the corporation are not situated in the same district, a copy of the liquidator's account must in addition be lodged with and lie for inspection at the office of   the magistrate or additional magistrate where the registered office is situated, and also where the corporation carried on business (s 406(1), (2) Companies Act).
2 S 406(3) Companies Act.

13.20 At any time before the confirmation of the liquidator's account any person interested in the corporation may lay before the Master any objection in writing with reasons therefor.[1]

1 S 407(1) Companies Act.

Confirmation of the liquidator's account

13.21 After an account has been open for inspection the Master must confirm the account.[1] The confirmation of the Master has the effect of a final judgment[2] save as against someone permitted by the court to re-open the account after its confirmation but before the liquidator commences with the distribution.[3] The court is prohibited from authorising the re-opening of any duly confirmed account except as is provided in section 408 of the Companies Act.

1 S 408 Companies Act.
2 *SA Clay Industries Ltd v Katzenellenbogen NO* 1957 1 SA 220 (W); *Central Africa Building Society v Pierce NO* 1969 1 SA 445 (RA) 455; see also *Kilroe-Daley v Barclays National Bank Ltd* 1984

4 SA 609 (A).
3 S 408 Companies Act. See *Rapp & Maister Holdings Ltd v Ruflex Holdings (Pty) Ltd* 1972 3 SA 835 (T); *Rulten NO v Herald Industries (Pty) Ltd* 1982 3 SA 600 (D) 610.

Distribution of the assets

13.22 Immediately after confirmation of the liquidator's account the liquidator must proceed to distribute the proceeds of the assets in terms of the account and/or collect from the creditors obliged to contribute and contributories the amounts for which they are liable.[1] The liquidator must give notice in the *Gazette* that the account has been confirmed and that a dividend will be paid to creditors or that a contribution will be collected.[2] Where the liquidator's account which is confirmed is not a final one only an interim dividend is paid to creditors.

1 S 409(1) Companies Act.
2 S 409(2) Companies Act.

13.23 The liquidator must without delay lodge with the Master receipts for the dividends paid to creditors and deposit any unpaid dividends in the Guardian's Fund within two months of the confirmation of the account.[1]

1 S 410(1), (2) Companies Act; failure in this regard by the liquidator is *prima facie* evidence of the unlawful disposition of a dividend and the Master   may institute proceedings against the liquidator to answer for his default (s 410(3) Companies Act).

"Release" of the liquidator

13.24 Although the liquidator is not formally released after completion of the liquidation process, he may on due performance of his duties apply in writing to the Master for a certificate that he has performed all his duties under the Act and complied with all the requirements of the Master.[1]

1 S 385 Companies Act.

14

Composition, deregistration and dissolution

Composition

14.01 No provision is made for a compromise by a corporation in terms of section 311 of the Companies Act.[1] A procedure similar to composition proceedings in sequestration is available, provided the corporation which is being wound up is unable to pay its debts.

In the winding up of a corporation unable to pay its debts the members may, at any time after the first meeting of creditors,[2] submit to the liquidator a written offer of composition, signed by the members holding more than 50 percent of members' interest in the corporation.[3] If the liquidator is of the opinion that creditors will probably accept the offer, he must post a copy of the offer together with his report thereon to every proved creditor.[4] If the liquidator decides that there is no likelihood that creditors will accept the offer, he must inform the members,[5] who may then appeal to the Master.[6]

A certain amount of risk is attached to the making of an offer of composition as, contrary to the position in company law,[7] the offer of composition or the fulfilment thereof may not be made subject to the setting aside of the winding up order or the consent of the creditors to the setting aside of the winding up of the corporation.[8]

1 *Kidson AR and Others* 1986 1 PH E2 (E); De la Rey 3 *Tran LCB* (1986) 107. However, for further discussion of the availability of a section 311 compromise, see Henning 1987 *JJS* 218; Henning and Bonnet 1991 *THRHR* 274; Bonnet and Henning 1991 *JSAL* 537; Henning 1992 *JJS* 90.
2 *De Wit v Boathavens CC (King Intervening)* 1989 1 SA 606 (C).
3 S 72(1).
4 S 119(2) Insolvency Act read with s 72(2)(a) Close

Corporations Act. The copy must be sent by registered post or be delivered to each creditor.
5 S 119(3) Insolvency Act read with s 72(2)(b)(i) Close Corporations Act requires notice to the 'corporation', which is represented by the liquidator. It is however submitted that notice to the members who signed the offer is required.
6 S 119(3), (4) Insolvency Act.
7 See s 311 Companies Act.
8 S 119(7) Insolvency Act read with s 72(2).

14.02 If the offer is to be submitted to creditors, the liquidator must simultaneously with the dispatch of the copy of the offer, convene a meeting of creditors for the purpose of considering the offer.[1]

The offer of composition may not contain any condition whereby any creditor will obtain as against another creditor any benefit to which he would not have been entitled upon the distribution of the estate in the ordinary way.[2] The offer of composition may also not be made subject to the condition that the winding up order will be set aside.[3] If the offer provides for the giving of any security, the nature of the security must be fully specified; if a surety bond or guarantee is to be given, every surety must be named.[4]

1 S 119(5) Insolvency Act. Such a meeting is a general meeting (see 12.25 above) and the meeting may consider any other matter mentioned in the notice. The meeting must be convened for a date not earlier than 14 days and not more than

28 days after the date on which the notice is posted or delivered to any creditor.
2 S 119(7) Insolvency Act.
3 S 119(7) Insolvency Act read with s 72(2)(b)(iii).
4 S 119(7) Insolvency Act.

14.03 At the meeting of creditors, the offer must be accepted by creditors whose votes amount to not less than three-fourths in value and three-fourths in number[1]

of proved creditors. If the offer is accepted and payment has been made or security been given as specified in the offer, the corporation is entitled to a certificate of acceptance from the Master.

If a corporation has obtained a certificate from the Master[2] showing that payment has been made or security given for the payment of not less than 50 cents in the rand of every claim proved or to be proved, the winding up may be set aside.[3] It is submitted that where a composition is accepted providing for payment of less than 50 cents in the rand, the court can also set aside the winding up.[4]

Where a plan of distribution providing for the payment in full of all proved claims has been confirmed by the Master, the corporation may apply to court for its winding up to be set aside.[5]

The rights of preferent and secured creditors are not affected by a composition except in so far as such creditor has expressly and in writing waived his preference.[6]

1 As to the calculation of these votes, see s 52 Insolvency Act and 12.27 above.
2 In terms of s 119(7) Insolvency Act.
3 S 124(1) Insolvency Act read with s 72.
4 In terms of s 354 Companies Act.
5 S 124(5) Insolvency Act read with s 72.
6 S 72 and s 72(2)(a) read with s 120(1) Insolvency Act.

Deregistration

14.04 Deregistration means the cancellation of the registration of the corporation's founding statement,[1] resulting in the loss, by the association of members forming the corporation, of legal personality and corporate status. Deregistration does not terminate the existence of the corporation; upon deregistration the association of persons sustaining the corporation merely loses its corporate personality. The existence of a corporation is terminated by dissolution after completion of the winding up procedure.[2]

1 S 1, definition of "deregistration".
2 See 14.09 below. See also Williams 1990 *SALJ* 610, which deals with companies.

14.05 Should members wish to have a corporation deregistered, a resolution must be passed and signed by all members. The resolution should state that, as the corporation is not carrying on business and as it has neither assets nor liabilities, members therefore resolve that the registrar be requested to deregister the corporation.[1]

1 S 26(2).

14.06 The registrar may also of his own accord, if he has reasonable cause to believe that a corporation is not carrying on business or is not in operation, set the deregistration process in motion by serving a letter by certified post on the corporation. If the registrar is not within 60 days from the date of his letter informed that the corporation is carrying on business or is in operation, he may, unless good cause is shown to the contrary, deregister the corporation.[1]

1 S 26(1). For the procedure which the registrar has to follow before deregistering a corporation, see s 26(2) and (3).

14.07 The deregistration of a corporation does not affect any liability of a member of the corporation to the corporation or to any other person, and such liability may be enforced as if the corporation were not deregistered.[1] If a corporation is deregistered while having outstanding liabilities, the persons who are members of such corporation at the time of deregistration, are jointly and severally liable for such liabilities.[2]

1 S 26(4).
2 S 26(5) which has been amended by the deletion of the *automatic* liability of *former* members for the debts and liabilities of the corporation upon its deregistration. The real protection for creditors is assumed to be found in various other sections such as s 51 *Payments by corporation to mem-* bers, s 52 *Prohibition of loans and furnishing of security to members and others by the corporation*, s 63 *Joint liability for debts of corporation*, s 64 *Liability for reckless or fraudulent carrying on of business of corporation* and s 65 *Powers of Court in case of abuse of separate juristic personality of corporation*.

14.08 The registrar may, on application by any interested person and if satisfied that a corporation was at the time of its deregistration carrying on business or was in operation or that it is otherwise just that the registration of the corporation be restored, restore the said registration.[1] The application for restoration must be made on the prescribed form (CK3). As a matter of practice, the registrar requires that the application be accompanied by—

□ an affidavit setting out the facts and circumstances leading to the deregistration, justifying the restoration of the corporation on the register, and showing that the deponent has an interest in such restoration;

□ proof of publication of an advertisement in a newspaper circulating where the corporation carried on its business, advising that the application will be made and that objection to the restoration must be lodged with the registrar within 30 days.

The registrar must give notice of the restoration of the registration of a corporation in the *Gazette*, and as from the date of such notice the corporation shall continue to exist and be deemed to have continued in existence as from the date of deregistration as if it were not deregistered.[2]

1 S 26(6).
2 S 26(7).

Dissolution

14.09 When the affairs of a corporation have been completely wound up, the Master sends a certificate to that effect to the registrar, who then gives notice of the dissolution in the *Gazette*.[1] The date of dissolution is the date on which the registrar records the dissolution of the corporation.[2] The dissolution of a corporation may be declared void by a court upon the application of the liquidator or any other interested person.[3]

1 S 419(1) and (2) Companies Act. A copy of the Master's certificate is also forwarded to the liquidator.
2 S 419(3) Companies Act.
3 S 420 Companies Act. See also Williams 1990 *SALJ* 610, which deals with companies.

Specimen documents

Contents

1

Draft association agreement

ZEE CLOSE CORPORATION

Registration number CK 86/00001/23

ASSOCIATION AGREEMENT

MEMORANDUM OF AGREEMENT ENTERED INTO BETWEEN:
(Names of members of Close Corporation)
(jointly referred to as the "members")
being the present members of
ZEE CLOSE CORPORATION
and
ZEE CLOSE CORPORATION

herein represented by .... whom the parties acknowledge and accept as being duly authorised thereto.

DEFINITIONS

1.

1.1 In this agreement, unless the context otherwise indicates, words and expressions:

1.1.1 defined in the Close Corporations Act, 1984 (Act 69 of 1984) shall have the meanings so defined;

1.1.2 importing the singular shall include the plural and vice versa;

1.1.3 importing the masculine shall include the female and neutral genders; and

1.1.4 importing natural persons shall include juristic persons.

1.2 Unless the context otherwise indicates the following words and expressions shall mean:

the "Act"	the Close Corporations Act 69 of 1984;
the "CC"	ZEE CLOSE CORPORATION in respect of which the matters herein set out are regulated by this agreement;
"member"	any one of the members of the CC;
"Registrar"	the Registrar of Close Corporations.

BASIS OF AGREEMENT

2.

2.1 The members between themselves and as between them and the CC and the CC as between it and the members, jointly and severally, enter into and bind themselves in terms of this agreement in the manner and for the purposes as set out in the Act and in regard to such other matters as herein set out.

2.2 In accordance with the provisions of section 44(5) of the Act a new member of the CC shall be bound by this agreement as if he has signed it as a party hereto.

2.3 Any amendment to or termination of this agreement may only be effected in writing signed by each member.

2.4 The parties hereto bind themselves thereto not to disclose any of the contents of this agreement to any person who is not a member of the CC.

INTEREST AND CERTIFICATES OF INTEREST

3.

3.1 Every member of the CC on becoming a member shall, without payment, be entitled to a certificate signed by or on behalf of every member of the CC stating the percentage of such member's interest in the CC and to further certificates reflecting any subsequent changes in such interest.

3.2 If a certificate of interest is defaced, lost or destroyed, another certificate may be issued on payment of the amount determined by the CC from time to time on condition that the member applying therefor is able to produce proof to the satisfaction of the CC of such defacing, loss or destruction and indemnifies the CC against such claims as may arise in consequence of the issue of the further certificate.

LIEN

4.

4.1 As from the moment a person becomes a member the CC acquires and retains a lien over the interest of such member in the CC for all monies owing by such member to the CC, in respect of any debt, obligation or undertaking to the CC and irrespective of whether the time for payment, performance or execution has arrived or not. The lien referred to in this clause operates also as a lien over any payment payable by the CC to a member (other than in his capacity as creditor or as employee or officer of the CC).

4.2 The CC may realize, in such manner as it thinks fit, any interest over which the CC has a lien after 14 (FOURTEEN) days notice in writing had been given to the member holding such interest stating the intention to realize the interest if payment is not made of the amount then payable before the expiration of that period.

4.3 The nett proceeds of the sale of the interest, after deducting reasonable expenses, shall be applied in payment of the amounts then payable and the balance shall be paid to the person registered as member at the date of the sale.

TRANSFER OF INTEREST

5.

A member may not transfer an interest in the CC otherwise than in accordance with the following conditions:

5.1 An interest in the CC may be transferred by a member to all members of the CC who are willing to purchase the particular interest, in which case the interest shall be allocated to such members in the manner set out in this clause. No interest may be transferred to any person not being a member of the CC as long as the CC itself on unanimous resolution of its members other than the member disposing of the interest or, failing that, any member or, failing that, any person nominated by the members other than the member disposing of the interest as being somebody who is to be recommended as new member, is prepared to purchase the interest at the price to be determined in the manner herein set out.

5.2 In order to determine whether the CC or any members or persons to be nominated as contemplated in 5.1 are prepared to purchase the interest, the member who wants to transfer the interest (hereinafter referred to as the "seller") shall give written notice (hereinafter referred to as a "Notice of Transfer") to the CC that he intends transferring the interest. This notice of transfer shall authorize the CC to act as agent of the seller to sell the interest in accordance herewith. The said authority may be revoked only if agreed to by all the members.

5.3 The seller shall state in the notice of transfer the value which he places on the interest as being the fair purchase price of the interest.

Alternative 5.3

(in which event also consider clause 17)

"5.3 The seller shall state in the notice of transfer the value which he places on the interest being the nett asset value of his interest in the CC plus only in the case of –

5.3.1 the interest of a deceased member or a member who has reached the retirement age set by the CC, if any, the full pro rata goodwill value attributable to such member's interest; or

5.3.2 the interest of a member who due to ill health or incapacity beyond his control but not being induced by abuse of alcohol or of any other substance inhibiting his normal faculties, had not been able to attend to his duties in the CC for a total of 180 (ONE HUNDRED AND EIGHTY) days in any one calendar year, $2/3$ (TWO THIRDS) of the pro rata goodwill value attributable to such member's interest."

5.4 If the members other than the seller are unanimously of the opinion that the value thus placed on the interest is too high, they must forthwith so inform the seller. If the other members and the seller cannot agree on the fair value of the interest within 14 (FOURTEEN) days of the date on which notice of transfer was given to the CC, the CC shall forthwith instruct an independent accounting officer to place a value on the interest and the amount so determined shall be taken as the fair value of the interest. The seller shall be responsible for all expenses reasonably incurred by the CC as a result of the instruction to determine the fair value.

5.5 After determining the fair value of the interest in any of the ways referred to in the preceding sub-clause, the CC shall immediately take up the interest or, failing that, offer it at the fair value to all members of the CC other than the seller in proportion as nearly as the circumstances admit to the percentage interest held by the members.

5.6 If, within a period of 30 (THIRTY) days after the fair value had been determined the CC had resolved to purchase the interest or had found members or other persons nominated by the members who are prepared to purchase the interest, the CC shall immediately notify the seller that the interest had been taken whereupon the seller shall be obliged against payment of the fair value to transfer the interest to the CC or the members or other persons concerned as the case may be.

5.7 If despite the aforesaid irrevocable authority by the seller to the CC to sell his interest he fails to sign the Amended Founding Statement (CK2), the CC may record the resultant changes in the holding of interests, lodge the Amended Founding Statement signed by the CC on behalf of the seller with the Registrar and keep the purchase price of the interest in trust for the seller. Receipt by the CC of the purchase price shall discharge the purchaser of the duty to pay for the interest.

5.8 In the event of the CC not being able, within 30 (THIRTY) days after the fair value of the interest had been determined, to purchase the interest itself or to find a member or other person who is willing to purchase the interest or if the CC failed to give notice to the seller to that effect, the seller shall be entitled for a period of 30 (THIRTY) days to sell at any price and to any person such interest and to give transfer of the interest to that person.

5.9 Notwithstanding anything to the contrary herein provided, the members may by unanimous consent in writing agree that some or all the foregoing provisions of this clause be waived and that such alternative procedure as may be decided on shall be followed.

TERMINATION

6.

6.1 A member shall on his death cease to have any right to his interest in the CC and his executor shall be the only person recognised by the CC as having any title to such interest. The executor shall be obliged, notwithstanding the provisions of section 35 of the Act, to offer such interest for sale in the manner provided for in the preceding clause failing which the CC may act as if the executor had given the notice of transfer referred to therein.

6.2 A member who due to ill health or incapacity beyond his control had not been able to attend to his duties in the CC for a total of 180 (ONE HUNDRED AND EIGHTY) days in any one calendar year or who as a result of abuse of alcohol or any other substance impairing his normal faculties has repeatedly and regularly been unable to give his normal attention to his duties in the CC or who is in persistent breach of the provisions of this agreement or who has been guilty of gross misconduct or neglect concerning any of the affairs of the CC, shall upon the unanimous resolution of the members other than the member concerned that the relevant state of affairs exist, cease to have any right to his interest in the CC other than to offer such interest for sale in the manner provided for in the preceding clause, failing which the CC may act as if such member had given the notice of transfer referred to therein.

6.3 A member whose interest has been attached or sold in execution shall cease to have any right to his interest other than to offer such interest for sale in the manner provided in the preceding clause failing which the CC may act as if such member or the person who had become entitled to such member's interest had given the notice of transfer referred to therein.

6.4 A member who surrendered his estate or whose estate has been sequestrated shall cease to have any right to his interest in the CC other than that his trustee may sell the interest in the manner provided for in section 34 of the Act, or offer the interest for sale in the manner provided for in the preceding clause failing which the CC may act as if the trustee had given the notice of transfer referred to therein.

MEETINGS

7.

7.1 A meeting of members shall be held at such regular intervals as the members may from time to time resolve but a meeting of members shall be held to consider and approve the annual financial statements of the CC not later than 21 (TWENTY ONE) days after completion of the annual financial statements which the CC shall cause to be completed not later than 9 (NINE) months after the end of its financial year.

7.2 A meeting of members may be convened in terms of any resolution by the CC or by any member by giving notice to every other member stating the purpose for such meeting.

7.3 The notice of a meeting of members shall state a reasonable place, time and date for the meeting.

7.4 No business shall be transacted at any meeting of members unless a quorum of members is present at the time when the meeting proceeds to business which shall be not less than $3/4$ (THREE QUARTERS)/$1/2$ (ONE HALF) of the members present in person or by proxy.

7.5 If within 15 (FIFTEEN) minutes from the time appointed for the meeting a quorum is not present, the meeting shall stand adjourned to a day 7 (SEVEN) days after the date of the meeting. Notice of such adjournment shall be given forthwith by the CC to all members in the same manner as a notice of meetings are to be given. If at such adjourned meeting a quorum is not present within 15 (FIFTEEN) minutes from the time appointed for the meeting the members present in person or by proxy, shall be a quorum.

7.6 If a chairman has been appointed for meetings of the CC he shall act as chairman at every meeting of the CC. If at any meeting such chairman is not present within 10 (TEN) minutes after the time appointed for holding the meeting or is unwilling to act as chairman or if no such chairman has been appointed, the members present shall elect one of their number to be chairman.

7.7 The chairman may, with the consent of a meeting, adjourn the meeting from time to time and from place to place. No business shall be transacted at any adjourned meeting other than the business unfinished at the meeting from which the adjournment took place.

7.8 At any meeting of members a motion put to the vote of the meeting shall be decided on a show of hands. A declaration by the chairman that a resolution has, on a show of hands, been carried or carried unanimously or by a particular majority or defeated, and an entry to that effect in the minutes of the proceedings of the CC, shall be conclusive evidence of the fact, without proof of the number or proportion of the votes recorded in favour of, or against such resolution.

7.9 A resolution shall be passed on show of hands and on a poll if the majority percentage interest in the CC have voted in favour of the resolution.

7.10 A resolution may be adopted in writing in that the proposal reflecting the written resolution is confirmed by the signature of each member and is so recorded in the minute book of the CC.

7.11 On a vote being taken the chairman shall at no time be entitled to a second or casting vote.

7.12 On a vote, votes may be given either personally or by proxy.

7.13 The instrument appointing a proxy shall be in writing under the hand of the appointer or of his agent duly authorised in writing. A proxy need not be a member of the CC and a member may not appoint more than 1 (ONE) proxy.

7.14 The instrument appointing a proxy and the power of attorney or other authority, if any, under which it is signed or a notarially certified copy of such power or authority shall be deposited at the registered office of the CC not less than 1 (ONE) hour before the time for holding the meeting at which the person named in the instrument proposes to vote, and in default the instrument of proxy shall be invalid. No instrument appointing a proxy shall be valid after the expiration of 6 (SIX) months from the date when it was signed, unless so specifically stated in the proxy itself.

7.15 The instrument appointing a proxy shall be substantially in the following form:

"

ZEE CLOSE CORPORATION

I ....

of ....

being a member of the abovementioned close corporation hereby appoint

.... of

....

.... or

failing him the chairman of the meeting as my proxy to speak on behalf and to vote for me and on my behalf at the meeting of members of the close corporation to be held on the .... day of .... 19 ....
and at any adjournment thereof.

Unless otherwise instructed, my proxy may vote as he thinks fit.

SIGNED this .... day of ....
19 ....

....
Signature ''

MINUTES
8.

A report of the proceedings at a meeting of members and every resolution in writing signed by each member shall be recorded in a minute book kept for that purpose at the registered office of the CC within 14 (FOURTEEN) days or, in the case of a resolution in writing, within 14 (FOURTEEN) days after the date on which the last member signed such resolution.

ADDITIONAL REMUNERATION AND EXPENSES
9.

A member shall be compensated for all travelling and other expenses which he may have incurred properly and necessarily in connection with the affairs of the CC.

PAYMENTS TO MEMBERS AND RESERVES
10.

10.1 The members shall decide on the payments to members each year but may from time to time make such interim payments as appear to them to be justified by the profits of the CC.

10.2 Payments to members may be made in no circumstances other than –

10.2.1 if, after such payments made, the CC's assets, fairly valued, will exceed all its liabilities;

10.2.2 if the CC is able to pay its debts as they become due in the ordinary course of its business; and

10.3 Any payment made to and received by a member in contravention of the provisions of the preceding sub-clause and of section 51 of the Act shall be recoverable by and repayable to the CC as security for which the CC may invoke its lien over a member's interest in the CC.

10.4 Notice of any payment to members that may have been decided upon shall be given to those entitled to share therein.

10.5 The members entrusted with the management of the CC may deduct from the payments payable to any member all such claims or sums of money which may be due from time to time to the CC. No payment to be made to members shall bear interest against the CC, and any payment remaining unclaimed for a period of 5 (FIVE) years as from the resolution to make the payment may be forfeited by resolution of the members for the benefit of the CC.

10.6 Every payment may be paid by cheque or otherwise as the members entrusted with the management of the CC may from time to time determine, and shall either be sent by post to the last registered address of the member entitled thereto or be given to him personally. The receipt or endorsement on the cheque or other instrument of payment by the member or his duly authorised agent shall be a good discharge as against the CC in respect thereof.

10.7 The CC shall not be responsible for the loss in transmission of any cheque or other instrument of payment sent through the post to the registered address of any member, whether or not it was so sent at his request.

ACCOUNTING RECORDS AND FINANCIAL STATEMENTS
11.

11.1 The members shall cause such accounting records to be kept as are prescribed by section 56 of the Act.

11.2 The accounting records shall be kept at the registered office of the CC or at such other place or places as the members may think fit, and shall at all times be open for inspection by every member.

11.3 The members shall within 9 (NINE) months of the end of the CC's financial year, in accordance with section 58 of the Act, cause to be completed and presented to and approved and signed by every member such annual financial statements as are referred to in that section.

ACCOUNTING OFFICER
12.

An accounting officer shall be appointed in accordance with section 59 of the Act.

NOTICES
13.

13.1 A notice by the CC may be given to a member either personally or by sending it through the post in a prepaid letter addressed to the member at the address (if any) within South Africa supplied by him for this purpose.

13.2 Whenever a notice is to be given the notice may be given by the CC to the persons entitled to an interest in consequence of the death or insolvency of a member by sending it through the post by a prepaid letter addressed to them in their official capacity at the address in South Africa supplied for that purpose by them. Until such address has been so supplied, notice may be given in any manner in which the same might have been given had the death or insolvency not occurred.

13.3 Notice of every meeting of members shall be given to –

13.3.1 every member of the CC, except those members who have not supplied the CC with an address within South Africa for the giving of notices to them; and

13.3.2 every person entitled to an interest in consequence of the death or insolvency of a member; and

13.3.3 the accounting officer of the CC.

No other person is entitled to receive notice of meetings of members.

13.4 Any notice given by post shall be deemed to have been served at the time when the letter containing the notice is posted.

13.5 A notice given to any member shall be binding on all persons claiming on his death or any transmission of his interests.

MANAGEMENT

14.

14.1 Each member of the CC by law stands in a fiduciary relationship to the CC so that, without derogation from the generality of the duty thereby created, each member shall –

14.1.1 act honestly and in good faith in relation to the CC;

14.1.2 avoid any material conflict between his own interests and those of the CC and in particular shall not while a member or for a period of 2 (TWO) years after he ceased to be a member, compete in any way with the CC in its business activities whether in his own name or together with or as agent for any other person or as agent, director or member of any company, corporation, close corporation, society or any other body of persons.

14.2 Subject to the provisions of section 47 of the Act as to persons disqualified from managing the business of the CC, the business of the CC shall be managed –

14.2.1 by the members jointly;

14.2.2 by the following persons to the exclusion of other members of the CC, with the responsibilities as stated:

14.3 The persons responsible for the management of the CC may exercise all the powers of the CC subject only to the following limitations and those contained elsewhere in this agreement:

14.3.1 the persons who are to devote their full time and attention to the business of the CC are –

14.3.2

14.4 Notwithstanding the provisions of the preceding sub-clause, the members may from time to time appoint one or more of their body or some other person to the office of manager or in an executive office for such period and with such powers and authorities to be exercised for such purposes and upon such terms and conditions and at such remuneration (whether by way of salary, or commission, or participation in profits, or partly in one way, and partly in another) as they may think fit, whether in terms of a written service agreement or not.

15.

Only on the authority of a resolution by the members and subject to the provisions of this agreement may a member:

15.1 use money or assets of the CC or bind the credit of the CC or incur any debt for the account of the CC otherwise than in the ordinary course of business;

15.2 do anything whereby his interest in the CC, otherwise than in accordance with the provisions of this agreement, shall be alienated, pledged or encumbered.

16.

In accordance with the provisions of section 52 of the Act the CC shall not, directly or indirectly, make a loan to any member, any other CC in which one or more members together hold more than 50% (FIFTY PERCENT) interest or any company or other juristic person (other than a CC) controlled by one or more members and shall not provide any security, including any guarantee, to any person in connection with any obligation of any such member, other CC, company or juristic person.

17.

Notwithstanding anything to the contrary herein contained, the members as between them and the CC shall, in the event of the death of a member or the ill health of a member in the sense contemplated in clause 5.3.2 hereof, be obliged to take over the interest of such member in the CC at a fair market value (including any goodwill factor involved), provided that the amount so payable and any amount owing by the CC to such member or deceased member, as the case may be, shall be paid in full in not less than 4 (FOUR) years by means of instalments not more than 1 (ONE) year apart at a rate of not less than 1/4 (ONE QUARTER) of the amount due per year. (Provision for interest ?)

18.

18.1 Subject to provisions to the contrary herein or in any written agreement between the parties, each member shall –

18.1.1 advance funds to the CC pro rata to his interest in the CC to the extent determined by members holding at least 75% (SEVENTY FIVE PER CENT) interest in the CC; and

18.1.2 provide such security for the due discharge of the commitments of the CC as may be required by the bankers or other creditors of the CC and as resolved to by members holding at least 75% (SEVENTY FIVE PER CENT) interest in the CC.

18.2 If a member fails to observe the provisions of this clause he shall be obliged, if so resolved by members holding not less than 75% (SEVENTY FIVE PER CENT) interest in the CC, to offer his interest for sale in accordance with this agreement as a seller.

SIGNED at .... on this

.... day of .... 19 ....

AS WITNESSES:

1. ....

2. ....

SIGNED at .... on this

.... day of .... 19 ....

AS WITNESSES:

1. ....

2. ....

on behalf of
ZEE CLOSE CORPORATION

2
Specimen certificate of member's interest

Close Corporations Act 1984
(Section 31)

Date: ....

Certificate Number: ....

1. Full name of corporation: CC
2. Registration number: ....
3. Shortened form of name: ....
4. Literal translation of name: CC
5. Registered office: ....

....

....

6. Postal address: ....

....

....

Full name of member	Identity number of member	Postal address of member	Size of interest*
			*Current percentage

This is to certify that the above-mentioned is a member of this corporation and that such member currently holds the above-mentioned interest in the corporation.

Signed by or on behalf of each member of the corporation on the date appearing opposite each signature.

Signature	Date	Signature	Date

3
Specimen member's interest transfer form

Close Corporations Act 1984

1. Full name of corporation: CC
2. Registration number: ....
3. Registered office: ....
....
....
....

4. Postal address: ....
....
....
....

Full name of member	Identity number of member	Postal address of member	Size of interest

I, the undersigned, hereby transfer the above interest from the name of the aforesaid person to the person(s) named below.

Signature of transferor: ....

Date of signature: ....

Transfer of the above interest is hereby accepted.

Signature of transferee: ....

Date of signature: ....

4
Specimen application for liquidation of a corporation

Notice of motion

IN THE MAGISTRATE'S COURT FOR THE DISTRICT OF ....

HELD   AT   ....

In the ex parte application of

.... CLOSE CORPORATION   Applicant

Registration number CK ..../............................/23

NOTICE OF MOTION

BE PLEASED to take notice that application will be made on behalf of the above applicant on .... day of .... 19 .... at .... h .... or as soon thereafter as the matter may be heard for an order declaring:

(a) that the applicant be liquidated;

(b) that the costs of this application be costs in the liquidation;

(c) that such further or alternative relief be granted as the Honourable Court may regard as reasonable.

AND FURTHER TAKE NOTICE that the affidavit of ...., hereto annexed, shall be used in support of the said application.

KINDLY place the matter on the roll accordingly.

SIGNED at .... this ....day of .... 19 ....

....
Attorneys for applicant

To: The Clerk of the Court

....

and

To: The Master of the Supreme Court

....

Specimen supporting affidavit

IN THE MAGISTRATE'S COURT FOR THE DISTRICT OF ....

HELD   AT   ....

In the ex parte application of

.... CLOSE CORPORATION   Applicant

Registration number CK ..../.........................../23

AFFIDAVIT

I, the undersigned, ...

hereby declare under oath as follows:

1.

The applicant is .... CLOSE CORPORATION, a close corporation duly incorporated and registered in accordance with the Close Corporations Act 69 of 1984 under registration number CK ..../............/23 with its registered office and main place of business at ...., situate within the magisterial district of .... The member of the applicant being myself and .... have made a contribution towards the assets of the corporation by members in an amount of R.. The said .... and I have a member's interest of 50% each in the applicant.

2.

The applicant is herein represented by myself in accordance with a resolution adopted by members having more than half of the total number of votes of members at a meeting called for the purpose of considering the winding up of the corporation by the court, which resolution was adopted and signed by both of the only members of the corporation, a copy of which resolution is annexed hereto marked "A".

3.

The business conducted by the applicant is that of ....

4.

The Applicant is presently unable to pay its debts and is in fact insolvent in that as at the date hereof the financial position of the applicant to my best belief and knowledge appears to be as follows:

ASSETS

Shopfittings at book value	R...................................
Stock at cost	R...................................
Debtors less bad debts	R...................................
Bank account	R...................................
	....

LIABILITIES

Receiver of Revenue (general sales tax)	R...................................
Creditors	R...................................
Bank overdraft	R...................................
Salaries and expenses	R...................................
Arrear rental	R...................................
Members' loan accounts	R...................................
	....

Shortfall	....

5.

The applicant is at present in fact trading at a loss and has no real prospect of trading at a profit in the near future, accordingly the longer the applicant remains in business the more it will be to the detriment of its creditors.

6.

On the .... 19 .... the applicant adopted the resolution as intended in section 68(a) of the Close Corporations Act 1984, as has been referred to in paragraph 2 above, resolving that the corporation be wound up by the court; the resolution has been signed by the only two members of the applicant and appears as annexure "A" hereto.

7.

Proper security as required in terms of section 346(3) of the Companies Act, as made applicable to the applicant as a close corporation in terms of section 66 of the Close Corporations Act 1984, has been furnished to the Master of the Supreme Court as will appear from his certificate hereto annexed marked "B".

8.

....

In the circumstances I respectfully pray that it may please the Honourable Court to grant an order as set out in the Notice of Motion.

I certify that the deponent acknowledges that he knows and understands the contents of the above declaration, that he has no objection to taking the prescribed oath and considers it to be binding on his conscience.

THUS done before me at .... on this .... day of .... 19 ....

....
FULL NAMES:
COMMISSIONER OF OATHS
EX OFFICIO
ADDRESS:

Annexure "A"

Resolution of members that the corporation be wound up by the court

....CC

Registration number CK......./...................../23

MINUTES OF A MEETING OF MEMBERS HELD AT ....

on .... 19........ at .... h ....

RESOLUTION

in terms of section 68(a) of the

Close Corporations Act 69 of 1984

All members being present it is unanimously –

1. resolved that the meeting having been called for the purpose of considering the winding up of the corporation it is hereby resolved that the corporation be wound up by the Court in terms of section 68(a) of the Close Corporations Act 69 of 1984.

2. resolved further that .... be authorised to perform all acts, to take all steps and to sign all documents which may be necessary to give effect to resolution 1 above.

Signature of members	Date	Percentage interest and votes
1.	....	....
2.	....	....

5
Specimen order of court –
order for provisional liquidation

IN THE MAGISTRATE'S COURT FOR THE DISTRICT OF ....

HELD AT ....

Case Number ....

In the ex parte application of

.... CLOSE CORPORATION   Applicant

Registration number CK ..../............................/23

Having heard the application brought on behalf of the Applicant and after reading the documents filed

IT IS ORDERED

1. That the above-named applicant close corporation is hereby placed in provisional liquidation;

2. That a rule nisi is hereby issued calling on all interested parties to advance reasons, if any, before this court at ....h .... on .... 19 .... why the applicant should not be placed in final liquidation;

3. That service of this rule nisi be effected on the applicant close corporation at its registered office, to all known creditors of the applicant close corporation by registered post and forthwith be published in each of the Government Gazette and .... newspaper.

BY THE COURT

CLERK OF THE COURT

6
Specimen order of court
– final liquidation order

IN THE MAGISTRATE'S COURT FOR THE DISTRICT OF ....

HELD AT ....

Case Number ....

In the ex parte application of

.... CLOSE CORPORATION   Applicant

Registration number CK ..../.........................../23

Having heard the application brought on behalf of the Applicant and after reading the rule *nisi* issued by this Court on .... 19 ....,

duly served and advertised as ordered, and as no grounds were advanced against the said rule *nisi* on the return date:

IT IS ORDERED

1. That the aforementioned rule *nisi* is hereby confirmed and that the applicant close corporation is hereby placed in final liquidation;

2. That the costs of this application be costs in the liquidation.

BY THE COURT

CLERK OF THE COURT

Close Corporations Act
No. 69 of 1984

Arrangement of sections

CLOSE CORPORATIONS ACT
NO. 69 OF 1984

[ASSENTED TO 19 JUNE 1984]   [DATE OF COMMENCEMENT: 1 JANUARY 1985]

(English text signed by the State President)

as amended by

Close Corporations Amendment Act, No. 38 of 1986
Close Corporations Amendment Act, No. 64 of 1988
Close Corporations Amendment Act, No. 17 of 1990
Close Corporations Amendment Act, No. 81 of 1992

ACT

To provide for the formation, registration, incorporation, management, control and liquidation of close corporations; and for matters connected therewith.

1. Definitions.— In this Act, unless the context otherwise indicates—

"accounting records", in relation to a corporation, includes accounts, deeds, writings and such other documents as may be prescribed;

"association agreement", in relation to any corporation or the members thereof, means an association agreement which has been entered into in terms of section 44 by the members of the corporation, including any such agreement which has been altered or added to as contemplated in subsection (3) of section 49, or an agreement which has replaced it as contemplated in that subsection;

"Companies Act" means the Companies Act, 1973 (Act No. 61 of 1973);

"company" means a company as defined in section 1(1) of the Companies Act;

"corporation" means a close corporation referred to in section 2(1) which has been registered under Part III of this Act;

"Court", in relation to—

(a) any corporation and any matter referred to in section 7, means any court having jurisdiction in terms of that section;

(b) any matter referred to in section 50, 65 or 73(1), means any court having jurisdiction in respect thereof; and

(c) any offence under this Act, means any court having jurisdiction in respect of that offence;

"deregistration", in relation to a corporation, means the cancellation of the registration of the corporation's founding statement; and **"deregister"** has a corresponding meaning;

"**director**", in relation to a company, means a director as defined in section 1(1) of the Companies Act;

"**founding statement**", in relation to a corporation, means the founding statement of the corporation referred to in section 12 which has been registered in terms of section 13, and also any amended founding statement in respect of that corporation registered in terms of section 15(1) or (2);

"**holding company**", in relation to a company, means a holding company as defined in section 1(1) of the Companies Act;

"**Master**" means the Master of the Supreme Court, and in relation to—

(a) a corporation in respect of which application is made to a Court for a winding-up order, the Master having jurisdiction in the area of jurisdiction of the Court where application is made;

(b) a corporation being wound up by a Court, the Master having jurisdiction in the area of jurisdiction of the Court which issued the winding-up order;

(c) a corporation other than a corporation referred to in paragraph (a) or (b), the Master having jurisdiction in the area in which the registered office of that corporation is situated;

"**member**", in relation to a corporation, means a person qualified for membership of a corporation in terms of section 29 and designated as a member in a founding statement of the corporation, including, subject to the provisions of this Act, a trustee, administrator, executor or curator, or other legal representative, referred to in paragraph (c) of subsection (2) of section 29, in respect of any such person who is insolvent, deceased, mentally disordered or otherwise incapable or incompetent to manage his affairs, but excluding any such person who has in terms of this Act ceased to be a member;

"**member's interest**" or "**interest**", in relation to a member of a corporation, means the interest of the member in the corporation expressed in accordance with section 12 (e) as a percentage in the founding statement of the corporation;

"**Minister**", in relation to any matter to be dealt with in the office of a Master in connection with the winding-up of a corporation, means the Minister of Justice and, in relation to any other matter, means the Minister of Trade and Industry;
[Definition of "Minister" substituted by s. 1 of Act No. 38 of 1986.]

"**officer**", in relation to—

(a) a corporation, means any manager or secretary thereof, whether or not such manager or secretary is also a member of the corporation;

(b) a company, means an officer as defined in section 1(1) of the Companies Act;

"**prescribe**" means prescribe by regulation; and "**prescribed**" has a corresponding meaning;

"**Registrar**" means the Registrar of Close Corporations referred to in section 4;

"registration", in relation to—

(a) any corporation, means the registration of the founding statement of the corporation referred to in section 12;

(b) the founding statement or any amended founding statement of a corporation, means the registration thereof in terms of section 13 or section 15(1) or (2), as the case may be;

(c) any matter in connection with a corporation, or any member thereof, particulars of which are specified in terms of this Act in a founding statement of the corporation, means the specifying of particulars thereof in any such statement; and

(d) any other matter in connection with which any duty or power in relation to the registration thereof is in terms of this Act imposed on or granted to the Registrar, means the registration thereof by him in accordance with any applicable provision of this Act; and **"registered"** has a corresponding meaning;

"Registration Office" means the Close Corporations Registration Office referred to in section 3;

"regulation" means any regulation made under this Act;

"subsidiary", in relation to a company, means a subsidiary as defined in section 1(1) of the Companies Act;

"this Act" includes the regulations.

PART I
FORMATION AND JURISTIC PERSONALITY OF CLOSE CORPORATIONS

2. Formation and juristic personality of close corporations.—(1) Any one or more persons, not exceeding ten, who qualify for membership of a close corporation in terms of this Act, may form a close corporation and secure its incorporation by complying with the requirements of this Act in respect of the registration of its founding statement referred to in section 12.

(2) A corporation formed in accordance with the provisions of this Act is on registration in terms of those provisions a juristic person and continues, subject to the provisions of this Act, to exist as a juristic person notwithstanding changes in its membership until it is in terms of this Act deregistered or dissolved.

(3) Subject to the provisions of this Act, the members of a corporation shall not merely by reason of their membership be liable for the liabilities or obligations of the corporation.

(4) A corporation shall have the capacity and powers of a natural person of full capacity in so far as a juristic person is capable of having such capacity or of exercising such powers.

PART II
ADMINISTRATION OF ACT

3. Registration Office and register.—(1) For the registration of corporations under this Act there shall be an office in Pretoria called the Close Corporations Registration Office.

(2) Registers of names and registration numbers and such other matters concerning corporations as may be prescribed, shall be kept in the Registration Office.

4. Registrar.—(1) The Minister shall, subject to the laws governing the public service, appoint a Registrar of Close Corporations, who shall—

(a) exercise the powers and perform the duties assigned to the Registrar by this Act; and

(b) subject to the directions of the Minister, be responsible for the administration of the Registration Office.

(2) The Minister may likewise appoint a Deputy Registrar and an Assistant Registrar, who shall, subject to the control of the Registrar, exercise any power or perform any duty conferred or imposed in terms of this Act on the Registrar, and whenever the Registrar is for any reason unable to perform his functions the Deputy Registrar shall act in his stead.

(3) The Registrar may delegate any of the powers and entrust any of the duties assigned to him by this Act to any officer or employee in the public service.

5. Inspection and copies of documents in Registration Office.—(1) Any person may, on payment of the prescribed fee (including an additional fee if any document is not collected personally at the Registration Office)—

(a) inspect any document kept under this Act by the Registrar in respect of any corporation; or

(b) obtain a certificate from the Registrar as to the contents or part of the contents of any such document open to inspection; or

(c) obtain a copy of or extract from any such document.

(2) If the Registrar is satisfied—

(a) that any such inspection, certificate, copy or extract is required on behalf of a foreign government accredited to the Government of the Republic; and

(b) that no fee is payable in the foreign country concerned in respect of a corresponding inspection, certificate, copy or extract required on behalf of the Government of the Republic,

no fee referred to in subsection (1) shall be payable.

(3) If the Registrar is satisfied that any such inspection, certificate, copy or extract is required for purposes of research by or under the control of an institution for higher education, he may permit such inspection or furnish such certificate, copy or extract without payment of fees.

6. Payment of fees.—(1) The payment of any fee, additional fee or other money payable to the Registrar in terms of this Act shall, subject to the provisions of subsection (3), be effected—

(a) by affixing revenue stamps to any document concerned, which stamps may be cancelled by a Receiver of Revenue or the Registrar; or

(b) by impressing a stamp on any document concerned by means of a die approved by the Commissioner for Inland Revenue; or

(c) in such other manner as the Registrar may direct.

(2) No document, form, return or notice in respect of which any fee is payable or any payment is required to be done in terms of this Act, shall be complete unless proof of payment of the required fee or other money has been lodged with the Registrar.

(3) For the purposes of subsection (1) the decision of the Registrar as to the manner in which in any particular case, or category of cases determined by him, any fee, additional fee or other money is in terms of this Act to be paid, shall be final.

(4) Any fees and other moneys payable in terms of this Act to the Registrar, shall be debts due to the State recoverable by the Minister in any competent court.

7. Courts having jurisdiction in respect of corporations. – For the purposes of this Act the courts having jurisdiction in any matter, including winding up, in respect of any corporation, shall be any magistrate's court, and any provincial or local division of the Supreme Court of South Africa, within whose area of jurisdiction the registered office or main place of business of the corporation is situate or, in relation to any such matter in respect of which a magistrate's court has in any particular case on account of any provision of the Magistrates' Courts Act, 1944 (Act No. 32 of 1944), no jurisdiction, any provincial or local division of the Supreme Court of South Africa within whose area of jurisdiction any such office or place of business is situate.

[S. 7 substituted by s.1 of Act No. 64 of 1988.]

8. Security for costs in legal proceedings by corporations.—When a corporation in any legal proceedings is a plaintiff or applicant or brings a counterclaim or counterapplication, the court concerned may at any time during the proceedings if it appears that there is reason to believe that the corporation or, if it is being wound up, the liquidator thereof, will be unable to pay the costs of the defendant or respondent, or the defendant or respondent in reconvention, if he is successful in his defence, require security to be given for those costs, and may stay all proceedings till the security is given.

9. Transmission of copies of Court orders to Registrar and Master.—When a Court makes any order in terms of this Act in relation to any corporation, the Registrar or clerk of the Court shall without delay by certified post transmit a copy of the order to the Registrar and, if such order relate to the winding-up of any corporation, a copy thereof to the Master as well.

10. Regulations.—(1) The Minister may make regulations—

    (a) providing for the conduct and administration of the Registration Office, and prescribing the practice and procedure to be observed therein;

    (b) prescribing the practice and procedure to be observed in the office of the Master in connection with the winding-up of corporations;

    (c) providing for the reproduction of any records relating to corporations in the Registration Office or the office of the Master by means of microfilm, microcard, miniature photographic process or any other process deemed suitable by the Minister;

(*d*) providing for the use for official purposes and the admissibility in evidence in any proceedings, whether in a court of law or otherwise of any reproduction contemplated in paragraph (*c*);

(*e*) providing for the keeping and preservation of any records, or any reproductions thereof contemplated in paragraph (*c*), in the Registration Office or the office of the Master, the removal from such offices of such records or reproductions and the preservation thereof in any other place, and prescribing the circumstances under which such records or reproductions may be destroyed;

(*f*) prescribing how records required under this Act to be kept by a corporation may be kept, and prescribing the circumstances under which such records may be destroyed;

(*g*) prescribing the procedure to be followed with respect to any matter in connection with the winding-up of corporations;

(*h*) prescribing the form and the contents of any return, notice or document provided for by this Act;

(*i*) prescribing when an additional copy or copies of documents to be lodged under this Act shall require to be lodged, and whether such additional copy or copies shall be in the form of a copy or copies certified in a defined manner or shall be in duplicate original form;

(*j*) with the concurrence of the Minister of Finance, prescribing the matters in respect of which fees shall be payable, the persons by whom and to whom the fees shall be payable and the tariff of such fees;

(*k*) providing for a table of fees, subject to taxation by the Master, which shall be payable to a liquidator as remuneration;

(*l*) prescribing a tariff of remuneration payable to any person performing on behalf of a liquidator any act relating to the winding-up of a corporation which the liquidator is not required to perform personally, and prohibiting the charging or recovery of remuneration at a higher tariff than the tariff so prescribed;

(*m*) providing for the appointment by the Registrar in specified circumstances of an inspector to investigate the affairs of a corporation, for the powers of an inspector in conducting any such investigation, for the duty of any member, officer, employee or accounting officer of a corporation to make available books and documents in his custody or under his control and to afford such assistance as an inspector may require in connection with any such investigation; for reporting by an inspector to the Registrar; for the making available by the Registrar of any such report to other persons; for the admissibility of any such report as evidence in legal proceedings; and for defraying the expenses of, and in connection with, any such investigation;

[Para. (*m*) substituted by s. 2 of Act No. 38 of 1986.]

(*n*) as to any other matter required or permitted by this Act to be prescribed; and

(*o*) generally, as to any matter which he considers it necessary or expedient to prescribe in order that the purposes of this Act may be achieved.

(2) Regulations made under subsection (1) may prescribe penalties for any contravention thereof or failure to comply therewith, not exceeding a fine of R300 or imprisonment for a period of six months or both such fine and such imprisonment.

11. Functions of standing advisory committee on company law in relation to corporations.—(1) The standing advisory committee on company law, appointed in terms of section 18 of the Companies Act, may from time to time make recommendations to the Minister in regard to any amendments to this Act which may appear to it to be advisable, and shall advise the Minister on any matter pertaining to this Act referred to it by the Minister.

(2) The standing advisory committee shall constitute and maintain a standing sub-committee for the purpose of considering and of advising it on such matters relating to corporations as may be referred by it to the sub-committee.

(3) The provisions of—

(a) the Companies Act and regulations made thereunder in relation to standing sub-committees of the standing advisory committee, and the members thereof, shall apply in respect of the standing sub-committee referred to in subsection (2) as if that sub-committee were constituted under subsection (4) of section 18 of the said Act; and

(b) subsections (2) and (5) (in so far as they relate to the calling of persons to assist the standing advisory committee) of the said section 18 shall apply in respect of the standing advisory committee in the exercising by it of any power granted to it in terms of subsection (1) of this section.

PART III

REGISTRATION, DEREGISTRATION AND CONVERSION

12. Founding statement.—Any person qualified for membership in terms of section 29 or, subject to section 28, any number of such persons who intend to form a corporation, shall draw up a founding statement in the prescribed form in one of the official languages of the Republic, which shall be signed by or on behalf of every person who is to become a member of the corporation upon its registration and which shall, subject to the provisions of this Act, contain the following particulars:

(a) The full name of the corporation: Provided that a literal translation of that name into the other official language of the Republic, or a shortened form of that name or such translation thereof, may in addition be given;

(b) the principal business to be carried on by the corporation;

(c) (i) a postal address for the corporation; and

(ii) the address (not being the number of a post office box) of the office of the corporation referred to in section 25(1);

(d) the full name of each member, his identity number or, if he has no such number, the date of his birth, and his residential address;
[Sub-s. (d) substituted by s. 1 of Act No. 81 of 1992.]

(e) the size, expressed as a percentage, of each member's interest in the corporation;

(f) particulars of the contribution of each member to the corporation in accordance with section 24(1), including—

(i) any amounts of money; and

(ii) a description, and statement of the fair value, of any property (whether corporeal or incorporeal) or any service referred to in section 24(1);

(g) (i) the name and postal address of a qualified person who or firm which has consented in writing to his or its appointment as accounting officer of the corporation; and

(ii) the date of the end of the financial year of the corporation.

13. Registration of founding statement.—If a founding statement referred to in section 12 complying with the requirements of this Act is lodged with the Registrar in triplicate in the manner prescribed, and if the business to be carried on by the corporation is lawful, the Registrar shall upon payment of the prescribed fee register such statement in his registers and shall give notice of the registration in the *Gazette*.
[S. 13 substituted by s. 3 of Act No. 38 of 1986.]

14. Certificate of incorporation.—(1) Upon the registration of such founding statement the Registrar shall assign a registration number to the corporation concerned and endorse under his hand on the statement a certificate that the corporation is incorporated.

(2) A certificate of incorporation given by the Registrar in terms of subsection (1) or section 27(4)(c), or a copy thereof, as the case may be, shall upon its mere production, in the absence of proof of fraud or error, be conclusive evidence that all the requirements of this Act in respect of registration of the corporation concerned and of matters precedent and incidental thereto have been complied with, and that the corporation concerned is duly incorporated under this Act.
[Sub-s. (2) substituted by s. 4 of Act No. 38 of 1986.]

15. Registration of amended founding statement.—(1) If any change is made or occurs in respect of any matter particulars of which are stated in a founding statement of a corporation in accordance with paragraph (b), (d), (e) or (f) of section 12, the corporation shall, subject to the provisions of section 29(3)(c) and (d), within 28 days after such change lodge with the Registrar for registration in his registers an amended founding statement, in triplicate in the prescribed form together with the prescribed fee, signed by or on behalf of every member of the corporation and by or on behalf of any person who will become a member on such registration, and which contains particulars and the date of the change.
[Sub-s. (1) substituted by s. 2(a) of Act No. 81 of 1992.]

(2) If any change is made or occurs in respect of any matter particulars of which are so stated in accordance with paragraph (a), (c) or (g) of section 12, an amended founding statement shall in accordance with the requirements of subsection (1) be lodged with the Registrar for registration, and any such change shall only take effect

when such statement has been so registered in the relevant registers, or upon a later date mentioned in such statement.

Provided that a statement in the prescribed form which upon registration thereof shall form part of the founding statement or amended founding statement, shall, instead of an amended founding statement, be lodged with the Registrar for registration if any such change is made or occurs in respect of—

(a) any matter of which particulars are so stated in accordance with paragraph (c) of section 12, in which case the accounting officer may sign such statement on behalf of the members if the corporation has approved of the said change and the accounting officer so certifies in writing; or

(b) the name or address of the duly appointed accounting officer, in which case the accounting officer may sign such statement on behalf of the members, and the said change shall take effect upon the date mentioned in the statement.

[Proviso to sub-s. (2) inserted by s. 2(*b*) of Act No. 81 of 1992.]

(2A) If a founding statement is altered or something is added thereto by an order of court referred to in section 49, the provisions of subsection (1) in relation to the lodging of an amended founding statement therein referred to, shall *mutatis mutandis* apply in respect of such founding statement.

[Sub-s. (2A) inserted by s. 5(*a*) of Act No. 38 of 1986.]

(3)(*a*) If a corporation fails to lodge an amended founding statement in terms of and in accordance with the provisions of subsection (1), (2) or (2A), as the case may be, the Registrar may on his own initiative or on application by any member or creditor of the corporation serve on the members of the corporation in accordance with section 25(2)(*a*) a reminder by certified post to make good the default within 28 days of the date of the reminder.

[Para. (*a*) substituted by s. 5(*b*) of Act No. 38 of 1986]

(*b*) if the members concerned fail to comply with any such reminder, the Registrar may direct those members by written notice, so served on the members by certified post, to make good the default within 28 days of the date of the notice.

(*c*) If the members concerned fail to comply with any such direction, the Registrar may by further written notice so served on the members by registered post, impose on the members, or any of them, a penalty not exceeding five rand per day from the date upon which the reminder referred to in paragraph (*a*) was sent.

(*d*) When the Registrar has served a notice referred to in paragraph (*c*) on the members, he may not less than 21 days after the date of that notice forward a certified copy thereof to the clerk of the magistrate's court in whose area of jurisdiction the registered office of the corporation is situated, who shall record it, and thereupon such notice shall have the effect of a civil judgment of that magistrate's court against every such member for the amount of the penalty in question.

(*e*) On application by one or more of the members concerned the court in question may reduce or rescind the penalty, or exempt any one or some of the members from the effect of the notice.

16. Keeping of copies of founding statements by corporations.—(1) A corporation shall keep a copy of its founding statement and any proof of its registration at the registered office of the corporation.

(2) A document referred to in subsection (1) shall during the business hours of the corporation be open to inspection by any person upon payment to the corporation, in the case of a person who is not a member of the corporation, of one rand or such lesser amount as the corporation may determine.

(3) A member or officer of a corporation who refuses access for the purposes of an inspection in terms of subsection (2) to a person entitled thereto, shall be guilty of an offence.

17. No constructive notice of particulars in founding statement and other documents.—No person shall be deemed to have knowledge of any particulars merely because such particulars are stated, or referred to, in any founding statement or other document regarding a corporation registered by the Registrar or lodged with him, or which is kept at the registered office of a corporation in accordance with the provisions of this Act.

18. Meaning of "name" in sections 19, 20 and 21.—For the purposes of sections 19, 20 and 21 "name", in relation to a corporation, unless the context otherwise indicates, means the full name of that corporation, or a literal translation of that name into the other official language of the Republic, or a shortened form of that name or any such translation thereof, referred to in section 12(*a*).

19. Undesirable names.—(1) The Registrar may refuse to register a founding statement of a corporation referred to in section 12, or an amended founding statement which relates to a change of name referred to in section 15(2), if the name or changed name of the corporation, as the case may be, is in the opinion of the Registrar undesirable.

(2) The provisions of subsection (1) shall not be construed as imposing a duty on the Registrar to consider the desirability of a name of a corporation mentioned in each founding statement or amended founding statement lodged for registration.

20. Order to change name.—(1) If within a period of one year after the registration of a founding statement of a corporation it appears to the Registrar that a name mentioned in the founding statement is undesirable, he shall order the corporation concerned to change such name.

(2) Any interested person may—

(*a*) within a period of one year referred to in subsection (1), on payment of the prescribed fee apply in writing to the Registrar for an order directing the corporation to change its name on the ground of undesirability or that such name is calculated to cause damage to the applicant; or

(*b*) within a period of two years after the registration of a founding statement apply to a Court for an order directing the corporation to change its name on the ground of undesirability or that such name is calculated to cause damage to the applicant, and the Court may on such application make such order as it deems fit.
[Sub-s. (2) substituted by s. 3(*a*) of Act No. 81 of 1992.]

(3) The Registrar may, after application has been made in terms of paragraph (a) of subsection (2), in writing order the corporation concerned to change its name if, in the opinion of the Registrar, it is or has become undesirable.

(3A) Any person feeling aggrieved by any decision or order of the Registrar under this section may, within one month after the date of such decision or order, apply to a competent provincial or local division of the Supreme Court for relief, and the Court may consider the merits of any such matter, receive further evidence and make any order it deems fit.

(3B) No prescribed fee mentioned in section 15(1) shall be payable in respect of the registration of an amended founding statement by virtue of an order under subsection (3) of this section.

[Sub-s. (3A) and (3B) inserted by s. 3(b) of Act No. 81 of 1992.]

(4) A corporation which fails within any period mentioned in an order under subsection (1) or (3) to comply with any such order, shall be guilty of an offence.

(5) No provision of this Act shall be construed as affecting the rights of any person at common law to bring an action against any corporation for passing off any business, goods or services as those of another person.

21. Effect of change of name.—(1) A change in terms of this Act of a name of a corporation shall not affect any right or obligation of the corporation or any legal proceedings instituted by or against the corporation, and any legal proceedings that could have been continued or commenced by or against the corporation prior to the change of name may, notwithstanding such change of name, after the change be continued or commenced by or against the corporation, as the case may be.

(2) Upon the production by a corporation of a certified copy of a founding statement reflecting a change of name of that corporation to any registrar or other officer charged with the maintenance of a register under any law, and on compliance with all the requirements pursuant to any such law as to the form of application (if any) and the payment of any required fee, such registrar or other officer shall make in his register all such alterations as are necessary by reason of the change of name in respect of the corporation.

22. Formal requirements as to names and registration numbers.—(1) The abbreviation CC or BK, in capital letters, shall be subjoined to the English or Afrikaans name, as the case may be, of a corporation which it uses.

(2) A corporation shall refer to the registration number of the corporation on all prescribed documents and correspondence sent by the corporation to the Registration Office.

(3) If a corporation is being wound up, the statement "In Liquidation" shall for the duration of such winding-up be subjoined to the name of the corporation which it uses.

22A. Any person carrying on business under a name or title—

(a) to which the abbreviation "CC" or "BK", as the case may be, is subjoined; or

(b) of which the words "close corporation" or "beslote korporasie" or any abbreviation thereof form part in a way which indicates incorporation as a close corporation in terms of this Act, shall, unless duly incorporated as a close corporation in terms of this Act, be guilty of an offence.

[S. 22A inserted by s. 4 of Act No. 81 of 1992.]

23. Use and publication of names.—(1) Every corporation—

(a) shall display its registered full name (or a registered literal translation thereof into the other official language of the Republic) and registration number in a conspicuous position and in characters easily legible on the outside of its registered office and every office or place in which its business is carried on;

(b) shall have that name (or such translation thereof) and registration number mentioned in legible characters in all notices and other official publications of the corporation, and in all bills of exchange, promissory notes, endorsements, cheques and orders for money, goods or services purporting to be signed by or on behalf of the corporation, and all letters, delivery notes, invoices, receipts and letters of credit of the corporation; and

[Sub-s. (b) substituted by s. 5 of Act No. 81 of 1992.]

(c) shall use a registered shortened form of that name only in conjunction with that name or such literal translation thereof.

(2) If any member of, or any other person on behalf of, a corporation—

(a) issues or authorizes the issue of any such notice or official publication of the corporation, or signs or authorizes to be signed on behalf of the corporation any such bill of exchange, promissory note, endorsement, cheque or order for money, goods or services; or

(b) issues or authorizes the issue of any such letter, advertisement, delivery note, invoice, receipt or letter of credit of the corporation,

without the name of the corporation, or such registered literal translation thereof, and its registration number being mentioned therein in accordance with subsection (1)(b), he shall be guilty of an offence, and shall further be liable to the holder of the bill of exchange, promissory note, cheque or order for money, goods or services for the amount thereof, unless the amount is duly paid by the corporation.

(3) Any corporation which fails to comply with any provision of subsection (1) shall be guilty of an offence.

24. Contributions by members.—(1) Every person who is to become a member of a corporation upon its registration, shall make to the corporation an initial contribution of money, of property (whether corporeal or incorporeal), or of services rendered in connection with and for the purposes of the formation and incorporation of the corporation, and particulars of such contribution shall be stated in the founding statement of the corporation referred to in section 12, as required by paragraph (f) of that section.

(2) The amount or value of the members' contributions, or of the contribution of any one or more members, may from time to time by agreement among all the members—

(a) be increased by additional contributions of money or property (whether corporeal or incorporeal) to the corporation by existing members or, in terms of section 33(1)(b), by a person becoming a member of a registered corporation; or

(b) be reduced, provided that a reduction by way of a repayment to any member shall comply with the provisions of section 51(1).

(3) Particulars of any increase or reduction of a member's contribution in terms of subsection (2) shall be furnished in an amended founding statement referred to in section 15(1).

(4) Money or property referred to in subsection (1) or (2)(*a*) shall, in order to vest ownership thereof in the corporation, be paid, delivered or transferred, as the case may be, to the corporation within a period of 90 days—

(*a*) after the date of registration of the corporation, in the case of an initial contribution referred to in subsection (1); or

(*b*) after the date of the registration of an amended founding statement in connection with any additional contribution referred to in subsection (2)(*a*).

(5) An undertaking by a member to make an initial or an additional contribution to a corporation shall be enforceable by the corporation in legal proceedings.

25. Postal address and registered office.—(1) Every corporation shall have in the Republic a postal address and an office to which, subject to subsection (2), all communications and notices to the corporation may be addressed.

(2) Any—

(*a*) notice, order, communication or other document which is in terms of this Act required or permitted to be served upon any corporation or member thereof, shall be deemed to have been served if it has been delivered at the registered office, or has been sent by certified or registered post to the registered office or postal address, of the corporation; and

(*b*) process which is required to be served upon any corporation or member thereof shall, subject to applicable provisions in respect of such service in any law, be served by so delivering or sending it.

26. Deregistration.—(1) If the Registrar has reasonable cause to believe that a corporation is not carrying on business or is not in operation, he shall serve on the corporation at its postal address a letter by certified post in which the corporation is notified thereof and informed that if he is not within 60 days from the date of his letter informed in writing that the corporation is carrying on business or is in operation, the corporation will, unless good cause is shown to the contrary, be deregistered.

(2) After the expiration of the period of 60 days mentioned in a latter referred to in subsection (1), or upon receipt from the corporation of a written statement signed by or on behalf of every member to the effect that the corporation has ceased to carry on business and has no assets or liabilities, the Registrar may, unless good cause to the contrary has been shown by the corporation, deregister that corporation.

(3) Where a corporation has been deregistered, the Registrar shall give notice to that effect in the *Gazette*, and the date of the publication of such notice shall be deemed to be the date of deregistration.

(4) The deregistration of a corporation shall not affect any liability of a member of the corporation to the corporation or to any other person, and such liability may be enforced as if the corporation were not deregistered.

(5) If a corporation is deregistered while having outstanding liabilities, the persons who are members of such corporation at the time of deregistration shall be jointly and severally liable for such liabilities.

[Sub-s. (5) substituted by s. 6(1) of Act No. 38 of 1986.]

(6) The Registrar may on application by any interested person, if he is satisfied that a corporation was at the time of its deregistration carrying on business or was in operation, or that it is otherwise just that the registration of the corporation be restored, restore the said registration.

(7) The Registrar shall give notice of the restoration of the registration of a corporation in the *Gazette*, and as from the date of such notice the corporation shall continue to exist and be deemed to have continued in existence as from the date of deregistration as if it were not deregistered.

27. Conversion of companies into corporations.—(1) Any company having ten or fewer members all of whom qualify for membership of a corporation in terms of section 29 of this Act, may be converted into a corporation, provided that every member of the company becomes a member of the corporation.

(2) In respect of a conversion referred to in subsection (1), there shall be lodged with the Registrar—

(a) an application for conversion, in the prescribed form, signed by all the members of the company, containing a statement that upon conversion the assets of the corporation, fairly valued, will exceed its liabilities, and that after conversion the corporation will be able to pay its debts as they become due in the ordinary course of its business;

(b) a statement in writing by the auditor of the company that he has no reason to believe that a material irregularity contemplated in subsection (3) of section 26 of the Public Accountants' and Auditors' Act, 1951 (Act No. 51 of 1951), has taken place or is taking place in relation to the company or, where steps have been taken in terms of that subsection, that such steps and other proceedings in terms of the subsection have been completed; and

(c) a founding statement referred to in section 12 lodged in accordance with section 13.

(3) For the purposes of the founding statement referred to in subsection (2)(c)—

(a) there shall, in regard to the requirements of section 12 (f), be a statement of the aggregate of the contributions of the members, which shall be for an amount not greater than the excess of the fair value of the assets to be acquired by the corporation over the liabilities to be assumed by the corporation by reason of the conversion: Provided that the corporation may treat any portion of such excess not reflected as members' contributions, as amounts which may be distributed to its members;

(b) the members' interests stated in terms of section 12(e) need not necessarily be in proportion to the number of shares in the company held by the respective members at the time of the conversion.

(4) If the provisions of subsection (2) have been complied with, the Registrar shall, if he is satisfied that the company concerned has complied materially with the requirements of the Companies Act—
[Substituted by s. 6 of Act No. 81 of 1992.]

(a) register the founding statement in accordance with the provisions of section 13;

(b) satisfy himself that, simultaneously with such registration, the registration of the memorandum and the articles of association of the company concerned is cancelled in accordance with the provisions of the Companies Act;

(c) endorse on the founding statement a certificate of incorporation as provided by section 14(1): Provided that such certificate shall state the fact that the corporation has been converted from a company and shall mention the name and registration number of the former company; and

[Para. (c) substituted by s. 7 of Act No. 38 of 1986.]

(d) give notice in the *Gazette* of the conversion.

(5)(a) On the registration of a corporation converted from a company, the assets, rights, liabilities and obligations of the company shall vest in the corporation.

(b) Any legal proceedings instituted by or against the company before the registration may be continued by or against the corporation, and any other thing done by or in respect of the company shall be deemed to have been done by or in respect of the corporation.

(c) The conversion of a company into a corporation shall in particular not affect—

(i) any liability of a director or officer of the company to the company on the ground of breach of trust or negligence, or to any other person pursuant to any provision of the Companies Act; or

(ii) any liability of the company, or of any other person, as surety.

(d) The juristic person which prior to the conversion of a company into a corporation existed as a company, shall notwithstanding the conversion continue to exist as a juristic person but in the form of a corporation.

[Para. (d) added by s. 2(1) of Act No. 64 of 1988.]

(6) The corporation shall forthwith after its conversion from a company, give notice in writing of the conversion to all creditors of the company at the time of conversion, and to all other parties to contracts or legal proceedings in which the company was involved at the time of the conversion.

(7) Upon the production by a corporation which has been converted from a company of a certified copy of its founding statement referred to in subsection (4)(a), to any registrar or other officer charged with the maintenance of a register under any law, and on compliance with all the requirements pursuant to any such law as to the form of application (if any) and the payment of any required fee, such registrar or officer shall make in his register all such alterations as are necessary by reason of the conversion of the company into a corporation: Provided that no transfer or stamp duties shall be payable in respect of such alterations in registers.

(8) If the accounting officer mentioned in the founding statement of a converted corporation is not the person who or firm which has acted as auditor for the company, the appointment of that person or firm shall lapse upon the conversion into a corporation.

(9) If a corporation is converted into a company in accordance with the provisions of the Companies Act, the registration of the founding statement of the corporation shall be cancelled simultaneously with the registration of the memorandum and articles of association of the company in terms of that Act.

PART IV

MEMBERSHIP

28. Number of members.—A corporation may at its incorporation have one or more members, but at no time shall the number of members exceed ten.

29. Requirements for membership.—(1) Subject to the provisions of subsection 2(*b*) and (*c*), only natural persons may be members of a corporation and no juristic person or trustee of a trust *inter vivos* in that capacity shall directly or indirectly (whether through the instrumentality of a nominee or otherwise) hold a member's interest in a corporation.

[Sub-s. (1) substituted by s. 3(1) of Act No. 64 of 1988.]

(1A) The provisions of subsection (1) shall not apply to the membership of a corporation of a natural person who holds that membership for the benefit of a trust *inter vivos* if immediately before 13 April 1987 a natural person held membership of the corporation for the benefit of that trust: Provided that—

(*a*) no juristic person shall directly or indirectly be a beneficiary of that trust;

(*b*) the member concerned shall, as between himself and the corporation, personally have all the obligations and rights of a member;

(*c*) the corporation shall not be obliged to observe or have any obligation in respect of any provision of or affecting the trust or any agreement between the trust and the member concerned of the corporation; and

(*d*) if at any time the number of natural persons at that time entitled to receive any benefit from the trust shall, when added to the number of members of the corporation at that time, exceed 10, the provisions of, and exemption under, this subsection shall cease to apply and shall not again become applicable notwithstanding any diminution in the number of members or beneficiaries.

[Sub-s. (1A) added by s. 1 of Act No. 17 of 1990.]

(2) The following persons shall qualify for membership of a corporation:

(*a*) Any natural person entitled to a member's interest;

(*b*) a natural or juristic person, *nomine officii*, who is a trustee of a testamentary trust entitled to a member's interest, provided that—

  (i) no juristic person is a beneficiary of such trust; and

  (ii) if the trustee is a juristic person, such juristic person is not directly or indirectly controlled by any beneficiary of the trust; and

(*c*) a natural or juristic person, *nomine officii*, who, in the case of a member who is insolvent, deceased, mentally disordered or otherwise incapable or incompetent to manage his affairs, is a trustee of his insolvent estate or an administrator, executor or curator in respect of such member or is otherwise a person who is his duly appointed or authorized legal representative.

(3)(*a*) The membership of any person qualified therefor in terms of subsection (2) shall commence on the date of the registration of a founding statement of the corporation containing the particulars required by section 12 in regard to such person and his member's interest.

(*b*) Where any person is to become a member of a registered corporation the existing member or members of the corporation shall ensure that the requirements of section 15(1) regarding the lodging of an amended founding statement with the Registrar are complied with.

(*c*) A trustee of an insolvent estate, administrator, executor or curator, or other legal representative, referred to in subsection (2)(*c*), in respect of any member of a corporation, who is not obliged or who does not intend to transfer the interest of the member in the corporation in accordance with the provisions of this Act within 28 days of his assuming office to any other person, shall within that period, or any extended period allowed by the Registrar on application by him, request the existing member or members of the corporation to lodge with the Registrar in accordance with section 15(1) an amended founding statement designating him, *nomine officii*, as representative of the member of the corporation in question.

(*d*) Where the corporation has no other member, any such representative himself shall, in the circumstances contemplated in paragraph (*c*), act on behalf of the corporation in accordance with the provisions of section 15(1), read with the said paragraph (*c*).

(*e*) The provisions of paragraphs (*c*) and (*d*) shall not affect the power of such representative, as from the date of his assuming office, and whether or not any such amended founding statement has been lodged, to represent the member concerned in all matters in which he himself as a member could have acted, until the interest of that member in the corporation has in accordance with the provisions of this Act been transferred to any other qualified person.

(4) A corporation is not concerned with the execution of any trust in respect of any member's interest in the corporation.

30. Nature of member's interest.—(1) The interest of any member in a corporation shall be a single interest expressed as a percentage.

(2) Two or more persons shall not be joint holders of the same member's interest in a corporation.

31. Certificate of member's interest.—Each member of a corporation shall be issued with a certificate, signed by or on behalf of every member of that corporation, and stating the current percentage of such member's interest in the corporation.

32. Representation of members.—(1) A minor who is a member of a corporation, other than a minor whose guardian has lodged a written consent referred to in section 47(1)(*a*)(ii), shall be represented in the corporation by his guardian.

(2) A married woman, whether subject to the marital power of her husband or not, shall require no representation or assistance to act as a member of a corporation.

(3) A member subject to any other legal disability shall be represented in the corporation by his duly appointed or authorized legal representative referred to in paragraph (*c*) of subsection (2) of section 29.

33. Acquisition of member's interest by new member.—(1) A person becoming a member of a registered corporation shall acquire his member's interest required for membership—

    (*a*) from one or more of the existing members or his or their deceased or insolvent estates; or

(b) pursuant to a contribution made by such person to the corporation, in which case the percentage of his member's interest is determined by agreement between him and the existing members, and the percentages of the interests of the existing members in the corporation shall be reduced in accordance with the provisions of section 38(b).

(2) The contribution referred to in subsection (1)(b) may consist of an amount of money, or of any property (whether corporeal or incorporeal) of a value agreed upon by the person concerned and the existing members.

34. Disposal of interest of insolvent member.—(1) Notwithstanding any provision to the contrary in any association agreement or other agreement between members, a trustee of the insolvent estate of a member of a corporation may, in the discharge of his duties, sell that member's interest—

(a) to the corporation, if there are one or more members other than the insolvent member;

(b) to the members of the corporation other than the insolvent member, in proportion to their member's interests or as they may otherwise agree upon; or

(c) subject to the provisions of subsection (2), to any other person who qualifies for membership of a corporation in terms of section 29.

(2) If the corporation concerned has one or more members other than the insolvent, the following provisions shall apply to a sale in terms of subsection (1)(c) of the insolvent member's interest:

(a) The trustee shall deliver to the corporation a written statement giving particulars of the name and address of the proposed purchaser, the purchase price and the time and manner of payment thereof;

(b) for a period of 28 days after the receipt by the corporation of the written statement the corporation or the members, in such proportions as they may agree upon, shall have the right, exercisable by written notice to the trustee, to be substituted as purchasers of the whole, and not a part only, of the insolvent member's interest at the price and on the terms set out in the trustee's written statement; and

(c) if the insolvent member's interest is not purchased in terms of paragraph (b), the sale referred to in the trustee's written statement shall become effective and be implemented.

35. Disposal of interest of deceased member.—Subject to any other arrangement in an association agreement, an executor of the estate of a member of a corporation who is deceased shall, in the performance of his duties—

(a) cause the deceased member's interset in the corporation to be transferred to a person who qualifies for membership of a corporation in terms of section 29 and is entitled thereto as legatee or heir or under a redistribution agreement, if the remaining member or members of the corporation (if any) consent to the transfer of the member's interest to such person; or

(b) if any consent referred to in paragraph (a) is not given within 28 days after it was requested by the executor, sell the deceased member's interest—

(i) to the corporation, if there is any other member or members than the deceased member;

    (ii) to any other remaining member or members of the corporation in proportion to the interests of those members in the corporation or as they may otherwise agree upon, or

    (iii) to any other person who qualifies for membership of a corporation in terms of section 29, in which case the provisions of subsection (2) of section 34 shall *mutatis mutandis* apply in respect of any such sale.

36. Cessation of membership by order of Court.—(1) On application by any member of a corporation a Court may on any of the following grounds order that any member shall cease to be a member of the corporation:

  (a) Subject to the provisions of the association agreement (if any), that the member is permanently incapable, because of unsound mind or any other reason, of performing his part in the carrying on of the business of the corporation;

  (b) that the member has been guilty of such conduct as taking into account the nature of the corporation's business, is likely to have a prejudicial effect on the carrying on of the business;

  (c) that the member so conducts himself in matters relating to the corporation's business that it is not reasonably practicable for the other member or members to carry on the business of the corporation with him; or

  (d) that circumstances have arisen which render it just and equitable that such member should cease to be a member of the corporation:

Provided that such application to a Court on any ground mentioned in paragraph (a) or (d) may also be made by a member in respect of whom the order shall apply.

(2) A Court granting an order in terms of subsection (1) may make such further orders as it deems fit in regard to—

  (a) the acquisition of the member's interest concerned by the corporation or by members other than the member concerned; or

  (b) the amounts (if any) to be paid in respect of the member's interest concerned or the claims against the corporation of that member, the manner and times of such payments and the persons to whom they shall be made; or

  (c) any other matter regarding the cessation of membership which the Court deems fit.

37. Other dispositions of members' interests. – Every disposition by a member of a corporation of his interest, or a portion thereof, in the corporation, other than a disposition provided for in section 34, 35 or 36, whether to the corporation, any other member or any other person qualifying for membership in terms of section 29, shall be done—

  (a) in accordance with the association agreement (if any); or

  (b) with the consent of every other member of the corporation:

Provided that no member's interest shall be acquired by the corporation unless it has one or more other members.

38. Maintenance of aggregate of members' interests.—The aggregate of the members' interests in a corporation expressed as a percentage shall at all times be one hundred per cent, and for that purpose—

(a) any transfer of the whole, or a portion, of a member's interest shall be effected by the cancellation or the reduction, as the case may be, of the interest of the member concerned and the allocation in the name of the transferee, if not already a member, of a member's interest of the percentage concerned, or the addition to the interest of an existing member of the percentage concerned;

(b) when a person becomes a member of a registered corporation pursuant to a contribution made by him to the corporation, the percentage of his member's interest shall be agreed upon by him and the existing members, and the percentages of the interests of the existing members shall be reduced proportionally or as they may otherwise agree; and

(c) any member's interest acquired by the corporation shall be added to the respective interests of the other members in proportion to their existing interests or as they may otherwise agree.

39. Payment by corporation for members' interests acquired.—(1) Payment by a corporation in respect of its acquisition of a member's interest in the corporation shall be made only—

(a) with the previously obtained written consent of every member of the corporation, other than the member whose interest is acquired, for the specific payment;

(b) if, after such payment is made, the corporation's assets, fairly valued, exceed all its liabilities;

(c) if the corporation is able to pay its debts as they become due in the ordinary course of its business; and

(d) if such payment will in the particular circumstances not in fact render the corporation unable to pay its debts as they become due in the ordinary course of its business.

(2) For the purposes of subsection (1) "payment" shall include the delivery or transfer of any property.

40. Financial assistance by corporation in respect of acquisition of members' interests.—A corporation may give financial assistance (whether directly or indirectly and whether by means of a loan, guarantee, the provision of security or otherwise) for the purpose of, or in connection with, any acquisition of a member's interest in that corporation by any person, only—

(a) with the previously obtained written consent of every member of the corporation for the specific assistance;

(b) if, after such assistance is given, the corporation's assets, fairly valued, exceed all its liabilities;

(c) if the corporation is able to pay its debts as they become due in the ordinary course of its business; and

(d) if such assistance will in the particular circumstances not in fact render the corporation unable to pay its debts as they become due in the ordinary course of its business.

41. Publication of names of members.—(1) A corporation shall not send to any person any business letter bearing a registered name of the corporation, unless the forenames (or the initials thereof) and surname of every member thereof is stated thereon.

(2) Any corporation which contravenes any provision of subsection (1) shall be guilty of an offence.

PART V

INTERNAL RELATIONS

42. Fiduciary position of members. – (1) Each member of a corporation shall stand in a fiduciary relationship to the corporation.

(2) Without prejudice to the generality of the expression "fiduciary relationship", the provisions of subsection (1) imply that a member—

(a) shall in relation to the corporation act honestly and in good faith, and in particular—

(i) shall exercise such powers as he may have to manage or represent the corporation in the interest and for the benefit of the corporation; and

(ii) shall not act without or exceed the powers aforesaid; and

(b) shall avoid any material conflict between his own interests and those of the corporation, and in particular—

(i) shall not derive any personal economic benefit to which he is not entitled by reason of his membership of or service to the corporation, from the corporation or from any other person in circumstances where that benefit is obtained in conflict with the interests of the corporation;

(ii) shall notify every other member, at the earliest opportunity practicable in the circumstances, of the nature and extent of any direct or indirect material interest which he may have in any contract of the corporation; and

(iii) shall not compete in any way with the corporation in its business activities.

(3)(a) A member o f a corporation whose act or omission has breached any duty arising from his fiduciary relationship shall be liable to the corporation for—

(i) any loss suffered as a result thereof by the corporation; or

(ii) any economic benefit derived by the member by reason thereof.

(b) Where a member fails to comply with the provisions of subparagraph (ii) of paragraph (b) of subsection (2) and it becomes known to the corporation that the member has an interest referred to in that subparagraph in any contract of the corporation, the contract in question shall, at the option of the corporation, be voidable: Provided that where the corporation chooses not to be bound a Court may on application by any interested person, if the Court is of the opinion that in the circumstances it is fair to order that such contract shall nevertheless be binding on the parties, give an order to that effect, and may make any further order in respect thereof which it may deem fit.

(4) Except as regards his duty referred to in subsection (2)(a)(i), any particular conduct of a member shall not constitute a breach of a duty arising from his fiduciary relationship to the corporation, if such conduct was preceded or followed by the written approval of all the members where such members were or are cognisant of all the material facts.

43. Liability of members for negligence.—(1) A member of a corporation shall be liable to the corporation for loss caused by his failure in the carrying on of the business of the corporation to act with the degree of care and skill that may reasonably be expected from a person of his knowledge and experience.

(2) Liability referred to in subsection (1) shall not be incurred if the relevant conduct was preceded or followed by the written approval of all the members where such members were or are cognisant of all the material facts.

44. Association agreements.—(1) The members of a corporation having two or more members may at any time enter into a written association agreement signed by or on behalf of each member, which regulates—

(a) any matter which in terms of this Act may be set out or agreed upon in an association agreement; and

(b) any other matter relating to the internal relationship between the members, or the members and the corporation, in a manner not inconsistent with the provisions of this Act.

(2) A corporation shall keep any association agreement at the registered office of the corporation where any member may inspect it and may make extracts therefrom or copies thereof.

(3) Whether or not an association agreement exists, any other agreement, express or implied, between all the members of a corporation on any matter that may be regulated by an association agreement shall be valid, provided that such express or implied agreement—

(a) is not inconsistent with any provision of an association agreement;

(b) does not affect any person other than the corporation or a member who is a party to it; and

(c) ceases to have any effect when any party to it ceases to be a member of the corporation.

(4) Subject to the provisions of this Act, an association agreement or an agreement referred to in subsection (3) shall bind the corporation to every member in his capacity as a member of that corporation and, in such capacity, every member to the corporation and to every other member.

(5) A new member of a corporation shall be bound by an existing association agreement between the other members as if he has signed it as a party thereto.

(6) Any amendment to, or the dissolution of, an association agreement shall be in writing and signed by or on behalf of each member, including a new member referred to in subsection (5).

45. No access to or constructive notice of association agreements.—No person who is not a member of a corporation shall, except by virtue of a provision of this Act, be entitled to inspect any association agreement in respect of that corporation, and no person dealing with the corporation shall be deemed to have knowledge of any particular thereof merely because it is stated or referred to therein, whether or not the agreement is in accordance with section 44(2) kept at the registered office of the corporation.

46. Variable rules regarding internal relations.—The following rules in respect of internal relations in a corporation shall apply in so far as this Act or an association agreement in respect of the corporation does not provide otherwise:

(a) Every member shall be entitled to participate in the carrying on of the business of the corporation;

(b) subject to the provision of section 47, members shall have equal rights in regard to the management of the business of the corporation and in regard to the power to represent the corporation in the carrying on of its business: Provided that the consent in writing of a member holding a member's interest of at least 75 per cent, or of members holding together at least that percentage of the members' interests, in the corporation, shall be required for—

    (i) a change in the principal business carried on by the corporation;

    (ii) a disposal of the whole, or substantially the whole, undertaking of the corporation;

    (iii) a disposal of all, or the greater portion of, the assets of the corporation; and

    (iv) any acquisition or disposal of immovable property by the corporation;
          [Para. (b) amended by s. 8 of Act No. 38 of 1986.]

(c) differences between members as to matters connected with a corporation's business shall be decided by majority vote at a meeting of members of the corporation;

(d) at any meeting of members of a corporation each member shall have the number of votes that corresponds with the percentage of his interest in the corporation;

(e) a corporation shall indemnify every member in respect of expenditure incurred or to be incurred by him—

    (i) in the ordinary and proper conduct of the business of the corporation; and

    (ii) in regard to anything done or to be done for the preservation of the business or property of the corporation; and

(f) payments by a corporation to its members by reason only of their membership in terms of section 51(1) shall be of such amounts and be effected at such times as the members may from time to time agree upon, and such payments shall be made to members in proportion to their respective interests in the corporation.

47. Disqualified members regarding management of business of corporation.—
(1) Notwithstanding any other provision of this Act or in any association agreement or any other agreement between members to the contrary, the following persons

shall, if they are members, be disqualified from taking part in the management of the business of a corporation:

(a) Any person under legal disability, except—

   (i) a married woman, whether subject to the marital power of her husband or not; and

   (ii) a minor who has attained at least the age of 18 years and whose guardian has lodged with the corporation a written consent to the minor's participation in the management of the business of the corporation;

(b) save under authority of a Court—

   (i) an unrehabilitated insolvent;

   (ii) any person removed from an office of trust on account of misconduct;

   (iii) any person who has at any time been convicted of theft, fraud, forgery or uttering a forged document, perjury, any offence under the Prevention of Corruption Act, 1958 (Act No. 6 of 1958), or any offence involving dishonesty or in connection with the formation or management of a company or a corporation, and has been sentenced therefor to imprisonment for at least six months without the option of a fine; and

(c) any person who is subject to any order of a court under the Companies Act disqualifying him from being a director of a company.

(2) Any person disqualified under the provisions of subsection (1)(b) or (c) who directly or indirectly takes part in or is concerned with the management of the business of any corporation, shall be guilty of an offence.

48. Meetings of members.—(1) Any member of a corporation may by notice to every other member and every other person entitled to attend a meeting of members, call a meeting of members for any purpose disclosed in the notice.

(2) Unless an association agreement provides otherwise—

(a) a notice referred to in subsection (1) shall, as regards the date, time and venue of the meeting, fix a reasonable date and time, and a venue which is reasonably suitable for all persons entitled to attend the particular meeting;

(b) three-fourths of the members present in person at the meeting, shall constitute a quorum; and

(c) only members present in person at the meeting may vote at that meeting.
    [Para. (c) added by s. 9(c) of Act No. 38 of 1986.]

(3)(a) A corporation shall record a report of the proceedings at a meeting of its members within 14 days after the date on which the meeting was held in a minute book which shall be kept at the registered office of the corporation.

(b) A resolution in writing, signed by all the members and entered into the minute book, shall be as valid and effective as if it were passed at a meeting of the members duly convened and held.

49. Unfairly prejudicial conduct.—(1) Any member of a corporation who alleges that any particular act or omission of the corporation or of one or more other members is unfairly prejudicial, unjust or inequitable to him, or to some members including him, or that the affairs of the corporation are being conducted in a manner unfairly prejudicial, unjust or inequitable to him, or to some members including him, may make an application to a Court for an order under this section.

(2) If on any such application it appears to the Court that the particular act or omission is unfairly prejudicial, unjust or inequitable as contemplated in subsection (1), or that the corporation's affairs are being conducted as so contemplated, and if the Court considers it just and equitable, the Court may with a view to settling the dispute make such order as it thinks fit, whether for regulating the future conduct of the affairs of the corporation or for the purchase of the interest of any member of the corporation by other members thereof or by the corporation.

(3) When an order under this section makes any alteration or addition to the relevant founding statement or association agreement, or replaces any association agreement, the alteration or addition or replacement shall have effect as if it were duly made by agreement of the members concerned.

(4) A copy of an order made under this section which—

(a) alters or adds to a founding statement shall within 28 days of the making thereof be lodged by the corporation with the Registrar for registration; or

(b) alters or adds to or replaces any association agreement, shall be kept by the corporation at its registered office where any member of the corporation may inspect it.

(5) Any corporation which fails to comply with any provision of subsection (4) shall be guilty of an offence.

50. Proceedings against fellow-members on behalf of corporation.—(1) Where a member or a former member of a corporation is liable to the corporation—

(a) to make an initial contribution or any additional contribution contemplated in subsection (1) and (2)(a), respectively, of section 24; or

(b) on account of—

(i) the breach of a duty arising from his fiduciary relationship to the corporation in terms of section 42; or

(ii) negligence in terms of section 43,

any other member of the corporation may institute proceedings in respect of any such liability on behalf of the corporation against such member or former member after notifying all other members of the corporation of his intention to do so.

(2) After the institution of such proceedings by a member the leave of the Court concerned shall be required for a withdrawal of the proceedings or for any settlement of the claim, and the Court may in connection with such withdrawal or settlement make such orders as it may deem fit.

(3) If a Court in any particular case finds that the proceedings, if unsuccessful, have been instituted without *prima facie* grounds, it may order the member who

has instituted them on behalf of the corporation, himself to pay the costs of the corporation and of the defendant in question in such manner as the Court may determine.

51. Payments by corporation to members.—(1) Any payment by a corporation to any member by reason only of his membership, may be made only—

(a) if, after such payment is made, the corporation's assets, fairly valued, exceed all its liabilities;

(b) if the corporation is able to pay its debts as they become due in the ordinary course of its business; and

(c) if such payment will in the particular circumstances not in fact render the corporation unable to pay its debts as they become due in the ordinary course of its business.

(2) A member shall be liable to a corporation for any payment received contrary to any provision of subsection (1).

(3) For the purposes of this section—

(a) without prejudice to the generality of the expression "payment by a corporation to any member by reason only of his membership", that expression—

(i) shall include a distribution, or a repayment of any contribution, or part thereof, to a member;

(ii) shall exclude any payment to a member in his capacity as a creditor of the relevant corporation and, in particular, a payment as remuneration for services rendered as an employee or officer of the corporation, a repayment of a loan or of interest thereon or a payment of rental; and

(b) "payment" shall include the delivery or transfer of any property.

52. Prohibition of loans and furnishing of security to members and others by corporation.—(1) A corporation shall not, directly or indirectly, make a loan—

(a) to any of its members;

(b) to any other corporation in which one or more of its members together hold more than a 50 per cent interest; or

(c) to any company or other juristic person (except a corporation) controlled by one or more members of the corporation,

and shall not provide any security to any person in connection with any obligation of any such member, or other corporation, company or other juristic person,

(2) The provisions of subsection (1) shall not apply in respect of the making of any particular loan or the provision of any particular security with the express previously obtained consent in writing of all the members of a corporation.

(3) Any member of a corporation who authorises or permits or is a party to the making of any loan or the provision of any security contrary to any provision of this section—

(a) shall be liable to indemnify the corporation and any other person who had no actual knowledge of the contravention against any loss directly resulting from the invalidity of such loan or security; and

(b) shall be guilty of an offence.

(4) For the purposes of this section—

(a) "loan" includes—

    (i) a loan of any property; and

    (ii) any credit extended by a corporation where the debt concerned is not payable or is not being paid in accordance with normal business practice in respect of the payment of debts of the same kind;

(b) one or more members of a corporation shall only be deemed to control a company or other juristic person as contemplated in subsection (1)(c), if the circumstances envisaged in section 226(1A)(b) of the Companies Act in relation to a director or manager or his nominee, or directors or managers or their nominees, referred to in that section, and a company or body corporate, are present in respect of any such member or his nominee, or such members or their nominees, and any such company or other juristic person; and

(c) "security" includes a guarantee.

PART VI
EXTERNAL RELATIONS

53. Pre-incorporation contracts.—(1) Any contract in writing entered into by a person professing to act as an agent or a trustee for a corporation not yet formed, may after its incorporation be ratified or adopted by such corporation as if the corporation had been duly incorporated at the time when the contract was entered into.

(2) The ratification or adoption by a corporation referred to in subsection (1) shall be in the form of a consent in writing of all the members of the corporation, given within a time specified in the contract or, if no time is specified, within a reasonable time after incorporation.

54. Power of members to bind corporation.—(1) Subject to the provisions of this section, any member of a corporation shall in relation to a person who is not a member and is dealing with the corporation, be an agent of the corporation for the purposes of the business of the corporation stated in its founding statement or actually being carried on by it.

(2) Any act of a member shall bind a corporation, if—

(a) such act is expressly or impliedly authorized by the corporation, or is subsequently ratified by it; or

(b) such act is performed for the carrying on, in the usual way, of business of the kind stated in a founding statement of the corporation or actually being carried on by the corporation at the time of the performance of the act, unless the member so acting has in fact no power to act for the corporation in the particular matter and the person with whom he deals has, or ought reasonably to have, knowledge of the fact that the member has no such power.

(3) Where any act of a member of a corporation is performed for a purpose apparently not connected with the ordinary course of the business of the corporation stated

in its founding statement or actually being carried on by it at the time of the performance of the act, the corporation shall not be bound by such act, unless it has in fact been authorized or is ratified as contemplated in subsection (2)(*a*) by the corporation.

(4) Where any association agreement restricts the power of any member to represent a corporation, or where any member is disqualified under section 47 from participating in the management of the business of a corporation, no act in contravention of the restriction or performed by such disqualified person shall be binding on the corporation with respect to any person who has, or ought reasonably to have, knowledge of such restriction or disqualification.

(5) Where the consent in writing of a member or members of a corporation is in any particular case required in terms of the proviso to section 46(*b*), no act in contravention of such requirement shall be binding on the corporation with respect to any person who has, or ought reasonably to have, knowledge of the fact that the particular act is performed in contravention of such requirement.

[Sub-s. (5) substituted by s. 10 of Act No. 38 of 1986.]

55. Application of sections 37 and 226 of Companies Act, 1973.—(1) If the relationship between any company and any corporation is such that the corporation, if it were a company, would be a holding company of such company, the provisions of section 37 of the Companies Act regarding—

(*a*) the employment of funds of a company in a loan to; or

(*b*) the provision of any security by a company to another person in connection with an obligation of,

its holding company, or a company which is a subsidiary of that holding company but is not a subsidiary of itself, shall *mutatis mutandis* apply in relation to any such employment of funds or provision of security by any such company in respect of any such corporation and in respect of any company which would be a subsidiary of the corporation were it a company, but which is not a subsidiary of the first-mentioned company.

(2) In the application in terms of subsection (1) of the provisions of subsection (3)(*b*) of the said section 37 of the Companies Act any reference therein to a director or officer, or a former director or officer, of a holding company, shall be construed as a reference to any member or officer, or former member or officer, of a corporation envisaged in subsection (1).

(3) If the relationship between any company and any corporation is as envisaged in subsection (1), the provisions of section 226 of the Companies Act regarding the making by a company of any loan to, or the provision of security by a company to another person in connection with any obligation of—

(*a*) any director or manager of the company's holding company or of another company which is a subsidiary of its holding company; or

(*b*) another company or another juristic person controlled by one or more directors or managers of the company's holding company or of a company which is a subsidiary of its holding company,

[Para. (*b*) substituted by s. 2(*a*) of Act No. 17 of 1990.]

shall *mutatis mutandis* apply in relation to any such loan or provision of security by any such company in respect of—

 (i) any member or officer of any such corporation, or any director or officer of another company which would be a subsidiary of any such corporation were the corporation a company; and

 (ii) another company or another juristic person controlled by one or more members of any such corporation, or by one or more directors or managers of a company which would be a subsidiary of the corporation were it a company.

 [Para. (ii) substituted by s. 2(*b*) of Act No. 17 of 1990.]

(4) In the application in terms of subsection (3) of the provisions of subsection (5) of the said section 226 of the Companies Act any reference therein to any director or officer of a holding company, shall be construed as a reference to any member or officer of a corporation envisaged in subsection (1).

PART VII

ACCOUNTING AND DISCLOSURE

56. Accounting records.—(1) A corporation shall keep in one of the official languages of the Republic such accounting records as are necessary fairly to present the state of affairs and business of the corporation, and to explain the transactions and financial position of the business of the corporation, including—

(*a*) records showing its assets and liabilities, members' contributions, undrawn profits, revaluations of fixed assets and amounts of loans to and from members;

(*b*) a register of fixed assets showing in respect thereof the respective dates of any acquisition and the cost thereof, depreciation (if any), and where any assets have been revalued, the date of the revaluation and the revalued amount thereof, the respective dates of any disposals and the consideration received in respect thereof: Provided that in the case of a corporation which has been converted from a company in terms of section 27, the existing fixed asset register of the company shall be deemed to be such a register in respect of the corporation, and such particulars therein shall be deemed to apply in respect of it;

 [Preceding words substituted by s. 7 of Act No. 81 of 1992.]

(*c*) records containing entries from day to day of all cash received and paid out, in sufficient detail to enable the nature of the transactions and, except in the case of cash sales, the names of the parties to the transactions to be identified;

(*d*) records of all goods purchased and sold on credit, and services received and rendered on credit, in sufficient detail to enable the nature of those goods or services and the parties to the transactions to be identified;

(*e*) statements of the annual stocktaking, and records to enable the value of stock at the end of the financial year to be determined; and

(*f*) vouchers supporting entries in the accounting records.

(2) The accounting records relating to—

(a) contributions by members;

(b) loans to and from members; and

(c) payments to members,

shall contain sufficient detail of individual transactions to enable the nature and purpose thereof to be clearly identified.

(3) The accounting records referred to in subsection (1) shall be kept in such a manner as to provide adequate precautions against falsification and to facilitate the discovery of any falsification.

(4) The accounting records shall be kept at the place or places of business or at the registered office of the corporation and shall, wherever kept, be open at all reasonable times for inspection by any member.

(5)(a) Any corporation which fails to comply with any provision of any of the preceding subsections of this section, and every member thereof who is a party to such failure or who fails to take all reasonable steps to ensure compliance by the corporation with any such provision, shall be guilty of an offence.

(b) In any proceedings against any member of a corporation in respect of an offence consisting of a failure to take reasonable steps to secure compliance by a corporation with any provision referred to in paragraph (a), it shall be a defence if it is proved that the accused had reasonable grounds for believing and did believe that a competent and reliable person was charged with the duty of seeing that any such provision was complied with, and that such person was in a position to discharge that duty, and that the accused had no reason to believe that such person had in any way failed to discharge that duty.

57. Financial year of corporation.—(1)(a) A corporation shall fix a date on which, in each year, its financial year will end.

(b) The financial year of a corporation shall be its annual accounting period.

(2) The date referred to in subsection (1)(a) may, subject to the provisions of section 15(2), be changed by the corporation to any other date. Provided that the corporation may not change the date referred to in subsection (1)(a) more than once in any financial year.

[Proviso to para. (2) was added by s. 3(a) of Act No. 17 of 1990.]

(3) Subject to any increase or reduction of the duration of a financial year by reason of the provisions of subsection (4), the duration of each financial year of a corporation shall be 12 months ending on the date or other date referred to in subsection (1)(a) or (2).

(4) Notwithstanding the provisions of subsection (3)—

(a) the first financial year of a corporation shall commence on the date of its registration and shall end on the date referred to in subsection (1)(a) occurring not less than 3 nor more than 15 months after the date of registration: Provided that the first financial year of a corporation converted from a company in terms of section 27, shall end on the date on which the financial year of the company would have ended had it not been so converted; and

[Para. (a) amended by s. 11 of Act No. 38 of 1986.]

(*b*) in the case of a corporation which has in terms of subsection (2) changed the date referred to in subsection (1)(*a*), the financial year shall commence at the end of the previous financial year and shall end on the date as changed occurring not less than 3 or more than 18 months after the end of that previous financial year.

[Para. (*b*) substituted by s. 3(*b*) of Act No. 17 of 1990.]

58. Annual financial statements.—(1) The members of a corporation shall within nine months after the end of every financial year of the corporation cause annual financial statements in respect of that financial year to be made out in one of the official languages of the Republic.

[Sub-s. (1) amended by s. 4(*a*) of Act No. 64 of 1988.]

(2) The annual financial statements of a corporation—

(*a*) Shall consist of—

(i) a balance sheet and any notes thereon; and

(ii) an income statement or any similar financial statement where such form is appropriate, and any notes thereon;

(*b*) shall in conformity with generally accepted accounting practice appropriate to the business of the corporation, fairly present the state of affairs of the corporation as at the end of the financial year concerned, and the results of its operations for that year;

(*c*) shall disclose separately the aggregate amounts, at the end of the financial year, of contributions by members, undrawn profits, revaluations of fixed assets and amounts of loans to or from members, and the movements in these amounts during the year;

(*d*) shall be in agreement with the accounting records, which shall be summarised in such a form that—

(i) compliance with the provisions of this subsection is made possible; and

(ii) an accounting officer is enabled to report to the corporation in terms of section 62(1)(*c*) without it being necessary to refer to any subsidiary accounting records and vouchers supporting the entries in the accounting records:

Provided that nothing contained in this paragraph shall be construed as preventing an accounting officer, if he deems it necessary, from inspecting such subsidiary accounting records and vouchers; and

[Para. (*d*) added by s. 12(1)(*b*) of Act No. 38 of 1986.]

(*e*) shall contain the report of the accounting officer referred to in section 62(1)(*c*).

[Sub-s. (2) amended by s.4(*a*) of Act No. 64 of 1988. Para (*e*) added by s. 12 (1)(*b*) of Act No. 38 of 1986.]

(3) The annual financial statements shall be approved and signed by or on behalf of a member holding a member's interest of at least 51 per cent, or members together holding members' interests of at least 51 per cent, in the corporation.

[Sub-s. (3) substituted by s. 4(*b*) of Act No. 64 of 1988.]

(4)(*a*) Any member of a corporation who fails to take all reasonable steps to comply or to secure compliance with any provision of this section, shall be guilty of an offence.

(*b*) In any proceedings against any member of a corporation under paragraph (*a*) the defence referred to in section 56(5)(*b*) shall be available to him.
[Para. (*b*) substituted by s. 12(1)(*c*) of Act No. 38 of 1986.]

59. Appointment of accounting officers.—(1) Every corporation shall appoint an accounting officer in accordance with the provisions of this Act.

(2) The appointment of the first accounting officer of a corporation referred to in section 12(*g*)(i) shall take effect on the date of the registration of the corporation.

(3) If a vacancy occurs in the office of an accounting officer, whether as a result of removal, resignation or otherwise, the corporation shall within 14 days appoint another accounting officer and comply with the provisions of subsection (2) of section 15: Provided that the provisions of subsection (3) of the said section 15 shall apply where the said subsection (2) of that section has not so been complied with, whether or not an appointment of such other accounting officer has been made.

(4) A corporation shall inform its accounting officer in writing of his removal from office.

(5) (*a*) An accounting officer shall on resignation or removal from office forthwith inform every member of the corporation thereof in writing, and shall send a copy of the letter to the last known address of the registered office of the corporation and shall in addition forthwith by certified post inform the Registrar—

(i) that he has resigned or been removed from office;

(ii) of the date of his resignation or removal from office;

(iii) of the date up to which he performed his duties; and

(iv) that as at the time of his resignation or removal from office he was not aware of any matters in the financial affairs of the corporation which are in contravention of the provisions of this Act.
[Sub-s. (5)(*a*) substituted by s. 8 of Act No. 81 of 1992.]

(*b*) If an accounting officer who has been removed from office is of the opinion that he was removed for improper reasons, he shall forthwith by certified post inform the Registrar thereof, and shall send a copy of the letter to every member.

60. Qualifications of accounting officers.—(1) No person shall be appointed as or hold the office of an accounting officer of a corporation, unless he is a member of a recognized profession which—
[Substituted by s. 9(*a*) of Act No. 81 of 1992.]

(*a*) as a condition for membership, requires its members to have passed examinations in accounting and related fields of study which in the opinion of the Minister would qualify such members to perform the duties of an accounting officer under this Act;

(*b*) has the power to exclude from membership those persons found guilty of negligence in the performance of their duties or of conduct which is discreditable to their profession; and

(*c*) has been named in a notice referred to in subsection (2).

(2) The Minister may from time to time publish by notice in the *Gazette* the names of those professions whose members are qualified to perform the duties of an accounting officer in terms of this Act.

(3) A member or employee of a corporation, and a firm whose partner or employee is a member or employee of a corporation, shall not qualify for appointment as an accounting officer of such corporation unless all the members consent in writing to such appointment.

(4) A firm as defined in section 1 of the Public Accountants' and Auditors' Act, 1991 (Act No. 80 of 1991), and any other firm may be appointed as an accounting officer of a corporation, provided each partner in the latter firm is qualified to be so appointed.

[Sub-s. (4) substituted by s. 9(*b*) of Act No. 81 of 1992.]

61. Right of access and remuneration of accounting officers.—(1) An accounting officer of a corporation shall at all times have a right of access to the accounting records and all the books and documents of the corporation, and to require from members such information and explanations as he considers necessary for the performance of his duties as an accounting officer.

(2) The remuneration of an accounting officer shall be determined by agreement with the corporation.

62. Duties of accounting officers.—(1) The accounting officer of a corporation shall, not later than three months after completion of the annual financial statements—

(a) subject to the provisions of section 58(2)(*d*), determine whether the annual financial statements are in agreement with the accounting records of the corporation;

[Para. (*a*) substituted by s. 13(*a*) of Act No. 38 of 1986.]

(b) review the appropriateness of the accounting policies represented to the accounting officer as having been applied in the preparation of the annual financial statements;

[Para. (*b*) substituted by s. 13(1)(*a*) of Act No. 38 of 1986 and s. 4(*a*) of Act No. 17 of 1990.]

(c) report in respect of paragraphs (a) and (b) to the corporation.

(2)(a) If during the performance of his duties an accounting officer becomes aware of any contravention of a provision of this Act, he shall describe the nature of such contravention in his report.

(b) Where an accounting officer is a member or employee of a corporation, or is a firm of which a partner or employee is a member or employee of the corporation, his report shall state that fact.

(3) If an accounting officer of a corporation—

(a) at any time knows, or has reason to believe, that the corporation is not carrying on business or is not in operation and has no intention of resuming operations in the foreseeable future; or

(b) during the performance of his duties finds—

(i) that any change, during a relevant financial year, in respect of any particulars mentioned in the relevant founding statement has not been registered;

    (ii) that the annual financial statements indicate that as at the end of the finan-cial year concerned the corporation's liabilities exceed its assets; or

    (iii) that the annual financial statements incorrectly indicate that as at the end of the financial year concerned the assets of the corporation exceed its liabilities, or has reason to believe that such an incorrect indication is given,

        [Sub-para. (iii) added by s. 13(1)(*d*) of Act No. 38 of 1986.]

he shall forthwith by certified post report accordingly to the Registrar.

    (4) If an accounting officer of a corporation has in accordance with subparagraph (ii) or (iii) of paragraph (*b*) of subsection (3) reported to the Registrar that the annual financial statements of the corporation concerned indicate that as at the end of the financial year concerned the corporation's liabilities exceed its assets or that the annual financial statements incorrectly indicate that as at the end of the financial year concerned the assets of the corporation exceed its liabilities, or that he has reason to believe that such an incorrect indication is given, and he finds that any subsequent financial statements of the corporation concerned indicate that the situation has changed or has been rectified and that the assets concerned then exceed the liabilities or that they no longer incorrectly indicate that the assets exceed the liabilities or that he no longer has reason to believe that such an incorrect indication is given, as the case may be, he may report to the Registrar accordingly.

        [Sub-s. (4) added by s. 4(*b*) of Act No. 17 of 1990.]

PART VIII

LIABILITY OF MEMBERS AND OTHERS FOR DEBTS OF CLOSE CORPORATION

63. Joint liability for debts of corporation.—Notwithstanding anything to the con-trary contained in any provision of this Act, the following persons shall in the following circumstances together with a corporation be jointly and severally liable for the speci-fied debts of the corporation:

    (*a*) Where the name of the corporation is in any way used without the abbrevi-ation CC or BK as required by section 22(1), any member of the corporation who is responsible for, or who authorized or knowingly permits the omission of such abbreviation, shall be so liable to any person who enters into any transaction with the corporation from which a debt accrues for the corpor-ation while he, in consequence of such omission, is not aware that he is dealing with a corporation;

    (*b*) where any member fails to pay money or to deliver or transfer property to the corporation as required by section 24(4), he shall be so liable for every debt of the corporation incurred from its registration to the date of the actual payment, delivery or transfer of such money or property;

    (*c*) where the number of members of a corporation exceeds the maximum speci-fied in section 28 for a period of six months, every such member shall be so liable for every debt of the corporation incurred while the number of mem-bers so exceeded or continues to exeed such maximum;

    (*d*) where a juristic person or a trustee of a trust *inter vivos* in that capacity pur-ports to hold, whether directly or indirectly, a member's interest in the corpor-ation in contravention of any provision of section 29, such juristic person or trustee of a trust *inter vivos* and any nominee referred to in that section shall, notwithstanding the invalidity of the holding of such interest, be so liable for every debt of the corporation incurred during the time the contravention continues;

[Para. (*d*) substituted by s. 5(1) of Act No. 64 of 1988.]

(*e*)   where the corporation makes a payment in respect of the acquisition of a member's interest in contravention of any provision of section 39, every person who is a member at the time of such payment and who is aware of the making of such payment, including a member or a former member who receives or who received such payment, shall be so liable for every debt of the corporation incurred prior to the making of such payment unless, in the case of a member who is so aware, he proves that he took all reasonable steps to prevent the payment;

(*f*)   where the corporation gives financial assistance for the purpose of or in connection with any acquisition of a member's interest in contravention of any provision of section 40, every person who is a member at the time of the giving of such assistance and who is aware of the giving of such assistance, and the person who receives such assistance, shall be so liable for every debt of the corporation incurred prior to the giving of such assistance unless, in the case of a member who is so aware, he proves that he took all reasonable steps to prevent the payment;

(*g*)   where a person takes part in the management of the business of the corporation while disqualified from doing so in terms of section 47(1)(*b*) or (*c*), that person shall be so liable for every debt of the corporation which it incurs as a result of his participation in the management of the corporation; and

(*h*)   where the office of accounting officer of the corporation is vacant for a period of six months, any person who at any time during that period was a member and aware of the vacancy, and who at the expiration of that period is still a member, shall be so liable for every debt of the corporation incurred during such existence of the vacancy and for every such debt thereafter incurred while the vacancy continues and he still is a member.

64. Liability for reckless or fraudulent carrying-on of business of corporation.—(1) If it at any time appears that any business of a corporation was or is being carried on recklessly, with gross negligence or with intent to defraud any person or for any fraudulent purpose, a Court may on the application of the Master, or any creditor, member or liquidator of the corporation, declare that any person who was knowingly a party to the carrying on of the business in any such manner, shall be personally liable for all or any of such debts or other liabilities of the corporation as the Court may direct, and the Court may give such further orders as it considers proper for the purpose of giving effect to the declaration and enforcing that liability.

(2) Without prejudice to any other criminal liability incurred where any business of a corporation is carried on in any manner contemplated in subsection (1), every person who is knowingly a party to the carrying on of the business in any such manner, shall be guilty of an offence.

65. Powers of Court in case of abuse of separate juristic personality of corporation.—Whenever a Court on application by an interested person, or in any proceedings in which a corporation is involved, finds that the incorporation of, or any act by or on behalf of, or any use of, that corporation, constitutes a gross abuse of the juristic personality of the corporation as a separate entity, the Court may declare that the corporation is to be deemed not to be a juristic person in respect of such rights, obligations or liabilities of the corporation, or of such member or members thereof, or of such other person or persons, as are specified in the declaration, and the Court may give such further order or orders as it may deem fit in order to give effect to such declaration.

PART IX
Winding-Up

66. Application of Companies Act, 1973.—(1) The provisions of the Companies Act which relate to the winding-up of a company, including the regulations made thereunder, (except sections 337, 338, 344, 345, 346(2), 347(3), 349, 364, 365(2), 367 to 370, inclusive, 377, 387, 389, 390, 395 to 399, inclusive 400(1)(*b*), 401, 402, 417, 418, 419(4), 421, 423 and 424), shall apply *mutatis mutandis* and in so far as they can be applied to the liquidation of a corporation in respect of any matter not specifically provided for in this Part or in any other provision of this Act.

(2) For the purposes of subsection (1)—

(*a*) any reference in a relevant provision of the Companies Act, and in any provision of the Insolvency Act, 1936 (Act No. 24 of 1936), made applicable by any such provision—

(i) to a company, shall be construed as a reference to a corporation;

(ii) to a share in a company, shall be construed as a reference to a member's interest in a corporation;

(iii) to a member, director, shareholder or contributory of a company, shall be construed as a reference to a member of a corporation;

(iv) to an auditor of a company, shall be construed as a reference to an accounting officer of a corporation;

(v) to an officer or a secretary of a company, shall be construed as a reference to a manager or a secretary who is an officer of a corporation;

(vi) to a registered office of a company, shall be construed as a reference to a registered office of a corporation;

(vii) to a memorandum or articles of association of a company, shall be construed as a reference to a founding statement and an association agreement of a corporation, respectively;

(viii) to the Registrar of Companies, shall be construed as a reference to the Registrar;

(ix) to the Companies Act or the regulations made thereunder, or to any provision thereof, shall be construed as including a reference to this Act or the regulations made thereunder, or to any corresponding provision thereof, as the case may be;

    (x) to an insolvent estate, shall be construed as a reference to a corporation;

   (xi) to a provisional liquidator of a company, or to a liquidator of a company or a trustee of an insolvent estate, shall be construed as a reference to a provisional liquidator and to a liquidator of a corporation, respectively;

  (xii) to a sheriff of a province, shall be construed as including a reference to a messenger of a magistrate's court;

 (xiii) to a Registrar of a Court, shall be construed as including a reference to a clerk of a magistrate's court;

 (xiv) to a Court, shall be construed as a reference to a Court having jurisdiction under this Act; and

  (xv) to a Master, shall be construed as a reference to a Master having jurisdiction under this Act:

 (b) a reference to a special resolution—

    (i) referred to in sections 340(2), 350(1), 351(1), 352, 356(2), 357(3) and (4), 359(1), 362(1) and 363(1) of the Companies Act, shall be construed as a reference to a written resolution for the voluntary winding-up of a corporation in terms of section 67 of this Act; and

   (ii) referred to in section 422(1)(b) of the Companies Act, shall be construed as a reference to a written resolution signed by or on behalf of all the members of a corporation; and

 (c) it shall be deemed that the following paragraph has been substituted for paragraph (b) of section 358 of the Companies Act:

    "(b) where any other action or proceeding is being or about to be instituted against the company in any court in the Republic, apply to such court for an order restraining further proceedings in the action or proceeding".

67. Voluntary winding-up.—(1) A corporation may be wound up voluntarily if all its members so resolve at a meeting of members called for the purpose of considering the winding-up of the corporation, and sign a written resolution that the corporation be wound up voluntarily by members or creditors, as the case may be.

(2) A copy of the written resolution, in duplicate in the prescribed form, shall be lodged within 28 days after the date of the passing of the resolution, together with the prescribed fee, with the Registrar, who shall register such resolution if it complies with the provisions of subsection (1).

(3) If such copy of the written resolution is not so registered by the Registrar within 90 days from the date of the passing of the resolution, the resolution shall lapse and be void.

(4) A resolution in terms of this section shall not take effect until it has been registered by the Registrar.

68. Liquidation by Court.—A corporation may be wound up by a Court, if—

 (a) members having more than one half of the total number of votes of members, have so resolved at a meeting of members called for the purpose of considering the winding-up of the corporation, and have signed a written resolution that the corporation be wound up by a Court;

(*b*) the corporation has not commenced its business within a year from its registration, or has suspended its business for a whole year;

(*c*) the corporation is unable to pay its debts; or

(*d*) it appears on application to the Court that it is just and equitable that the corporation be wound up.

69. Circumstances under which corporation deemed unable to pay debts.—(1) For the purposes of section 68(*c*) a corporation shall be deemed to be unable to pay its debts, if—

(*a*) a creditor, by cession or otherwise, to whom the corporation is indebted in a sum of not less than two hundred rand then due has served on the corporation, by delivering it at its registered office, a demand requiring the corporation to pay the sum so due, and the corporation has for 21 days thereafter neglected to pay the sum or to secure or compound for it to the reasonable satisfaction of the creditor; or

(*b*) any process issued on a judgment, decree or order of any court in favour of a creditor of the corporation is returned by a sheriff, or a messenger of a magistrate's court, with an endorsement that he has not found sufficient disposable property to satisfy the judgment, decree or order, or that any disposable property found did not upon sale satisfy such process; or

(*c*) it is proved to the satisfaction of the Court that the corporation is unable to pay its debts.

(2) In determining for the purposes of subsection (1) whether a corporation is unable to pay its debts, the Court shall also take into account the contingent and prospective liabilities of the corporation.

70. Repayments by members.—(1) Subject to the provisions of this section, no member of a corporation shall in the winding-up of the corporation be liable for the repayment of any payment made by the corporation to him by reason only of his membership, if such payment complies with the requirements of section 51(1).

(2) In the winding-up of a corporation unable to pay its debts, any such payment made to a member by reason only of his membership within a period of two years before the commencement of the winding-up of the corporation, shall be repaid to the corporation by the member, unless such member can prove that—

(*a*) after such payment was made, the corporation's assets, fairly valued, exceeded all its liabilities; and

(*b*) such payment was made while the corporation was able to pay its debts as they became due in the ordinary course of its business; and

(*c*) such payment, in the particular circumstances, did not in fact render the corporation unable to pay its debts as they became due in the ordinary course of its business.

(3) A person who has ceased to be a member of the corporation concerned within the said period of two years, shall also be liable for any repayment provided for in subsection (2) if, and to the extent that, repayments by present members, together with all other available assets, are insufficient for paying all the debts of the corporation.

(4) A certificate given by the Master as to the amount payable by any member or former member in terms of subsection (2) or (3) to the corporation, may be forwarded by the liquidator to the clerk of the magistrate's court in whose area of jurisdiction the registered office of the corporation is situated, who shall record it, and thereupon such notice shall have the effect of a civil judgment of that magistrate's court against the member or former member concerned.

(5) The court in question may, on application by a member or former member referred to in subsection (3), make any order that it deems fit in regard to any certificate referred to in subsection (4).

71. Repayment of salary or remuneration by members.—(1) If a corporation being wound up is unable to pay its debts, and—

(a) any direct or indirect payment of a salary or other remuneration was made by the corporation within a period of two years before the commencement of its winding-up to a member in his capacity as an officer or employee of the corporation; and

(b) such payment was, in the opinion of the Master, not *bona fide* or reasonable in the circumstances,

the Master shall direct that such payment, or such part thereof as he may determine, be repaid by such member to the corporation.

(2) A person who has within a period of two years referred to in subsection (1)(a) ceased to be a member of a corporation referred to in that subsection may, under the circumstances referred to therein, be directed by the Master to make a repayment provided for in subsection (1), if, and to the extent that, any such repayments by present members are, together with all other available assets, insufficient for paying all the debts of the corporation.

(3) The provisions of subsections (4) and (5) of section 70 shall *mutatis mutandis* apply in respect of any repayment to a corporation in terms of subsection (1) or (2).

72. Composition. – (1) In the winding-up of a corporation unable to pay its debts, the members of the corporation may at any time after the first meeting of creditors submit to the liquidator a written offer of composition, signed by the members holding more than 50 per cent of members' interests in the corporation.

(2)(a) The provisions of sections 119, 120, 123 and 124(1) and (5) of the Insolvency Act, 1936 (Act No. 24 of 1936), shall *mutatis mutandis* apply in respect of the procedure and effect of any such composition, and the liquidator's functions thereunder.

(b) For the purposes of paragraph (a), any reference in any provision referred to therein—

(i) to an insolvent or insolvent estate, shall be construed as a reference to the corporation concerned;

    (ii) to a trustee, shall be construed as a reference to the liquidator of the corporation concerned; and

    (iii) to the rehabilitation of an insolvent, shall be construed as a reference to the setting aside of the winding-up of the corporation concerned.

73. Repayments, payments of damages and restoration of property by members and others.—(1) Where in the course of the winding-up of a corporation it appears that any person who has taken part in the formation of the corporation, or any former or present member, officer or accounting officer of the corporation has misapplied or retained or become liable or accountable for any money or property of the corporation, or has been guilty of any breach of trust in relation to the corporation, a Court may, on the application of the Master or of the liquidator or of any creditor or member of the corporation, inquire into the conduct of such person, member, officer or accounting officer and may order him to repay or restore the money or property, or any part thereof, with interest at such rate as the Court considers just, or to contribute such sum to the assets of the corporation by way of compensation or damages in respect of the misapplication, retention or breach of trust, as the Court considers just.

(2) The provisions of subsection (1) shall apply in respect of any person, member, officer or accounting officer referred to therein, notwithstanding the fact that such person may also be criminally responsible in respect of any conduct contemplated therein.

74. Appointment of liquidator.—(1) For the purposes of conducting the proceedings in a winding-up of a corporation, the Master shall appoint a suitable natural person as liquidator.

(2) The Master shall make an appointment as soon as is praticable after a provisional winding-up order has been made, or a copy of a resolution for a voluntary winding-up has been registered in terms of section 67(2).

(3) When the Master in the case of a voluntary winding-up by members makes an appointment, he shall take into consideration any further resolution at a meeting of members nominating a person as liquidator.

(4) In the case of a creditors' voluntary winding-up and a winding-up by the Court, the Master shall, subject to the provisions of section 76, if a person is nominated as co-liquidator at the first meeting of creditors, appoint such person as co-liquidator as soon as he has given security to the satisfaction of the Master for the proper performance of his duties.

75. Vacancies in office of liquidators.—(1) When a vacancy occurs in the office of a liquidator of a corporation, the Master may—

    (*a*) where the vacancy occurs in the office of a liquidator nominated by members or creditors, direct any remaining liquidator to convene a meeting of creditors or members, as the case may be, to nominate a liquidator to fill the vacancy;

    (*b*) in a case other than a case contemplated in paragraph (*a*), if he is of opinion that any remaining liquidator will be able to complete the winding-up, dispense with the appointment of a liquidator to fill the vacancy, and direct the remaining liquidator to complete the winding-up; or

(c) in any other case, appoint a liquidator to fill the vacancy.

(2) The provisions of the Companies Act relating to the nomination or appointment of a liquidator, as applied by section 66 of this Act, and of this Act, shall apply to the nomination or appointment of a liquidator to fill a vacancy in the office of liquidator.

76. Refusal by Master to appoint nominated person as liquidator.—(1) If a person who has been nominated as liquidator by any meeting of creditors or of members of a corporation was not properly nominated, or is disqualified from being nominated or appointed as liquidator pursuant to section 372 or 373 of the Companies Act, as applied by section 66 of this Act, or has failed to give within a period of 21 days as from the date upon which he was notified that the Master had accepted his nomination or within such further period as the Master may allow, the security mentioned in section 375(1) of the Companies Act, as so applied, or, if in the opinion of the Master the person nominated as liquidator should not be appointed as liquidator of the corporation concerned, the Master shall give notice in writing to the person so nominated that he declines to accept his nomination or to appoint him as liquidator, and shall in such notice state his reasons for declining to accept his nomination or to appoint him: Provided that if the Master declines to accept the nomination for appointment as liquidator because he is of the opinion that the person nominated should not be appointed as liquidator, it shall be sufficient if the Master states in that notice, as such reason, that he is of the opinion that the person nominated should not be appointed as liquidator of the corporation concerned.
[Sub-s. (1) amended by s. 14 of Act No. 38 of 1986.]

(2)(a) When the Master has so declined to accept the nomination of any person or to appoint him as liquidator, or when the Minister has under section 371(3) of the Companies Act, as applied by section 66 of this Act, set aside the appointment of a liquidator, the Master shall convene a meeting of creditors or members, as the case may be, of the corporation concerned for the purpose of nominating another person for appointment as liquidator.

(b) In the notice convening any said meeting the Master shall state that he has declined to accept the nomination for appointment as liquidator of the person previously nominated, or to appoint the person so nominated and, subject to the proviso to subsection (1), the reasons therefor, or that the appointment of the person previously appointed as liquidator has so been set aside by the Minister, as the case may be, and that the meetings are convened for the purpose of nominating another person for appointment as liquidator.

(c) The Master shall post a copy of such notice to every creditor whose claim against the company was previously proved and admitted.

(d) Any meeting referred to in paragraph (a) shall be deemed to be a continuation of the relevant first meeting of creditors or of members, or of any such meeting referred to in section 75, as the case may be.

(3) If the Master again so declines for any reason mentioned in subsection (1) to accept the nomination for appointment as liquidator by any meeting referred to in subsection (2), or to appoint a person so nominated—

(a) he shall act in accordance with the provisions of subsection (1); and

(b) if the person so nominated as sole liquidator has not or if all the persons so nominated have not been appointed by him, he shall appoint as liquidator or liquidators of the corporation concerned any other person or persons not disqualified from being liquidator of that corporation.

77. Resignation and absence of liquidator.— (1) At the request of a liquidator the Master may relieve him of his office upon such conditions as the Master may think fit.

(2) A liquidator shall not be absent from the Republic for a period exceeding 60 days, unless—

(a) the Master has before his departure from the Republic granted him permission in writing to be absent; and

(b) he complies with such conditions as the Master may think fit to impose.

(3) Every liquidator who is relieved of his office by the Master, or who is permitted to absent himself for a period exceeding 60 days from the Republic, shall give notice thereof in the *Gazette*.

78. First meeting of creditors and members.—(1) A liquidator shall as soon as may be and, except with the consent of the Master, not later than one month after a final winding-up order has been made by a Court or a resolution of a creditors' voluntary winding-up has been registered—

(a) summon a meeting of the creditors of the corporation for the purpose of—

(i) considering the statement as to the affairs of the corporation lodged with the Master;

(ii) the proving of claims against the corporation;

(iii) deciding whether a co-liquidator should be appointed and, if so, nominating a person for appointment; and

(iv) receiving or obtaining, in a winding-up by the Court or a creditors' voluntary winding-up, directors or authorization in respect of any matter regarding the liquidation; and

(b) summon a meeting of members of the corporation for the purpose of—

(i) considering the said statement as to the affairs of the corporation, unless the meeting of members when passing a resolution for the voluntary winding-up of the corporation has already considered the said statement; and

(ii) receiving or obtaining directions or authorization in respect of any matter regarding the liquidation.

(2)(a) The provisions of the law relating to insolvency in respect of voting, the manner of voting and voting by an agent at meetings of creditors, shall apply *mutatis mutandis* in respect of any meeting referred to in this section: Provided that in a winding-up by the Court a member or former member of a corporation shall have no voting right in respect of the nomination of a liquidator based on his loan account with the corporation or claims for arrear salary, travelling expenses or allowances due by the corporation, or claims paid by such member or former member on behalf of the corporation.

(b) The provisions of paragraph (a) shall *mutatis mutandis* apply in respect of a person to whom a right contemplated in that paragraph has been ceded.

79. Report to creditors and members.—Except in the case of a members' voluntary winding-up, a liquidator shall, as soon as practicable and, except with the consent of the Master, not later than three months after the date of his appointment, submit to a general meeting of creditors and members of the corporation concerned a report as to the following matters:

(a) The estimated amounts of the corporation's assets and liabilities;

(b) if the corporation has failed, the causes of the failure;

(c) whether or not he has submitted or intends to submit to the Master a report under section 400(2) of the Companies Act, as applied by section 66 of this Act;

(d) whether or not any member or former member appears to be liable—

   (i) to the corporation on the ground of breach of trust or negligence;

   (ii) to make repayments to the corporation in terms of section 70(2) or (3) or section 71(1) or (2);

   (iii) to either a creditor of the corporation or the corporation itself, as the case may be, by virtue of any provision of Part VIII of this Act;

(e) any legal proceedings by or against the corporation which may have been pending at the date of the commencement of the winding-up, or which may have been or may be instituted;

(f) whether or not further enquiry is in his opinion desirable in regard to any matter relating to the formation or failure of the corporation or the conduct of its business;

(g) whether or not the corporation has kept the accounting records required by section 56 and, if not, in what respects the requirements of that section have not been complied with;

(h) the progress and prospects in respect of the winding-up; and

(i) any other matter which he may consider fit, or in connection with which he may require the directions of the creditors.

80. Repayments by members or former members.—The liquidator of a corporation unable to pay its debts—

(a) shall ascertain whether members or former members of the corporation are liable in terms of section 70(2) or (3) to make repayments;

(b) shall ascertain whether circumstances justify an approach to the Master for a direction that members or former members of the corporation make repayments in terms of section 71(1) or (2);

(c) may, if necessary, enforce such repayments; and

(d) may, in the event of the death of such member or former member liable for or directed to make a repayment, or of the insolvency of his estate, claim the amount due from the estate concerned.

81. Duties of liquidator regarding liability of members to creditors or corporation.—(1) The liquidator of a corporation unable to pay its debts shall ascertain whether, on the facts reasonably available to him, there is reason to believe that any member or former member of the corporation, or any other person, has by virtue of any provision of Part VIII of this Act incurred any liability to a creditor of the corporation or to the corporation itself, as the case may be.

(2) If the liquidator finds that there is such reason in respect of any creditor who has proved a claim, he shall in writing inform such creditor accordingly, and if the creditor recovers the amount of his claim or part thereof from such member or former member, or from such other person, the liquidator shall take such recovery into account in determining the dividend payable to that creditor.

(3) In particular the liquidator shall determine whether an application to the Court in terms of section 64(1) is justified and advisable.

PART X
PENALTIES AND GENERAL

82. Penalties.—(1) Any corporation or a member or officer of a corporation or any other person convicted of any offence in terms of this Act, shall be liable to be sentenced, in the case of an offence referred to—

(a) in section 52, 56 or 64, to a fine not exceeding R2 000 or imprisonment for a period not exceeding two years, or to both such fine and such imprisonment;

(b) in section 58, to a fine not exceeding R1 000 or imprisonment for a period not exceeding one year, or to both such fine and such imprisonment;

(c) in section 20, 22A, 23 or 47, to a fine not exceeding R500 or imprisonment for a period not exceeding six months, or to both such fine and such imprisonment; and

   [Sub-s. (1)(c) substituted by s. 10 of Act No. 81 of 1992.]

(d) in section 16, 41 or 49, to a fine not exceeding R100 or imprisonment for a period not exceeding three months, or to both such fine and such imprisonment.

(2) The Court convicting any such corporation, member, officer or person for failure to perform any act required to be performed by it or him under this Act, may, in addition to any penalty which the Court imposes, order such corporation, member, officer or person to perform such act within such period as the Court may determine.

(3) Any person who, in respect of any offence under any provision of the Companies Act, or of the Insolvency Act, 1936 (Act No. 24 of 1936), which is made applicable by any provision of this Act, is convicted of any such offence under any such provision as so applied, shall be liable to be sentenced to the penalties which are imposed in respect of any such offence by any applicable provision of the said Companies Act or Insolvency Act, as the case may be.

83. Short title and commencement.—This Act shall be called the Close Corporations Act, 1984, and shall come into operation on a date fixed by the State President by proclamation in the *Gazette*.

PART
4

Regulations and forms

CLOSE CORPORATIONS ACT, 1984
ADMINISTRATIVE REGULATIONS

[NOTE: These regulations were published under Government Notice R.2487 in *Government Gazette* 9503 of 16 November 1984 and amended by Government Notice 540 in *Government Gazette* 10157 of 27 March 1986, Government Notice R.1447 in *Government Gazette* 10807 of 3 July 1987 (as corrected by Government Notice R.1730 in *Government Gazette* 10861 of 14 August 1987) and Government Notice 2098 in *Government Gazette* 11547 of 21 October 1988, Government Notices R.417 in *Government Gazette* 11739 of 10 March 1989, R.602 in *Government Gazette* 11792 of 31 March 1989, R.1392 in *Government Gazette* 11979 of 30 June 1989 and R.1664 in *Government Gazette* 14050 of 19 June 1992.]

No. R.2487   16 November 1984

CLOSE CORPORATIONS ACT, 1984
(ACT 69 OF 1984)

CLOSE CORPORATIONS ADMINISTRATIVE REGULATIONS

I, Kent Diederich Skelton Durr, Deputy Minister of Trade and Industry, hereby, on behalf of the Minister of Trade and Industry, by virtue of the powers vested in him by section 10 of the Close Corporations Act, 1984 (Act 69 of 1984), make the regulations contained in the Schedule.

K.D.S. DURR, Deputy Minister of Trade and Industry.

SCHEDULE

Definitions

1. In these regulations, unless the context otherwise indicates—

"**Act**" means the Close Corporations Act, 1984 (Act 69 of 1984);

"**forms**" means the prescribed forms contemplated in Schedule 4;

"**records**", in relation to a corporation, includes accounting records, books and papers as contemplated in section 56 of the Act.

Documents

2. (1) All documents lodged with the Registration Office, shall, unless the Registrar otherwise directs, be written in block capitals or be typewritten, lithographed or printed in legible characters with deep permanent black ink on one side only of strong white paper approximately 298 millimetres by 207 millimetres in size (international paper size A4): Provided that paper of different sizes and of different colours may be specified for forms to be lodged with the Registrar.

(2) Documents or copies of documents to be transmitted or returned to any corporation or person may, unless the Registrar otherwise directs in any particular case, be carbon copies of originals.

(3) The Registrar may reject any document that in his opinion is unsuitable for record-keeping purposes.

(4) All documents to be lodged with the Registration Office shall be in one of the official languages of the Republic.

(5) A copy of any document in the Registration Office reproduced by microfilm purporting to be certified by the Registrar or an officer or employee contemplated in section 4(3) of the Act shall, without proof of production of the original, upon the mere production thereof in proceedings, whether in a court of law or otherwise, be admissible as evidence in respect of the contents of such document.

(6) All forms to be lodged with the Registration Office shall comply with the printing specifications determined by the Registrar from time to time.

3. All communications to the Registrar may be made, or any document required to be sent or lodged with the Registrar may be transmitted by post or by a member or authorised agent of a corporation: Provided that Forms CK 1, CK 2 and CK 2A if not lodged personally with the Registration Office shall be transmitted by registered or certified post.

4. Any document lodged with the Registration Office in terms of regulation 2(1) may be reproduced by the Registrar by microfilm in accordance with the code of practice of the South African Bureau of Standards for the processing, testing and preservation of silver gelatin microfilm for archival purposes.

Office hours

5. The Registration Office shall be open to the public from 08h30 to 15h30 from Mondays to Fridays except on the following days:

(a) All days that are public holidays in terms of section 1 of the Public Holidays Act, 1952 (Act 5 of 1952), or that have been proclaimed public holidays in terms of section 2 of that Act; and

(b) days of which notice may from time to time be given by means of a placard posted in a conspicuous place at the Registration Office or in such other manner as the Registrar may think fit.

Forms and fees

6. (1) The forms contained in Schedule 4 to these regulations shall be used in all cases to which they apply and shall be modified as directed by the Registrar to meet other cases or as circumstances may require.

(2) The fees to be paid in terms of the Act and these regulations shall be those set out in Schedule 1 to these regulations.

Manner of payment of fees (section 6)

7. (1) Subject to the provisions of section 6(1)(a) and (b) of the Act, fees, additional fees or other moneys payable to the Registrar may, except where otherwise provided in these regulations, be paid to any office of the Receiver of Revenue.

(2) Proof of payment of such fees, additional fees or other moneys shall be affixed to the relevant form or document by means of adhesive paste or glue spread over the entire surface of the reverse side of the document to be affixed.

(3) The date of the payment of fees, additional fees or other moneys referred to in section 6(1) of the Act shall be the date, as the case may be—

(a) on the receipt issued in respect of a payment contemplated in subregulation (1); or

(b) upon which the revenue stamps referred to in paragraph (a) of section 6(1) of the Act are cancelled in accordance with the provisions of that paragraph; or

(c) impressed by means of a date stamp of the Registrar on a document upon which has been impressed a stamp referred to in paragraph (b) of the said section 6(1) or in respect of which a payment was made in a manner contemplated in paragraph (c) of the said section.

8. Fees in relation to inspection or copies of documents may be paid on an account, subject to such conditions as the Registrar may determine.

Inspection and copies of documents (section 5)

9. (1) Any person who applies personally to inspect any document or to obtain a copy of any document kept by the Registrar under the Act shall complete a form provided by the Registration Office.

(2) The prescribed fee for such inspection or copy shall be paid by affixing an uncancelled revenue stamp or a revenue franking machine impression to the form referred to in subregulation (1): Provided that the Registrar may allow such fee to be paid in the manner prescribed in regulation 8.

10. (1) Any person who does not personally inspect a document kept by the Registrar under the Act, or collect a copy thereof, may apply in writing to the Registrar for any information relating to the document or for a copy of such document.

(2) The additional prescribed fee shall be paid in respect of inspection of any documents relating to any one corporation by affixing uncancelled revenue stamps or a revenue franking machine impression to the written application or in the manner prescribed in regulation 7.

(3) In respect of copies of documents relating to any one corporation, the additional fee shall be paid in respect of each document and the provisions of subregulation (2) shall apply *mutatis mutandis*.

11. Any person who, whilst inspecting any document at the Registration Office, knowingly and without the consent of the Registrar—

(a) removes any document from the custody of the Registrar or from the Registration Office;

(b) makes or causes to be made any entry on such document;

(c) destroys or damages any such document; or

(d) alters or causes to be altered any entry on such document,

shall be guilty of an offence and liable on conviction to a fine not exceeding R300 or to imprisonment for a period not exceeding six months or to both such fine and such imprisonment.

12. (1) No person shall have in his possession any writing instrument other than a black lead pencil and a sheet of paper when making an inspection of any document at the Registration Office.

(2) Any person making an inspection of documents at the Registration Office who is knowingly in possession of a writing instrument in contravention of subregulation (1) shall be guilty of an offence and liable on conviction to a fine not exceeding R150 or to imprisonment for a period not exceeding three months or to both such fine and such imprisonment.

Preservation of records

13. (1) Any document lodged with the Registration Office or any microfilm thereof may, with the permission of the director referred to in section 1 of the Archives Act, 1962 (Act 6 of 1962), be transferred to the appropriate archives depot or to any intermediate depot, in accordance with the provisions of section 6 of the last-mentioned Act, or be destroyed, as the case may be.

(2) A corporation may reproduce or cause to be reproduced any record to be kept by it under the Act on microfilm: Provided that any record that may be reproduced on microfilm shall be reproduced in accordance with the code of practice of the South African Bureau of Standards for the processing, testing and preservation of silver gelatin microfilm for archival purposes.

(3) A reproduction of any original record of a corporation on microfilm shall be certified by a member or officer of the corporation to be a true and accurate reproduction of the original of such record and such certificate shall be substantially in the form contained in Schedule 2 to these regualtions.

(4) Any reproduction referred to in subregulations (2) and (3) shall for all purposes be deemed to be the original record of the corporation concerned, and a copy obtained by means of such reproduction and certified by a member or officer of that corporation as a true copy of such reproduction shall be admissible as evidence and shall therefore be as effective in law as if it were the original of the record concerned.

(5) A corporation shall, in accordance with the code of practice of the South African Bureau of Standards referred to in subregulation (2), take the necessary steps to ensure the safe preservation of any microfilm on which any record of the corporation has been reproduced.

Retention of records

14. (1) The minimum period of retention of any record that has to be kept by a corporation under the Act shall be the period specified in Schedule 3 to these regulations and such period shall, where applicable, run from the date of a particular record or the date of the last entry in a particular record referred to in the said Schedule.

(2) Notwithstanding the provisions of subregulation (1), the original of any record of a corporation that has been reproduced on microfilm and duly certified in terms of regulation 13(3) may be destroyed after a period of three years from the date on which the record concerned was so reproduced.

Reservation of name

14A. (1) The Registrar may, on written application on the prescribed form and on payment of the prescribed fee, reserve a name (approved by him) or literal translation into another official language of the Republic of a name of a corporation or a shortened form of the name or name so translated of a corporation, pending the registration of a founding statement or amended founding statement.

(2) A reservation referred to in subregulation (1), shall be valid for a period not exceeding two months.

(3) An application for reservation referred to in subregulation (1) shall consist of Form CK 7.

(4) The provisions of regulation 15(3) shall apply *mutatis mutandis* to the proof of payment of the appropriate prescribed fee in respect of Form CK 7.

[Regulation 14A inserted by Government Notice 2098 of 1988.]

Registration of founding statement (sections 12 and 13)

15. (1) The founding statement of a corporation shall consist of Form CK 1.

(2) The original and two copies of Form CK 1 shall be lodged for the registration and incorporation of a corporation.

(3) Proof of payment of the prescribed fee in terms of section 13 of the Act shall be affixed to the original Form CK 1 in the following manner:

(a) If payment has been made in accordance with regulation 7(1), in the manner prescribed in regulation 7(2); or

(b) if payment is made in accordance with section 6(1)(a) or (b) of the Act, by affixing the revenue stamps or impressing the stamp, as the case may be, on such form in the space provided.

(4) The written consent of the accounting officer to his appointment in that capacity shall be attached to Form CK 1.

[Subregulation (4) added by Government Notice R.1447 of 1987.]

(5) Form CK 7 containing particulars of the name reserved for the corporation, as approved by the Registrar, together with such other Forms CK 7, if any, containing particulars of the translated name and of the shortened form of the name or translated name, for the corporation, as approved by the Registrar shall, if applicable, be attached to Form CK 1.

[Subregulation (5) added by Government Notice 2098 of 1988.]

Registration of amended founding statement (section 15)

16. (1) An amended founding statement to be lodged in accordance with section 15 of the Act shall consist of Forms CK 2 and CK 2A.

(2) The original and two copies of Forms CK 2 and CK 2A shall be lodged for registration.

(3) The provisions of regulation 15(3) shall apply *mutatis mutandis* to the proof of payment of the appropriate prescribed fee in respect of Form CK 2.

(4) An amended founding statement shall be completed in full, even in respect of particulars which have not or are not going to be changed.

(5) If a new accounting officer is appointed his written consent to such appointment shall be attached to Form CK 2.

[Subregulation (5) added by Government Notice R.1447 of 1987.]

(6) If the name or translated name of a corporation or the shortened form of the corporation's name or translated name is to be changed, the Form CK 7 containing the new name of the corporation as approved by the Registrar, together with such other Forms CK 7, as the case may be, containing the new translated name or the shortened form of the corporation's name or translated name as approved by the Registrar shall, if applicable, be attached to Form CK 2.

[Subregulation (6) added by Government Notice 2098 of 1988.]

Conversion of companies into corporations (section 27)

17. (1) The following documents shall be lodged for the conversion of a company into a corporation:

(a) The original and one copy of Form CK 4:

(b) the written statement by the auditor of the company contemplated in section 27(2)(b) of the Act; and

(c) the original and two copies of Form CK 1.

(2) The provisions of regulation 15(3) shall apply *mutatis mutandis* to the proof of payment of the appropriate prescribed fee in respect of Form CK 1.

Restoration of the registration of a corporation (section 26(6))

18. (1) An application for the restoration of the registration of a corporation shall consist of Form CK 3.

(2) The following documents shall be lodged by an interested person applying for the restoration of the registration of a corporation:

(a) The original and one copy of Form CK 3; and

(b) the original and two copies of Forms CK 2 and CK 2A, if a change in respect of the matters particulars of which were stated in the founding statement in force at the time of the deregistration of the corporation has taken place or is going to take place with the restoration of the registration of the corporation.

(3) The provisions of regulation 15(3) shall apply *mutatis mutandis* to the proof of payment of the appropriate prescribed fee in respect of Forms CK 2 and CK 3.

Order of court for the alteration of or addition to a founding statement (section 49 (4))

19. (1) The following documents shall be lodged with the Registrar for registration if, in terms of section 49(4) of the Act an order of court alters or adds to a founding statement:

(a) A copy of the order of court under cover of Form CK 5; and

(b) the original and two copies of Forms CK 2 and CK 2A.

(2) The provisions of regulation 15(3) shall apply *mutatis mutandis* to the proof of payment of the appropriate prescribed fee in respect of Forms CK 2 and CK 5.

Voluntary winding-up (section 67)

20. (1) The original and one copy of Form CK 6 shall be lodged for registration if a corporation resolves in terms of section 67 of the Act that the corporation should be wound up voluntarily by members or creditors.

(2) The provisions of regulation 15(3) shall apply *mutatis mutandis* to the proof of payment of the appropriate prescribed fee in respect of Form CK 6.

Accounting officer

21. Any person who is a member of a profession whose members are qualified to perform the duties of an accounting officer in terms of section 60 of the Act and who signs any documents of or in respect of a corporation in his capacity as accounting officer of such corporation, shall state the name of the said profession of which he is a member beneath his signature.

Reporting by accounting officer

21A. If an accounting officer has in terms of section 62(3)(ii) or (iii) of the Act reported to the Registrar that the annual financial statements of the corporation concerned indicate that as at the end of the financial year concerned the corporation's liabilities exceed its assets or that the annual financial statements incorrectly indicate that as at the end of the financial year concerned the assets of the corporation exceed its liabilities, or that he has reason to believe that such an incorrect indication is given, and he finds that any subsequent financial statements indicate that the situation has changed or has been rectified and that the assets concerned then exceed the liabilities or that they no longer incorrectly indicate that the assets exceed the liabilities or that he no longer has reason to believe that such an incorrect indication is given, as the case may be, he may report accordingly to the Registrar.
[Regulation 21A inserted by Government Notice R.1447 of 1987.]

Lodging of additional copy of certain prescribed forms

22. (1) The Registrar may from time to time by written notice sent to a corporation or an officer thereof at the registered office or postal address of the corporation require the corporation or the officer thereof to lodge with him within a period stated in the notice, which shall not be less than 30 days, a copy of the prescribed Form CK 1, CK 2 or CK 2A by which the corporation gave notice in terms of section 12(c) of the Act of the situation of the corporation's registered office and of its postal address in force at the time of the lodging of that form.

(2) No fee shall be payable to the Registrar on the lodging of the copy referred to in subregulation (1).

(3) A corporation or the officer thereof to whom a notice referred to in sub-regulation (1) was sent and who failed to lodge or remained in default of lodging the copy required in that notice within the period stated in the notice shall be guilty of an offence and upon conviction liable to a fine of R100.

Standing advisory committee (section 11)

23. Where recommendations or submissions are made for the consideration of the standing advisory committee on company law contemplated in section 11 of the Act, 25 copies of each letter or memorandum shall be lodged with the Registrar of Close Corporations, P.O. Box 429, Pretoria, 0001.

Commencement

24. These regulations shall come into operation on 1 January 1985.

SCHEDULE 1

[Schedule 1 as last substituted by Government Notice R.417 of 10 March 1989.]

The following fees shall be payable under the Act and these Regulations. Payment shall be made as prescribed by Regulations 7 and 8:

Item	Service	Fees payable (R)	Corresponding form (if any)
1	Inspection of a corporation file in the Registration Office—		
	(a) personally by applicant	5,00	H191
	(b) on the written request of an applicant (* includes up to 12 photocopies of documents, thereafter R0,50 per copy — certification excluded)	10,00*	H191
2	(a) Photocopy of a document, approximately 298 mm by 210 mm in size or smaller (per copy)	0,50	H191
	(b) Photocopy on paper reproduced from microfilm (per copy)	0,50	H191
	(c) Photocopy on diazo reproduced from microfilm (per copy)	1,00	H191
3	Certification of a document or part of a document (per document)	5,00	H191
4	Issuing of a typed certificate in respect of the contents of a form or other document or part thereof	20,00	H191
5	Consideration of an objection to a name	300,00	–
6	Registration of a founding statement	100,00	CK1
7	Registration of an amended founding statement	30,00	CK2
8	Restoration of the registration of a corporation	150,00	CK3
9	Registration of an order of the Court	30,00	CK5
10	Registration of a resolution to wind up voluntarily	40,00	CK6
11	Reservation of name or a translated name or an abbreviated name	50,00	CK7

SCHEDULE 2
REPUBLIC OF SOUTH AFRICA
CLOSE CORPORATIONS ADMINISTRATIVE REGULATIONS
CERTIFICATE OF AUTHENTICITY BY MEMBER OR OFFICER OF
CLOSE CORPORATION
[Regulation 13(3)]

Microfilm Record No ....

Name of close corporation ....

....

Date ....

This is to certify that the microfilm record identified above is a true and accurate reproduction of the following category of original records of the above close corporation:

(List category of records)

....
Signature: Member/Officer

SCHEDULE 3

RETENTION PERIODS OF CORPORATION RECORDS

Item	Records	Retention period
1.	Founding statement (Form CK 1)	Indefinite.
2.	Amended founding statement (Forms CK 2 and CK 2A)	Indefinite.
3.	Minutes book as well as resolutions passed at meetings	Indefinite.
4.	Annual financial statements, including annual accounts and the report of the accounting officer	15 years
5.	Accounting records, including supporting schedules to accounting records and ancillary accounting records	15 years
6.	The microfilm image of any original record reproduced directly by the camera — the "camera master"	Indefinite.

BYLAE 4

Vorms CK 1 en CK 2 vervang by Goewermentskennisgewing R.1447 van 1987 soos verbeter by Goewermentskennisgewing R.1730 van 1987. Vorm CK 7 bygevoeg by Goewermentskennisgewing 2098 van 1988. Vorms CK 1, 2, 3, 5, 6 & 7 vervang by Goewermentskennisgewings R.602 en R.1392 van 1989. Vorms CK 1 en CK 2 vervang by Goewermentskennisgewing R.1664 van 1992. Vorm CK 2A bygevoeg by Goewermentskennisgewing R.1664 van 1992.

Forms CK 1 and CK 2 substituted by Government Notice R.1447 of 1987 as corrected by Government Notice R.1730 of 1987. Form CK 7 added by Government Notice 2098 of 1988. Forms CK 1, 2, 3, 5, 6 & 7 substituted by Government Notices R.602 and R.1392 of 1989. Forms CK 1 and CK 2 substituted by Government Notice R.1664 of 1992. Form CK 2A added by Government Notice R.1664 of 1992.

CLOSE CORPORATIONS ACT, 1984 — CK 1

Sections 12, 13, 14, 24, 27, 29, 47 and 60
Regulations 2, 5 and 17

Founding Statement

To be lodged in triplicate

Before filling in the form, first take note of the notes on the reverse side of page 2. Complete page 1 in one language only.

Affix Revenue Stamp or impress revenue franking machine impression here R100	REGISTRATION NUMBER OF CORPORATION	

Full name of corporation _____

Literal translation of name (if applicable) _____

Shortened form of name (if applicable) _____

Description of principal business _____

Number of members _____

Date of end of financial year _____

Aggregate members' contribution R ____

Postal address _____

Address of registered office (not post office box) _____

Name and postal address of accounting officer _____

Attach written consent to appointment

Full name of recognised profession of accounting officer _____

Membership/practice No _____

CERTIFICATE OF INCORPORATION
The founding statement has been registered and the corporation has been incorporated on

The above-named corporation has been converted from company: _____

_____ (Reg No _____)

	Data Processing
	Classification
	Recorded
REGISTRAR OF CLOSE CORPORATIONS DATE	Initials and date

CK 1

NAAM VAN KORPORASIE
NAME OF CORPORATION _____

_____

REGISTRASIENOMMER **REGISTRATION NUMBER**	

LEDE/MEMBERS

Ek/Ons* die lid/lede* wie se naam/name* op hierdie stigtingsverklaring aangeteken is, beves-
tig deur my/ons* handtekening(e)*/die handtekening(e)* van my/ons* gevolmagtigde(s)*
hiertoe dat die besonderhede hierin vervat, korrek is en versoek die inlywing van die korporasie (volmag aangeheg indien van toepassing).
*Skrap wat nie van toepassing is nie.

I/We* the members(s)* whose name(s)* is/are* recorded on this founding statement, confirm by my/our* signature(s)*/the signature(s)* of my/our* proxy(ies)* hereto that the particulars stated herein are correct and request the registration of the corporation (power
of attorney attached if applicable).
*Delete which is not applicable.

VIR SLEUTEL TOT BESONDERHEDE, KYK NOTA 6 OP KEERSY VAN BLADSY 2
FOR KEY TO PARTICULARS SEE NOTE 6 ON REVERSE SIDE OF PAGE 2

1	(a)		1	(a)
	(b)			(b)
2	(i)		2	(i)
2	(ii)	3 %	2	(ii)	3 %
4	R		4	R
5			5	
6			6	
7	8		7	8

1	(a)		1	(a)
	(b)			(b)
2	(i)		2	(i)
2	(ii)	3 %	2	(ii)	3 %
4	R		4	R
5			5	
6			6	
7	8		7	8

NOTAS/**NOTES**

1. Vorm CK 1 moet in blokhoofletters geskryf wees of getik, steengedruk of gedruk wees in leesbare letters met swaar vaste swart ink, en in drievoud ingedien word.
   Form CK 1 must be written in block capitals or be typewritten, lithographed or printed in legible characters with deep permanent black ink, and lodged in triplicate.

2. Vorm CK 1 wat nie aan die vereistes van die Wet, regulasies of hierdie notas voldoen nie, sal verwerp word.
   Form CK 1 which does not comply with the requirements of the Act, regulations or these notes, will be rejected.

3. Waar 'n persoon namens 'n lid teken, moet volmag aangeheg word.
   Where a person signs on behalf of a member, power of attorney must be attached.

4. Minderjarige kinders en ander handelingsonbevoegde persone moet deur hulle ouers, voogde of verteenwoordigers, na gelang van die geval, bygestaan word en die hoedanigheid moet vermeld word.
   Minor children and other persons under legal disability must be assisted by their parents, guardians or representatives as the case may be, and the capacity must be stated.

5. Indien geen identiteitsdokument uitgereik is nie, moet 'n skriftelike verklaring tot dien effekte aangeheg word.
   If no identity document has been issued, a written statement to this effect must be attached.

6. Besonderhede wat onder die opskrif "LEDE" verstrek moet word:
   Particulars to be furnished under the heading "MEMBERS":

   (1) (a) Van. (Indien regspersoon, meld naam en hoedanigheid en indien trustee, meld ook naam en besonderhede van testamentêre trust en indien 'n lid nomine officii as administrateur, eksekuteur, kurator, ens. optree, meld hoedanigheid.)
   (a) Surname. (If juristic person, mention name and capacity and if trustee, also mention name and particulars of testamentary trust and if acting nomine officii as trustee, administrator, executor, curator, etc. state capacity.)
   (b) Volle voorname/**Full forenames.**

   (2) Identiteitsnommer. ((i) Indien geen identiteitsdokument uitgereik is nie, verstrek geboortedatum en sien par. 5 hierbo.) ((ii) Indien regspersoon, meld registrasienommer.)
   Identity number. ((i) If no identity document has been issued, state date of birth and see par. 5 above.) ((ii) If juristic person, mention registration number.)

   (3) Grootte van belang uitgedruk as 'n persentasie.
   Size of interest expressed as a percentage.

   (4) Besonderhede van bydrae en billike geldwaarde daarvan (indien van toepassing).
   Particulars of contribution and fair monetary value thereof (if applicable).

   (5) Woonadres/**Residential address.**

   (6) Posadres/**Postal address.**

   (7) Handtekening van lid of verteenwoordiger (waar van toepassing).
   Signature of member or representative (where applicable).

   (8) Datum onderteken.
   Date of signature.

7. Indien daar 4 of minder lede is, moet bladsye 1 en 2 voltooi word. Bladsy 3 moet slegs voltooi word indien daar meer as 4 lede is.
   If there are 4 or less members, pages 1 and 2 only need be completed. Page 3 need only be completed if there are more than 4 members.

CK 1

NAAM VAN KORPORASIE
NAME OF CORPORATION _____

_____

REGISTRASIENOMMER **REGISTRATION NUMBER**	

LW: Hierdie bladsy moet slegs voltooi word indien die korporasie meer as 4 lede het.
NB: This page should only be completed if the corporation has more than 4 members.

LEDE (VERVOLG)/**MEMBERS (CONTINUED)**

1	(a)		1	(a)
	(b)			(b)
2	(i)		2	(i)
2	(ii)	3 %	2	(ii)	3 %
4		R	4		R
5			5	
6			6	
7		8	7		8

1	(a)		1	(a)
	(b)			(b)
2	(i)		2	(i)
2	(ii)	3 %	2	(ii)	3 %
4		R	4		R
5			5	
6			6	
7		8	7		8

1	(a)			
	(b)			
2	(i) ||||||||||||||
2	(ii)		3	%
4			R	
5				
6				
7			8	

1	(a)			
	(b)			
2	(i) ||||||||||||||
2	(ii)		3	%
4			R	
5				
6				
7			8	

CLOSE CORPORATIONS ACT, 1984

CK 2

Sections 13, 15, 24, 29, 47 and 60/Regulations 2 and 16

Amended Founding Statement

To be lodged in triplicate

Before completing the form, first take note of the notes on reverse side of page 2. Complete page 1 in one language only.

REGISTRATION NUMBER OF CORPORATION	CK / /23	Affix Revenue Stamp or impress revenue franking machine impression here

	R30.00 payable in respect of changes in particulars in Part A only.	Date of commencement of change

PART A

Full name of corporation _____

Previous name of corporation (if applicable) _____

Literal translation of name (if applicable) _____

Shortened form of name (if applicable) _____

Description of principal business _____

Date of end of financial year _____

Date of original incorporation _____

Number of members _____

Aggregate members' contribution   R _____

NOTE: For changes in particulars of accounting officer, postal address and registered office see Note 9 on reverse side of page 2.

PART B

MEMBERS

I/We* the member(s)* whose name(s)* is/are* recorded on this founding statement, confirm by my/our* signature(s)*/the signature(s)* of my/our* proxy(ies)* hereto that the particulars stated herein are correct and request the registration of the amended founding statement (power of attorney attached if applicable).
*Delete which is not applicable.

Amended Founding Statement registered	Data Processing Classification _____ Recorded Initials and date _____
REGISTRAR OF CLOSE CORPORATIONS DATE	

CK 2

NAAM VAN KORPORASIE
NAME OF CORPORATION _____

_____

| REGISTRASIENOMMER **REGISTRATION NUMBER** | CK / | /23 |

VIR SLEUTEL TOT BESONDERHEDE, KYK NOTA 10 OP KEERSY VAN BLADSY 2
FOR KEY TO PARTICULARS SEE NOTE 10 ON REVERSE SIDE OF PAGE 2

NOTAS/NOTES

1. Vorm CK 2 moet in blokhoofletters geskryf wees of getik, steengedruk of gedruk wees in leesbare letters met swaar vaste swart ink, en in drievoud ingedien word.
   Form CK 2 must be written in block capitals or be typewritten, lithographed or printed in legible characters with deep permanent black ink, and lodged in triplicate.

2. Vorm CK 2 wat nie aan die vereistes van die Wet, regulasies of hierdie notas voldoen nie, sal verwerp word.
   Form CK 2 which does not comply with the requirements of the Act, regulations or these notes, will be rejected.

3. Geen geld is betaalbaar ten opsigte van veranderings in besonderhede onder DEEL B nie.
   No fee is payable in respect of any changes in particulars under PART B.

4. Besonderhede wat nie verander nie, moet ook verstrek word.
   Particulars which do not change should also be furnished.

5. Verandering(s) van krag vanaf die datum van registrasie of op datum aangedui.
   Change(s) effective from date of registration or upon date indicated.

6. Waar 'n persoon namens 'n lid teken, moet volmag aangeheg word.
   Where a person signs on behalf of a member, power of attorney must be attached.

7. Minderjarige kinders en ander handelingsonbevoegde persone moet deur hulle ouers, voogde of verteenwoordigers, na gelang van die geval, bygestaan word en die hoedanigheid moet vermeld word.
   Minor children and other persons under legal disability must be assisted by their parents, guardians or representatives as the case may be, and the capacity must be stated.

8. Indien geen identiteitsdokument uitgereik is nie, moet 'n skriftelike verklaring tot dien effekte aangeheg word.
   If no identity document has been issued, a written statement to this effect must be attached.

9. Vorm CK 2A moet vir registrasie ingedien word indien veranderings plaasvind in die besonderhede van die rekeningkundige beampte, sy adres, die posadres van die korporasie en die ligging van sy geregistreerde kantoor.
   Form CK 2A should be lodged for registration if changes occur in the particulars of the accounting officer, his address, the postal address of the corporation and the situation of its registered office.

10. Besonderhede wat onder die opskrif "LEDE" verstrek moet word:
    Particulars to be furnished under the heading "MEMBERS":

    (1) (a) Van. (Indien regspersoon, meld naam en hoedanigheid en indien trustee, meld ook naam en besonderhede van testamentêre trust en indien 'n lid nomine officii as administrateur, eksekuteur, kurator ens. optree, meld hoedanigheid.)

    (a) **Surname. If juristic person, mention name and capacity and if trustee, also mention name and particulars of testamentary trust and if acting nomine officii as trustee, administrator, executor, curator, etc. state capacity.)**

    (b) Volle voorname/**Full forenames.**

    (2) Identiteitsnommer. ((i) Indien geen identiteitsdokument uitgereik is nie, verstrek geboortedatum en sien par. 8 hierbo.) ((ii) Indien regspersoon, meld registrasienommer.)
    Identity number. ((i) If no identity document has been issued, state date of birth and see par. 8 above.) ((ii) If juristic person, mention registration number.)

    (3) Grootte van belang uitgedruk as 'n persentasie.
    Size of interest expressed as a percentage.

    (4) Besonderhede van bydrae en billike geldwaarde daarvan (indien van toepassing).
    Particulars of contribution and fair monetary value thereof (if applicable).

(5) Woonadres/**Residential address.**

(6) Posadres/**Postal address.**

(7) Handtekening van lid of verteenwoordiger (waar van toepassing) en datum onderteken.
Signature of member or representative (where applicable) and date signed.

(8) Datum van verandering met aanduiding van item 1 – 6 wat verander.
Date of change with indication of item 1 – 6 which changes.

LW: Indien daar 4 of minder lede is moet bladsye 1 en 2 voltooi word. Bladsy 3 moet slegs voltooi word indien daar meer as 4 lede is.

NB: If there are 4 or less members pages 1 and 2 only need be completed. Page 3 need only be completed if there are more than 4 members.

CK 2

NAAM VAN KORPORASIE
NAME OF CORPORATION _____

_____

| REGISTRASIENOMMER
REGISTRATION NUMBER | CK | / | /23 |

LEDE (VERVOLG)/**MEMBERS (CONTINUED)**

1	(a)
	(b)

2	(i)	

| 2 | (ii) | 3 | % |

4	R

5	
6	
7	

8	1	2	3
	4	5	6

1	(a)
	(b)

2	(i)	

| 2 | (ii) | 3 | % |

4	R

5	
6	
7	

8	1	2	3
	4	5	6

1	(a)
	(b)

2	(i)	

| 2 | (ii) | 3 | % |

4	R

5	
6	
7	

8	1	2	3
	4	5	6

1	(a)
	(b)

2	(i)	

| 2 | (ii) | 3 | % |

4	R

5	
6	
7	

8	1	2	3
	4	5	6

1	(a)						
	(b)						
2	(i)						
2	(ii)			3			%
4				R			
5							
6							
7							
8	1		2		3		
	4		5		6		

1	(a)						
	(b)						
2	(i)						
2	(ii)			3			%
4				R			
5							
6							
7							
8	1		2		3		
	4		5		6		

CK 2

NAAM VAN KORPORASIE
NAME OF CORPORATION _____

REGISTRASIENOMMER **REGISTRATION NUMBER**	CK	/	/23

PERSONE WAT OPHOU OM LID TE WEES/**PERSONS WHO CEASE TO BE MEMBERS**

Volle naam en van van lid **Full name and surname of member**	Identiteitsnommer **Identity number**	Handtekening **Signature**

Lidmaatskap eindig op die datum van registrasie van die Gewysigde Stigtingsverklaring.
Membership ceases on the date of registration of the Amended Founding Statement.

WET OP BESLOTE KORPORASIES, 1984 **CK 2A**
CLOSE CORPORATIONS ACT, 1984
(Artikels 13, 15 en 60/Sections 13, 15 and 60)
(Regulasies 2 en 16/Regulations 2 and 16)

Gewysigde Stigtingsverklaring ten opsigte van Rekeningkundige Beampte en Adresse
Amended Founding Statement in respect of Accounting Officer and Addresses

Kennisgewing van aanstelling en verandering van naam en adres van rekeningkundige beampte en besonderhede van posadres en geregistreerde kantoor van korporasie/ **Notice of appointment and change of name and address of accounting officer and particulars of postal address and registered office of corporation**

(Moet in drievoud ingedien word/**To be lodged in triplicate**)

Voor voltooiing van die vorm, let op notas op keersy/**Before completing the form, take note of notes on reverse side**

REGISTRASIENOMMER VAN KORPORASIE **REGISTRATION NUMBER OF CORPORATION**	CK / /23

Volle naam van korporasie
Full name of corporation _____

DEEL 1/**PART 1** (Moet voltooi word/**To be completed**)

REKENINGKUNDIGE BEAMPTE/**ACCOUNTING OFFICER**

1. Naam en posadres van rekeningkundige beampte/nuwe rekeningkundige beampte*
Name and postal address of accounting officer/new accounting officer* _____

(Heg skriftelike toestemming tot aanstelling aan/**Attach written consent to appointment**)

Volle naam van erkende professie van rekeningkundige beampte
Full name of recognised profession of accounting officer _____

Lid/praktyknr
_____ **Membership/practice No** _____

2. Die rekeningkundige beampte het met ingang van
The accounting officer has with effect from _____

sy adres verander na
changed his address to _____

3. Die rekeningkundige beampte,
The accounting officer, _____

het met ingang van   sy naam verander en sal voortaan
has with effect from _____ **changed his name and will in**

bekend staan as
future be known as _____

*Skrap wat nie van toepassing is nie/**Delete which is not applicable**

Geteken deur of namens elke lid (in die geval van die aanstelling van nuwe rekeningkundige beampte
Signed by or on behalf of every member (in the case of the appointment of a new accounting officer)

_____

Geteken deur rekeningkundige beampte (in die geval van 2 en 3 hierbo)
Signed by accounting officer (in the case of 2 and 3 above) _____

NOTAS/NOTES

1. Vorm CK 2A moet in blokhoofletters geskryf wees of getik, steengedruk of gedruk wees in leesbare letters met swaar vaste swart ink, en in drievoud ingedien word.
   Form CK 2A must be written in block capitals or be typewritten, lithographed or printed in legible characters with deep permanent black ink, and lodged in triplicate.

2. Verandering(s) van krag vanaf die datum van registrasie of op 'n latere datum genoem.
   Change(s) effective from date of registration or upon a later date mentioned.

3. Waar 'n persoon anders as die rekeningkundige beampte namens 'n lid teken, moet volmag aangeheg word.
   Where a person other than the accounting officer signs on behalf of a member, power of attorney must be attached.

4. Besonderhede wat nie verander nie, moet ook verstrek word.
   Particulars which do not change should also be furnished.

5. Vorm CK 2A wat nie aan die vereistes van die Wet, regulasies of hierdie notas voldoen nie, sal verwerp word.
   Form CK 2A which does not comply with the requirements of the Act, regulations or these notes, will be rejected.

CK 2A

NAAM VAN KORPORASIE
NAME OF CORPORATION _____

REGISTRASIENOMMER REGISTRATION NUMBER	CK	/	/23

DEEL 2/**PART 2** (Moet voltooi word/**To be completed**)
ADRESSE/**ADDRESSES**

Die posadres en die ligging van die geregistreerde kantoor van die korporasie het/gaan verander*
The postal address and the situation of the registered office of the corporation have/will be changed*

(i) Posadres:
   Postal address: _____

   _____

(ii) Adres van geregistreerde kantoor (nie posbus nie):
   Address of registered office (not post office box): _____

   _____

Datum van verandering
Date of change _____

Geteken deur of namens elke lid
Signed by or on behalf of each member _____

Datum
Date _____

OF/**OR**

Deur die rekeningkundige beampte wat soos volg sertifiseer:
By the accounting officer who certifies as follows:

Ek
I _____

die behoorlik aangestelde rekeningkundige beampte van die korporasie
the duly appointed accounting officer of the corporation

sertifiseer dat die korporasie die wysigings in hierdie Deel aangedui,
certify that the corporation has approved the amendments indicated in this Part

goedgekeur het en dat ek gemagtig is om namens die korporasie kennis van die wysigings te gee.
and that I am authorised to give notice of the amendments on behalf of the corporation.

Handtekening van rekeningkundige beampte
Signature of accounting officer _____

Datum
Date _____

*Skrap wat nie van toepassing is nie/**Delete which is not applicable**

Alle veranderings geregistreer op
All changes registered on _____

REGISTRATEUR VAN BESLOTE KORPORASIES   DATUM
REGISTRAR OF CLOSE CORPORATIONS   **DATE**

CLOSE CORPORATIONS ACT, 1984
WET OP BESLOTE KORPORASIES, 1984

(Section 26(6) / Artikel 26(6))

CK 3

Application for the Restoration of the Registration of the Corporation
Aansoek om die Herstel van die Registrasie van die Korporasie

(To be lodged in duplicate / Moet in tweevoud ingedien word)

REGISTRATION NUMBER REGISTRASIENOMMER	Affix revenue stamp or impress revenue franking machine impression here R150 Plak inkomsteseël of plaas inkomstefrankeermasjienstempel hier

Full name of corporation
Volle naam van korporasie _____

_____

I/We,
Ek/Ons, _____

in my/our capacity/ies as
in my/ons hoedanigheid/hoedanighede as _____

_____

apply in terms of section 26(6) of the above-named Act for the restoration of the registration
doen ingevolge artikel 26(6) van bovermelde Wet aansoek om die herstel van die registrasie
of the corporation which was deregistered on
van die korporasie wat op _____
and of which notice was given in Government Gazette
gederegistreer is en waarvan kennis in Staatskoerant _____
of
van _____ , for the following reasons:
gegee is, en wel om die volgende redes:

_____

_____

_____

An amended founding statement, if necessary, is attached. / **'n Gewysigde stigtingsverklaring, indien nodig, gaan hierby.**
SIGNED
GETEKEN _____ DATE
DATUM _____

The registration of the corporation has been restored with effect from
Die registrasie van die korporasie is herstel met ingang van _____
as published in Government Gazette   of
soos gepubliseer in Staatskoerant _____ **van** _____

_____

REGISTRAR OF CLOSE CORPORATIONS   DATE
REGISTRATEUR VAN BESLOTE KORPORASIES   **DATUM**

(To be completed by corporation /
Moet deur korporasie ingevul word)

NAME
NAAM _____

POSTAL ADDRESS
POSADRES _____

_____

Office use / **Kantoorgebruik**
Data processing / **Dataverwerking**
(1) Recorded/**Opgeneem** Date and initials/ Datum en paraaf _____
(2) Corrections/**Regstelling** Date and initials/ Datum en paraaf _____

Printing specifications obtainable from the Registrar /
Drukspesifikasies verkrygbaar van die Registrateur.

CLOSE CORPORATIONS ACT, 1984
WET OP BESLOTE KORPORASIES, 1984
(Section 27 / Artikel 27)

CK 4

Application for Conversion / Aansoek om Omskepping
(To be lodged in duplicate / Moet in tweevoud ingedien word)

REGISTRATION NUMBER OF COMPANY REGISTRASIENOMMER VAN MAATSKAPPY	

Name of company
Naam van maatskappy _____

I/We, the undersigned, being all the members of the above-named company, apply for the conversion of this company into a corporation.
Ek/Ons, die ondergetekendes, synde al die lede van bogenoemde maatskappy, doen aansoek om die omskepping van hierdie maatskappy in 'n korporasie.

I/We state that—
Ek/Ons verklaar dat—

(a) every member of the company will become a member of the corporation; and
    elke lid van die maatskappy 'n lid van die korporasie sal word; en

(b) upon conversion the assets of the corporation, fairly valued, will exceed its liabilities, and that after conversion the corporation will be able to pay its debts as they become due in the ordinary course of its business.
    by omskepping die bates van die korporasie, billik gewaardeer, sy laste sal oorskry en dat na omskepping die korporasie in staat sal wees om sy skulde soos hulle in die gewone loop van sy besigheid verskuldig raak, te betaal.

The following documents are lodged herewith:
Die volgende dokumente word hierby ingedien:

(a) A statement in writing by the auditor as required by section 27(2)(b) of the Act; and
    'n Skriftelike verklaring deur die ouditeur soos vereis by artikel 27(2)(b) van die Wet; en

(b) a founding statement in terms of section 12 of the Act.
    'n stigtingsverklaring ooreenkomstig artikel 12 van die Wet.

SIGNATURE(S) / HANDTEKENING(E)   DATE(S) / DATUM(S)

_____   _____

_____   _____

_____   _____

_____   _____

_____   _____

_____   _____

_____   _____

NEW REGISTRATION NUMBER NUWE REGISTRASIENOMMER	

Printing specifications obtainable from the Registrar / Drukspesifikasies verkrygbaar by die Registrateur.

247

WET OP BESLOTE KORPORASIES, 1984   CK 5
CLOSE CORPORATIONS ACT, 1984
(Artikel 49(4)/Section 49(4))

Indiening van Hofbevel vir die Verandering van*/Vervanging van*/ Toevoeging tot* 'n Stigtingsverklaring
Lodging of Order of Court for the Alteration of*/Replacement of*/ Addition to* a Founding Statement

(Moet in tweevoud ingedien word/To be lodged in duplicate)

REGISTRASIENOMMER **REGISTRATION NUMBER**	Plak inkomsteseël of plaas inkomstefrankeermasjienstempel hier **R30** Affix revenue stamp or impress revenue franking machine impression here

Volle naam van korporasie
Full name of corporation _____

_____

Hofbevel vir die verandering van*/vervanging van*/toevoeging tot* 'n stigtingsverklaring
Order of Court for the alteration of*/replacement of*/addition to* a founding statement

gedateer
dated _____

word hierby ingedien.
is lodged herewith.

'n Gewysigde stigtingsverklaring gaan hierby.
An amended founding statement is attached.

GETEKEN
SIGNED _____

DATUM
DATE _____

*Skrap wat nie van toepassing is nie/ *Delete that which is not applicable.

Die bevel is geregistreer op/**The order was registered on** _____

REGISTRATEUR VAN BESLOTE KORPORASIES
REGISTRAR OF CLOSE CORPORATIONS

DATUM
DATE

(Moet deur korporasie ingevul word/To be completed by corporation)

NAAM
NAME _____

POSADRES
POSTAL ADDRESS _____

_____

_____

Drukspesifikasies verkrygbaar van die Registrateur/Printing specifications obtainable from the Registrar.

CLOSE CORPORATIONS ACT, 1984 CK 6
WET OP BESLOTE KORPORASIES, 1984
(Section 67 / Artikel 67)

Resolution: Voluntary Liquidation/Besluit: Vrywillige Likwidasie

(To be lodged in duplicate/ **Moet in tweevoud ingedien word**)

REGISTRATION NUMBER **REGISTRASIENOMMER**	Affix revenue stamp or impress revenue franking machine impression here **R40** Plak inkomsteseël of plaas inkomstefrankeermasjienstempel hier

Full name of corporation
Volle naam van korporasie _____

We, the undersigned, being all the members of the above-named corporation, resolved at a
Ons, die ondergetekendes, synde al die lede van bogemelde korporasie, het op 'n vergadering

meeting held on that the corporation be wound up voluntarily
gehou op _____ **besluit dat die korporasie vrywillig deur**

by members*/creditors*.
lede*/skuldeisers* gelikwideer word.

SIGNATURES/**HANDTEKENINGE** DATES/**DATUMS**

_____ _____

_____ _____

_____ _____

_____ _____

_____ _____

*Delete that which is not applicable/ *Skrap wat nie van toepassing is nie.**

The above-mentioned resolution was registered on:/
Bovermelde besluit is geregistreer op: _____

REGISTRAR OF CLOSE CORPORATIONS DATE
REGISTRATEUR VAN BESLOTE KORPORASIES **DATUM**

(To be completed by corporation/
Moet deur korporasie ingevul word)

NAME
NAAM _____

POSTAL ADDRESS
POSADRES _____

_____

Office use/ **Kantoorgebruik**
Data processing/ **Dataverwerking**
(1) Recorded/**Opgeneem** Date and initials/ **Datum en paraaf** _____
(2) Corrections/**Regstelling** Date and intials/ **Datum en paraaf** _____

Printing specifications obtainable from the Registrar/
Drukspesifikasies verkrygbaar by die Registrateur.

REPUBLIEK VAN SUID-AFRIKA
REPUBLIC OF SOUTH AFRICA
VORM/FORM CK 7

WET OP BESLOTE KORPORASIES, 1984/CLOSE CORPORATIONS ACT, 1984
(Regulasie 14A/Regulation 14A)

Geen koolpapier benodig nie.
No carbon paper required.

Aansoek om Reservering van Naam of Vertaalde Vorm of Verkorte Vorm
Application for Reservation of Name or Translated Form or Shortened Form
(Moet in tweevoud ingedien word/To be lodged in duplicate)

Registrasiekantoor vir Beslote Korporasies Posbus 429, Pretoria, 0001 Telegramadres: "MAATCOM" **Close Corporations Registration Office** **P.O. Box 429, Pretoria, 0001** **Telegraphic Address: "MAATCOM"**	Inkomsteseël of inkomstefrankeermasjien- stempel: R50 **Revenue stamp or revenue** **franking machine** **impression: R50**

A. Voorgestelde Naam ☐ of Vertaalde Vorm ☐ of Verkorte Vorm ☐
   Proposed Name   or Translated Form   or Shortened Form

(Dui aan met 'n kruisie/Indicate with a cross)

In voorkeurorde In order of preference	Vir Kantoorgebruik For Office Use	Paraaf en datum Initials and Date
1.	goedgekeur/afgekeur approved/not approved	
2.	goedgekeur/afgekeur approved/not approved	
3.	goedgekeur/afgekeur approved/not approved	
4.	goedgekeur/afgekeur approved/not approved	
5.	goedgekeur/afgekeur approved/not approved	
6.	goedgekeur/afgekeur approved/not approved	

Reservering is vir twee maande geldig tensy 'n korter tydperk aangedui word.
Reservation is valid for two months unless a shorter period is indicated.

B. Vergelykende Name (Vir Kantoorgebruik)/**Comparative Names (For Office Use)** _____

C. Het die voorgestelde naam enige verbintenis met 'n persoon, korporasie of maatskappy? Indien wel, wat is die naam en nommer (indien 'n korporasie of maatskappy) en die aard van die verbintenis (bv. lid, houer/filiaal/direkteur ens).
Is the proposed name associated with a person, corporation or a company? If so, what is the name and number (if a corporation or a company) and the nature of the association (e.g. member, holding/subsidiary/director etc).
Indien nie, rede(s) vir, of oorsprong van naam
If not, reason(s) for, or origin of name _____

D. Vernaamste besigheid van die korporasie/voorgestelde korporasie
Principal business of the corporation/proposed corporation _____

Naam van Aansoeker (drukskrif)
Name of Applicant (print)

_____

Handtekening van aansoeker/agent
Signature of applicant/agent

Adres waarheen vorm gepos moet word
Address to which form must be returned

_____

Datum/Date

Drukspesifikasies – A4-grootte. Wit "NCR" papier. Gepons met twee gate aan linkerkant.
Printing Specifications – A4 Size. White NCR paper. Punched with two holes left hand side.

Table of Statutes

Table of Statutes

Table of Cases

Table of Cases

Bibliography

Bibliography

Beck A

"Close corporations in plain language etc." Kerk 'n Nuwe lewe etc. etc.

Benade ML

Sakereidesbing etc. met vervat van etc. etc. etc. etc. Pretoria etc.
Romeins-Hollandse Reg 2/3.

Blackman MS

The relation decline and a state of our etc. etc. etc. etc.
of Cape Town, 1975.

Bonnet A

The figurative reproduction etc. etc.
van die Maatskappye etc. etc.
Durban: Law publishers 1963.

Bennet A en Honninghu...

Romeins-Hollandse etc. etc. etc. etc. etc.
gesigniturre etc. etc. etc. nuwe etc. etc. etc.

Brooke PEJ

"Examination of a theme's statement etc. etc. etc.
Model in Businesses etc.

Cilliers AC

Die figur etc. etc. Bespreek etc. etc. etc. etc. etc.

Cilliers H & Benade JurLed

Corporate etc. etc. YD etc. etc. Suidewetenr 1973.

De Koker L

Geentreklike op aventuur te steins etc. etc. etc. etc. etc.
optreksie in Romeins etc. etc. etc. etc. etc. etc. etc. etc.

De Koker L & Henning JJ

"Etike sapere van die etalikspoo etc. etc. etc. etc.
Kopprarée 1990 etc. etc. etc. etc. etc. etc. etc. etc.

De la Rey EM

Kerk "The law of insolvency in South etc. etc. etc. etc.
Bcadle xxprotation Probleme in verband met etc. etc. etc.
insolvency of that entire for Buewerkesk. Bloemfontein 1969.
The risk of being appointed as liquidator. 1990 SA Mercantile Law etc. etc.

Bibliography

Beck A

"Close corporations: some jurisdictional obstacles" 1987 *Modern Business Law* 47.

Benade ML

"Sekerheidstelling deur middel van aandele" 1964 *Tydskrif vir Hedendaagse Romeins-Hollandse Reg* 279.

Blackman MS

The fiduciary doctrine and its application to directors of companies PhD University of Cape Town 1970.

Bonnet A

Die likwidasie van beslote korporasies met besondere verwysing na die bepalings van die Maatskappywet en die Insolvensiewet 17 *Transactions of the Centre for Business Law* Bloemfontein 1992.

Bonnet A en Henning JJ

"Opsies vir 'n vergelyk met skuldeisers in die beslote korporasiereg – problematiek en remediëring" 1992 *Journal of South African Law* 537.

Brooks PEJ

"Ramifications of a member's duty not to compete with his corporation" 1988 *Modern Business Law* 46.

Cilliers AC

"Jurisdiksie - Wet op Beslote Korporasies, 1984" 1988 *De Rebus* 515.

Cilliers HS & Benade ML *et al*

Corporate law 2 ed Durban Butterworths 1992.

De Koker L

Gesamentlike en afsonderlike aanspreeklikheid in die maatskappye- en beslote korporasiereg 13 *Transactions of the Centre for Business Law* Bloemfontein 1990.

De Koker L & Henning JJ

"Enkele aspekte van die statutêre beheer oor die maksimum ledetal van beslote korporasies" 1990 *Tydskrif vir Hedendaagse Romeins-Hollandse Reg* 547.

De la Rey EM

Mars. The law of insolvency in South Africa 8 ed Wetton Juta 1988.

"Beslote korporasies. Probleme in verband met likwidasie en akkoord" 3 *Transactions of the Centre for Business Law* Bloemfontein (1986) 84.

"The risk of being appointed as liquidator" 1990 *SA Mercantile Law Journal* 95.

Du Plessis JJ

Maatskappyregtelike grondslae van die regsposisie van direkteure en besturende direkteure LLD University of the Orange Free State 1991.

Geach WD & Schoeman T

Guide to the Close Corporations Act and Regulations Cape Town Juta 1984.

Henning JJ

"Die aanspreeklikheid van 'n beslote korporasie vir die handelinge van 'n lid en enkele ander aspekte van eksterne verhoudings" 1984 *Journal for Juridical Science* 155.

"Aspekte van die verteenwoordiging van 'n beslote korporasie (Deel 1)" 1985 *De Rebus* 641.

"Aspekte van die verteenwoordiging van 'n beslote korporasie (Deel 2)" 1986 *De Rebus* 73.

"Aspekte van verteenwoordigingsbevoegdheid, misbruik van beheer, die Wysigingswet op Beslote Korporasies, 1986, ander tersaaklike wetgewing en besigheidstrusts" 3 *Transactions of the Centre for Business Law* Bloemfontein (1986) 25.

"Inter vivos trusts en die lidmaatskap van beslote korporasies. Verdere perspektiewe, 'n geslaagde aansoek en 'n amptelike caveat" 1987 *De Rebus* 485.

"Die beslote korporasie se rasse skrede vooruit" 1987 *Journal for Juridical Science* 104.

"Akkoord, skikking en reëling en die beslote korporasie in likwidasie" 1987 *Journal for Juridical Science* 218.

"Lenings aan en die voorsiening van sekuriteit vir beslote korporasies. Enkele anomalieë en die wysiging van artikels 226 en 55(3)" 1989 *Journal for Juridical Science* 65.

"Caveats rakende beslote korporasies in groepsverband" 1992 *Tydskrif vir Hedendaagse Romeins-Hollandse Reg* 287.

"Judicial management and corporate rescues in South Africa" 1992 *Journal for Juridical Science* 90.

Henning JJ & Bleimschein MFR

"The registrability of a close corporation not for gain" 1989 *Tydskrif vir Hedendaagse Romeins-Hollandse Reg* 251.

"Structuring a close corporation not for gain" 1990 *Tydskrif vir Hedendaagse Romeins-Hollandse Reg* 567.

Henning JJ & Bonnet A

"Likwidasie van beslote korporasies en reëlingskemas ingevolge artikels 311 en 389 van die Maatskappywet" 1991 *Tydskrif vir Hedendaagse Romeins-Hollandse Reg* 274.

Hyman A

Close corporation association agreements Pretoria Clevro 1985.

Joubert WA

"Rekeningkundige aspekte van beslote korporasies" 1984 *Accountancy SA* 541.

Joubert WA & Rademeyer A

"Finansiële en rekeningkundige aspekte van beslote korporasies" 1984 *Journal for Juridical Science* 185.

Larkin MP

"Regarding judicial disregarding of the company's separate identity" 1989 *SA Mercantile Law Journal* 283.

Laughton H

"Close corporation accounting - the company or partnership precedent" 1989 *Accountancy SA* 191.

Lessing JPG

"Puppet members of close corporations" 1989 *SA Mercantile Law Journal* 242.

"Company law-reform in New Zealand" 1990 *SA Mercantile Law Journal* 49.

Malan FR

Collective securities depositories and the transfer of securities Johannesburg Rand Afrikaans University 1983.

Malan JF

Beslote korporasiereg Johannesburg Lex Patria 1985.

McLennan JS

"Directors' fiduciary duties and the Companies Act" 1983 *South African Law Journal* 417.

"Misapplication of company funds - a proposal for reform" 1983 *South African Law Journal* 644.

"Contracting with close corporations" 1985 *South African Law Journal* 322.

Nagel CJ

"Wisselreg. Handtekening namens beslote korporasie op tjek - voorlopige vonnis" 1989 *De Jure* 183.

Naudé SJ

Die regsposisie van die maatskappydirekteur Butterworths Durban 1970.

"The need for a new legal form for small business" 1982 *Modern Business Law* 5.

"The South African close corporation" 1984 *Journal for Juridical Science* 117.

"Die toekoms van die beslote korporasie en die private maatskappy" 3 *Transactions of the Centre for Business Law* Bloemfontein (1986) 1.

Olivier PA

Aspekte van die reg insake trust en trustee met besondere verwysing na die Amerikaanse reg LLD University of Pretoria 1982.

Oosthuizen MJ

Beslote korporasies Johannesburg Lex Patria 1986.

Otto JM

"Likwidasie - watter hof het jurisdiksie?" 1987 *De Rebus* 555.

Ribbens DS

"Close corporators' fiduciary duties: The significance and impact of the distinction between horizontal and vertical fiduciary relations" 1985 *Modern Business Law* 132.

The personal fiduciary character of members' inter se relations in the incorporated partnership Lex Patria Johannesburg 1988.

Savvas BG

"Close corporations' liquidation: which court?" 1987 *De Rebus* 616.

Scott S

The law of cession 2 ed Wetton Juta 1991.

Smit JC

"Aantekening oor die praktyk" 1986 *De Rebus* 489.

Smith C

The law of insolvency 3 ed Durban Butterworths 1988.

South African Institute of Chartered Accountants

Close corporations. An introduction and a guide to some of the more important aspects of the Close Corporations Act, No 69 of 1984 (as amended) revised issue Johannesburg 1991.

Theron L

"Artikel 30 van die Maatskappywet 61 van 1973 en die besigheidstrust" 1990 *South African Law Journal* 673.

"Regulering van die besigheidstrust" 1991 *South African Law Journal* 277.

"Die besigheidstrust" 1991 *Journal of South African Law* 268.

Trichard A Organ K & Cilliers J

The purchase by a company of its own shares. The English rule vs the American rule 10 *Transactions of the Centre for Business Law* Bloemfontein University of the Orange Free State 1989.

Urquhart G

"The close corporation" 1984 *South African Company Law Journal* 41.

Van Loggerenberg D & Van den Berg E

"Section 7 of the Close Corporations Act of 1984" 1990 *South African Law Journal* 97.

Viljoen DJ

"Die trust as lid van die beslote korporasie: agtergrond en standpunte" 1987 *De Rebus* 409.

Williams RC

"Disinterring a body corporate: Sections 73(6) and 420 of the Companies Act 1973" 1990 *South African Law Journal* 610.

Wunsh B

"Inter vivos trusts and close corporations" 1987 *De Rebus* 457.

Index

Index

Par

E

F

H

I

J

L

Par

P

R

S

T